From the searing heat of the Zambezi Valley to the freezing cold of the Chimanimani Mountains in Rhodesia, from the bars in Port St Johns in the Transkei to the Drakensberg Mountains in South Africa, this is the story of one man's fight against terror, and his conscience.

Anyone living in Rhodesia during the 1960s and 1970s would have had a father, husband, brother or son called up in the defence of the war-torn, landlocked little country. A few of these brave men would have been members of the elite and secretive unit that struck terror into the hearts of the ZANLA and ZIPRA guerrillas infiltrating the country at that time – the Selous Scouts. These men were highly trained and disciplined, with skills to rival the SAS, Navy Seals and the US Marines, although their dress and appearance were wildly unconventional: civilian clothing with blackened, hairy faces to resemble the very people they were fighting against.

Twice decorated – with the Member of the Legion of Merit (MLM) and the Military Forces' Commendation (MFC) – Andrew Balaam was a member of the Rhodesian Light Infantry and later the Selous Scouts, for a period spanning twelve years. This is his honest and insightful account of his time as a pseudo operator. His story is brutally truthful, frightening, sometimes humorous and often sad.

In later years, after Rhodesia became Zimbabwe, he was involved with a number of other former Selous Scouts in the attempted coups in the Ciskei, a South African homeland, and Lesotho, an independent nation, whose only crimes were supporting the African National Congress. Training terrorists, or as they preferred to be called, 'liberation armies', to conduct a war of terror on innocent civilians, was the very thing he had spent the last ten years in Rhodesia fighting against. This is the true, untold story of these failed attempts at governmental overthrows.

The author, one of ten children, spent his early life moving between Bulawayo, in the then Southern Rhodesia, now known as Zimbabwe, and Livingstone in Northern Rhodesia, now known as Zambia. His love of wildlife, fishing and the African Bush came from spending a lot of his time as a youngster fishing on the banks of the Zambezi River.

In 1966 he was called up for National Service and decided to join the Rhodesian Army. That was the era of peace in Rhodesia, and after doing a stint in the Rhodesian Light Infantry he left to join the Rhodesia Railways. However, war was on the horizon, and eight months after leaving, he re-joined the Rhodesia Light Infantry. Two years later he joined the famous Selous Scouts, where he stayed until the end of the war. After, leaving Rhodesia he ended up in the Transkei with Ron Reid Daly and other former members of the Scouts.

BUSH WAR OPERATOR

MEMOIRS OF THE RHODESIAN LIGHT INFANTRY, SELOUS SCOUTS AND BEYOND

A.J. Balaam

Helion & Company

Helion & Company Limited
26 Willow Road
Solihull
West Midlands
B91 1UE
England
Tel. 0121 705 3393
Fax 0121 711 4075
Email: info@helion.co.uk
Website: www.helion.co.uk
Twitter: @helionbooks
Visit our blog http://blog.helion.co.uk/

Published by Helion & Company 2014. Reprinted 2016

Designed and typeset by Farr out Publications, Wokingham, Berkshire
Cover designed by Euan Carter, Leicester (www.euancarter.com)
Printed by Hobbs The Printers Ltd, Totton, Hampshire

Text and colour photographs © A.J. Balaam 2014
Maps by George Anderson © Helion & Company 2014

ISBN 978 1 909982 77 2

British Library Cataloguing-in-Publication Data.
A catalogue record for this book is available from the British Library.

For details of other military history titles published by Helion & Company Limited
contact the above address, or visit our website: http://www.helion.co.uk.

We always welcome receiving book proposals from prospective authors.

Contents

List of photographs

Photographs appear in central plate section

The main road into Port St Johns, where I was paraded after my arrest.   J

The training camp for the Ciskei Liberation Army was situated at
   the base of this hill.   J

The road leading to George Matanzima's house, now converted to holiday flats.   K

Quacha's Nek and surrounds with the mountains in the distance.   K

The area around Quacha's Nek – rugged and beautiful.   L

The main road I had to cross to get to the golf course.   L

In the background is the stream/water trap where I tried to clean
   up and shave.   M

Main entrance to King William's Town Golf Club.   M

The church in King William's Town. The house in the background
   is the priest's house where I was turned away.   N

The main entrance to the church – and the door I could not open.   N

The site of the public telephone I used to call my contact in Port
   St Johns. The old public telephone has now been replaced by
   more modern telephones.   O

The garage in King William's Town where I was picked up after
   the failed Palace attack. I was sitting on the wall. In those days
   there was no fence.   O

What used to be the police station – across the road from the public telephone. P

The railway bride over the Kei River where I was to cross back into
   Transkei after walking the 70 kilometres from Bisho.   P

List of maps

"I don't care how much they cost, pour this petrol on them and set them on fire."

—Author ordered to burn his Chelsea boots by Training Troop instructor Corporal Les Avery

"You look like a bag of shit with a rope tied round the middle."

—RSM WOI Robin Tarr to author

"Sorry, corporal, I am going to have to lock you up in the armoury for the next week or two while we practise for the colours parade. With you on the parade square we will never finish. The sight of you drives the RSM crazy."

—Colour Sergeant van Breda to author

"What do you mean you're lost? I tell what you do: put your head between your legs and blow. If you see a blue flame, you're heading in the right direction."

—Captain Reid-Daly to Corporal Trevor Mathews, Zambezi Valley

"Christ sake, corp, you can't take beer with you on patrol. The boss will shit himself if he finds out."

—Author to Corporal Paddy Ryan, Kanyemba, Zambezi Valley

Preface

War is not about jumping over logs and burning trucks, or kicking in doors and firing from the hip with grenades hanging from your teeth and a devil-may-care smile slapped on your face, as the enemy drop like flies. It is a heart-wrenching, soul-destroying, guilt-ridden and personality-changing experience. In guerrilla warfare there is no front line. The enemy has to be hunted down and eliminated, group by group, one by one. The pressure on both the hunter and the eliminator is incredible. Having performed the eliminator role in the Rhodesian Light Infantry Fire Force, and also with the Selous Scouts' column raids into Mozambique, I found the loneliness of the hunter/commander role in the Selous Scouts to be the far more demanding of the two. The hunter works alone for long periods of time, relying entirely on his senses to survive. With nobody to talk to and no human companionship of any kind, he soon loses the ability to communicate properly with his fellow humans. Once the ability to communicate has been lost, he no longer has a release valve for his anger and frustrations. Over time, the anger and frustration build up, leading to extremely violent outbursts of anger, as well as long periods of depression.

As a youngster I was taught that to kill another human being was the worst crime possible. The training I received in the army was, for want of a better word, an attempt to re-wire me. I had to push aside and smother everything I had been taught as a child, and try to replace right and wrong with an unthinking, robot-like obedience to whatever instruction I was given. Brainwashed and fanatical are labels often associated with Special Forces. I do not believe I was a fanatic, or brainwashed. I did what I had to do to survive.

This is my story.

Acknowledgements

A book will never reach its final conclusion without the help of many people and this book is no exception.

Firstly, to Cath, thank you for patiently listening as I struggled to put my thoughts down on paper.

Shelley and Stan, thank you for the donation of the laptop, which saved hours of painstaking writing in longhand.

Pete Mac and Willie van der Riet, thanks guys for refreshing my memory.

John and Kath Costello, grateful thanks for your help, without which this book would never have been written.

Neil Kriel, thank you for turning a blind eye while I was writing during working hours!

Craig Balaam – thanks for your help and encouragement in getting the ball rolling.

David Balaam, my brother, many thanks for driving me all over the country to obtain photos and jog my memory.

Liz Balaam, thank you for all your help and advice in proof-reading and editing the initial drafts and without which this book would never have been published.

Last but not least, my publisher Duncan Rogers and the team at Helion, and editor Chris Cocks for your hard work, advice and encouragement.

Maps

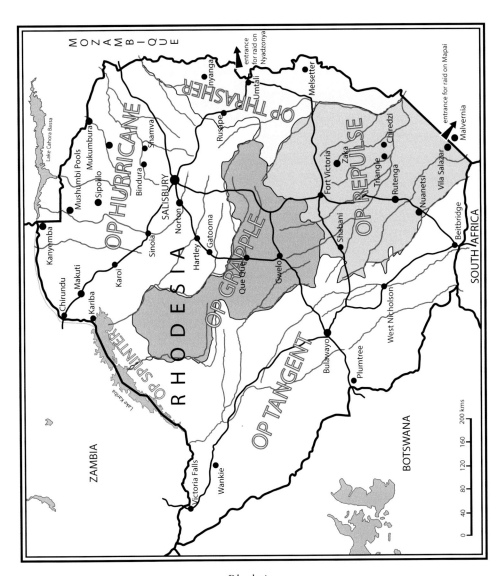

Rhodesia

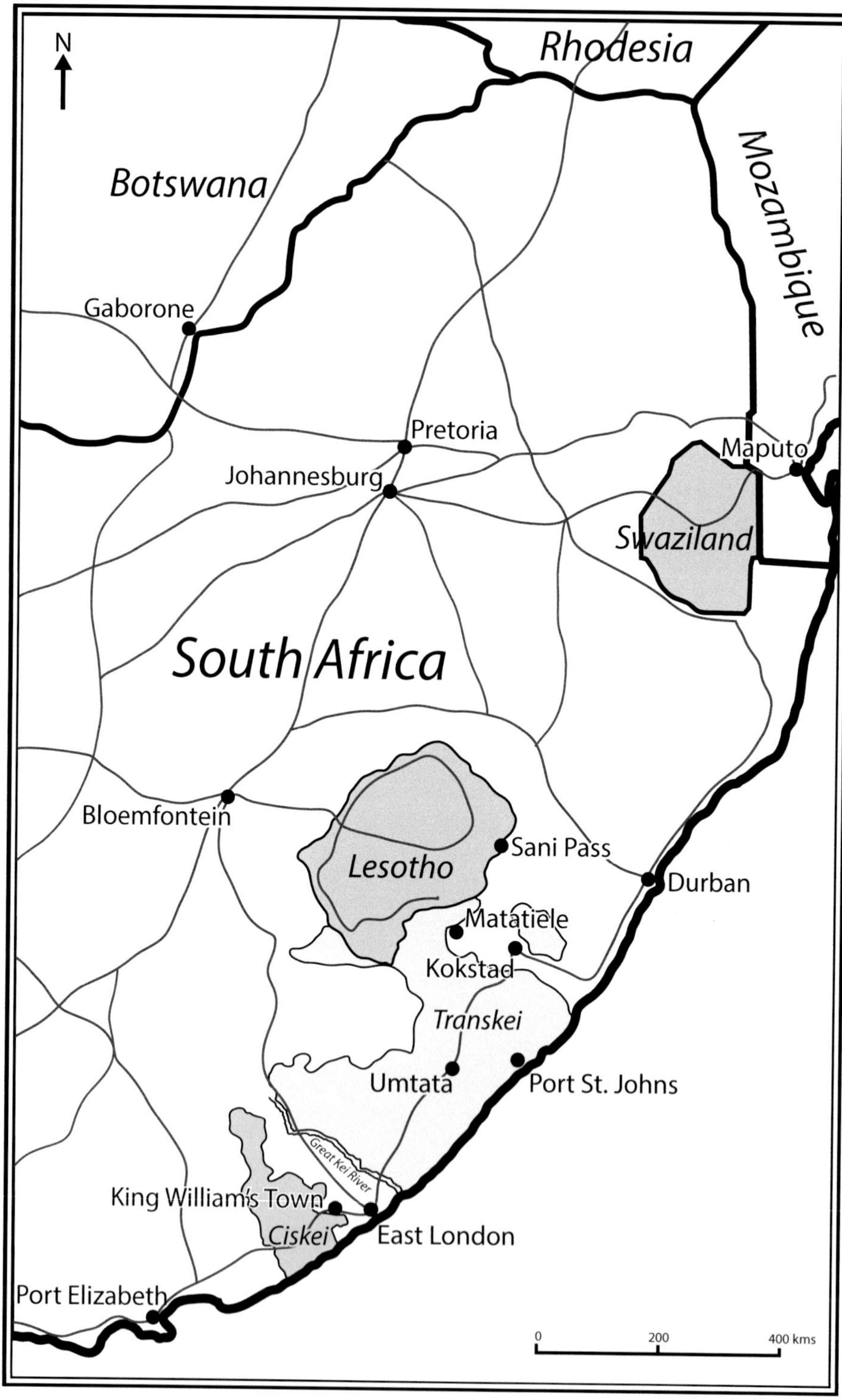

N

Rhodesia

Botswana

Mozambique

Gaborone

Pretoria

Johannesburg

Maputo

Swaziland

South Africa

Bloemfontein

Lesotho

Sani Pass

Durban

Matatiele

Kokstad

Transkei

Umtata

Port St. Johns

Great Kei River

King William's Town

Ciskei

East London

Port Elizabeth

| 0 | 200 | 400 kms |

South Africa

Prologue
Livingstone, Northern Rhodesia, 1960

It was a Friday morning and I was covered from head to toe in strong-smelling local African beer. I should have been at school. Instead I was running as fast as I could, beer spraying everywhere, dodging in and out of the trees, jumping the gullies and dry riverbeds as though they were not even there. Fear had given me wings. Running next to me, just as wet and smelly, was my black friend Robert, each of us carrying a bag of *masese* slung over our shoulders.

It was still very early in the morning. The smoke from hundreds of cooking fires was hanging in the trees and the smell of boiling maize and kaffir corn was strong in the air. Robert and I had just raided the local open-air beer-brewing factory, and were being chased by several pissed-off brewers.

If you wanted to catch fish in the Zambezi River, you had to have *masese*, the fresher the better. *Masese* is the dregs of the beer-brewing process. It smells strongly of yeast and consists of all the various grains used to make the beer. It settles to the bottom of the forty-four-gallon drums used by the locals to make beer, and is dynamite when it comes to catching fish. If you wanted it fresh, no more than a day or so old, then you had to visit the beer factory and buy it – this was one way of getting it. However, if you wanted fresh, fresh like I did, and had no money, you raided the factory, pushed over a forty-four-gallon drum of cold beer and gathered the dregs by hand. Then you filled up your bag and took off, normally closely pursued by unhappy brewers. The brewers were fat and overweight from drinking too much of their product and normally called it a day after a couple of hundred metres.

It was a still, warm evening. The rising moon painted a road of silver across the black mirror like water. The trees were silhouetted by the moon against the dark blue of the sky and took on weird, mystical shapes. In the distance I could hear the roar of the Victoria Falls, and closer, the occasional grunt of a hippo. Lying across from me on the other side of the fire was Robert. I was happy and content. Our fresh *masese* had worked wonders: our bags were full of fish, ready to sell to the white fishermen the next morning.

With a stomach full of fresh fish, hands waving in a vain attempt to keep the mosquitoes at bay, I relaxed. It had been a bad week. Then the black water exploded and I was staring down the throat of a foul-smelling, red-eyed, enraged hippo bull. A bad week had just got worse.

A few days earlier I had been in big trouble. Twelve years old, naked, my behind full of thick red welts, I tried to bring my crying under control. The bath was full of broken wooden coat hangers, the result of the hiding I had just received from my father for selling all the mango trees in our yard to some Indian gentleman to make mango chutney.

In a family of ten children money was always short. Although only twelve, I already had several business ventures on the go. My main business was selling fishing worms. Our house was situated on the main road to the nearby Zambezi River. During the fishing season, I did a roaring trade. In the off season, when business was a bit slack, I sold *vetkoeks* (fat cakes) and Swiss rolls that I made myself. Most of the money I made found its way back into the household. The way I figured it was: sell the mangos, most of which went rotten or were eaten by the fruit bats, take the money and buy groceries. Obviously my father did not agree with me.

My friend, comrade and master salesman in these business ventures was my black friend Robert.

My love, my life, was fishing and the Zambezi. The fact that I did not have any proper fishing rods did not bother me. Using a short, thin, wet tree branch, a four-metre length of fishing line, a hook, a sinker and a cork as a float, I caught more fish than most people, including those using the latest rods and reels available.

Soaking wet, shaking with fear, looking down into the glaring red pig eyes of the hippo bull from the tree I had somehow managed to climb, I wondered if a change of sport might not be a bad idea.

⚒

"Hey, Andy, you okay?"

Reluctantly, fighting every inch of the way, my mind was dragged back to the harsh reality of the present. Lifting my head, I muttered a faint, "Yeah, I'm okay," to my friend Vance Meyers.

Forcing open my now-stuck-together eyelids with dirty bruised fingers, I looked around. The shimmering grey amphitheatre of death was still there, as were the cicada beetles and their never-ending screeching. The heat haze imparted movement in an otherwise motionless landscape. The burnt black grass bent and swayed as though caught in a passing breeze, grey scorched earth rippled and rolled like a running stream of molten lava, the gaunt twisted branches on the leafless trees, like worshippers of old, seemed to stretch and bow as they implored the heavens for rain.

Closing my eyes, no longer wanting to look at what was, to me, a scene straight from hell, I rested my head on my knees and let my mind drift away.

⚘

The water, a deep greenish blue, looked cool and inviting. The spray from the bow of the government launch cutting through the water was whipped up by the slight breeze and gently deposited on our faces, legs and arms. We were on our way to Feira, a Portuguese army base situated on the banks of the Zambezi River, to play a football match.

The beer was cold, the white froth running down my chin onto my shirt. As usual we had lost the match hands down. None of us cared. We had come for the cold beer and brown Portuguese cigarettes. We had learnt from past experience that if you wanted cold beer and cigarettes, beating the home team was not the way to go. Sitting in the open-air bar, cooled by the breeze coming off the nearby Zambezi, supplied with cold beers as fast as we could drink them, we were relaxed and happy.

⚘

"Come on big boy, just a bit closer," I muttered to myself.

I was attempting to launch my latest business venture: crocodile hunting. Not for the meat, but for the skins. It was not an impromptu decision.

Several days earlier Robert had mentioned that an Indian gentleman in town was paying up to seven shillings and sixpence a square inch for crocodile skin, depending on the condition. This was a fortune as far as I was concerned. And I had been thinking about it ever since.

I knew how to catch crocodiles. Small ones, that is. My father had taught me that the best way was by hand, at night, using a torch. According to Robert, the small ones we had been catching for fun were too small. We needed to up our game and look at the four- to five-footers if we wanted to make money. A four- to five-foot crocodile was a completely different kettle of fish to the eighteen-inch-or-so size I had been catching. This was serious stuff: hands were out, spears were in.

The Zambezi was in full flood. Still dressed in my school uniform, minus my shoes and socks, I stared in awe. Over a kilometre wide, it rolled, heaved, twisted and turned in an awesome display of power, the brown, debris-strewn water destroying whatever stood in its path. The roar of the river was deep and menacing, almost drowning out the thunder of the nearby Victoria Falls. Having burst its banks, covering the roads in the area in several feet of water, the river had created huge floodplains. Into this sanctuary of calm water came crocodiles, large and small, together with the occasional hippo, not to mention thousands of fish, all trying to escape from the raging river. Branches bending, packed to breaking point, every tree for miles around was swamped by thousands of birds. The screeching and squabbling was never-ending as they fought and bickered over the millions of insects that had taken refuge in the trees trying to escape the floodwaters.

Into this water wonderland walked Robert and I.

The river was a lot higher than I thought it would be. Pushing my bicycle loaded with a bag of *masese*, followed by Robert carrying our fishing rods and a bag containing spare hooks, fishing line and a couple of knives, I cautiously moved down the now-submerged road looking for a fishing spot. Half an hour later, waist deep in what I knew to be crocodile-infested water, I had still found no piece of ground above water level large enough to hold Robert, the bicycle and me. I should have been scared but I was not. I knew the river well. I had learnt to swim it. It was like my back yard. I had grown up on its banks and I knew its many moods and inhabitants well.

It felt great, on dry ground, sun beating down, fishing lines in the water waiting for a bite. My whole body tingling, I was like a statue, stiff and unmoving, my makeshift wooden spear firmly clutched in my hand, my eyes burning from the sweat running down my forehead, as unblinking, I watched the crocodile edge ever closer to me.

The fishing had been good and we were catching fish hand over fist. As we caught a fish, we gutted it and threw the guts into the water. The reason for this was twofold. Firstly, without its innards the fish stayed fresh longer and secondly, the innards attracted catfish, which were a great favourite among the locals and very easy to sell.

Robert had first noticed the almost-five-foot-long crocodile when it was still fifty metres away. Lying just beneath the water, with only its eyes and nostrils breaking the surface, it could easily have passed for one of the hundreds of small logs floating in the floodplain. Attracted by the smell of blood and fish guts – its natural prey – it was on its way to investigate.

It was now time to convert my thoughts of all the money I could make by killing crocodiles into action. I lunged, the spear sank in and the water exploded. I hung on for dear life. Seconds later it was all over. I lay gasping for breath, laughing at the sheer pleasure of being alive. Tripping, falling and staggering around like a drunk, I made my way back to the piece of high ground that was our fishing spot.

In its effort to escape from my wooden spear that had pierced the soft skin behind it front leg, the crocodile had rolled. The spear had snapped like a match and, with a slap of its tail, the crocodile had disappeared and with it my dreams of becoming rich overnight. But the rock hurled with every ounce of strength that Robert had in his wiry body had connected with a sickening thud on the crocodile's head. While I had been sitting there feeling sorry for myself, Robert had kept his eyes on the water. He remembered something we had both been told by a local crocodile hunter: once injured, a crocodile would not stay in the water as he would be easy prey for his fellow crocodilians, and would head for the nearest piece of dry land in an effort to escape their attentions.

It was late, the sun a blinding orange ball in the sky, the water a reflection of the sky above, seemingly on fire, motionless. The birds sounded like an orchestra gone crazy, drowning out even the deep growl of the river. As I pushed my bicycle though the glowing orange water, with the crocodile tied to the crossbar, I was happy. I was going to get a hiding – that was for sure: it would take my long-suffering mother many hours to get the white school shirt white again. I did not care: I had got my first crocodile. The road to riches and fame was open and I was on my way.

⚕

It could not be. No way, I was dreaming. The sound persisted. The crack and thud of a helicopter's main rotor as it sliced its way through the air. Cautiously I lifted my head. What had seconds before been a motionless grey piece of hell, soon to become a cemetery, was now alive with jumping, waving figures.

Some of them were completely naked, having discarded their clothes in the belief that they would be cooler and need less water, therefore standing a better chance of survival. Luckily for them, the theory was never put to the test.

How long we had wandered around I have no idea. I have a dead spot, a mental block concerning the last few hours of our ordeal. I can remember the white phosphorus grenade spraying streams of white smoke into the sky … after that nothing. From here on in, the Rhodesian army, very British in structure and training, would concentrate more on the skills required to survive in the harshest of conditions and win battles and less on drill and the parade ground.

Part I

Rhodesian Light Infantry, 1967–74

1

Kanyemba, Zambezi Valley, November 1967

"Jesus Christ," I thought to myself, "what the fuck does this arsehole think he's doing?"

It was hot, unbelievably hot, not a breath of air, not a bird in the sky, even the mopane flies had taken cover. The trees were leafless, their gaunt branches pointing up to the searing bright sky as if imploring the gods for rain. The grey-blue soil and rocks baked hard by the summer sun acted as one huge solar panel, absorbing the incredible heat produced by the glaring sun, and slowly releasing it as darkness fell, making sure the temperature never dropped below 30°C, day or night.

Into this mountainous, waterless, furnace walked ten members of Support Group, Rhodesian Light Infantry (RLI), loaded down like pack mules, practising patrol formations. And loaded down like pack mules we were. We had no lightweight equipment of any kind; the blankets you slept with in barracks were the same ones you took to the bush, heavy and cumbersome. All our webbing, British by design, was old and uncomfortable, especially the packs. Lacking a frame and having no padding on the straps, they were a mobile torture chamber. When loaded down with four days' food, two blankets, hand grenades, trip flares and other odds and sods, it was not long before all the feeling in your arms was lost as the straps bit deep into your shoulder muscles, cutting off the blood supply.

Crouched under a leafless tree, head drooping, swearing at our patrol leader under my breath, soaking wet from sweat, arms hanging lifeless, I struggled to get my breathing under control and my heart felt as if it was going to burst. With my water bottle held in both shaking hands, I gulped down mouthful after mouthful, wasting just as much as I was drinking.

As far as I knew our task was simple. We were to ambush a group of terrorists who were supposed to be crossing the Zambezi River from Zambia into Rhodesia. The supposed crossing point was below a narrow gorge known as Hell's Gate. Why we had been dropped at Kanyemba airstrip many hot, waterless, mountainous miles from the ambush point was beyond me, as was the reason we were practising patrol formations in the incredible heat.

Everything was grey, the trees, the rocks, the soil, the mountains and the sky, all grey and all encompassed in a glimmering heat haze. One look at the lifeless panorama spread out in front of us should have set the alarm bells ringing. It did not. We were young and stupid, led by equally young and stupid non-commissioned officers. Our knowledge of the bush and survival skills were limited to what we had learnt while growing up. At that stage, the Rhodesian army taught little or nothing on surviving under extreme conditions, but this patrol would change all that.

Looking around at my fellow patrol members, I could see they were suffering in the heat as much as I was – heads hanging, shirts unbuttoned and soaking wet from sweat, flushed faces, packs and webbing lying on the ground, weapons leaning up out of reach against trees or rocks, whichever was the closest. It was late afternoon. We had stopped at the bottom of a ridge in a small valley. That we were lost I did not doubt. The whole day the grey ridge-like steps had been leading us downward into the waterless hell of the Zambezi Valley itself. Everything looked the same. The one grey ridge looked the same as the next, as did the countless dry riverbeds. This was a map-reader's nightmare. There was not a breath of air, not a bird in the sky, not an animal spoor on the game trail we were following, nothing, except the endless, mind-destroying screech of cicada beetles and the energy-sapping heat.

The practising of patrol formations had long since ceased. Bent over in order to try and relieve the pressure on my shoulders caused by the pack straps, I could see that, unfortunately, it was a case of too little too late. Looking around at my lifeless, exhausted, comrades, I could see the damage had already been done. Fighting back the urge to drink some of the warm water I had left in my water bottles, I walked over to where the patrol leader and several other sergeants were hunched over the map. There was much pointing at the map and the surrounding countryside, especially the ridges, which now hedged us in on all sides. I would have loved to have had a look at the map myself and offer an opinion. I had not been in the army long, but I already knew that to offer an opinion without being asked was a shortcut to trouble. I had offered a couple of uninvited opinions on my first recruit course: unfortunately they were not received in the spirit in which they were given, and I found myself failing my first recruit course. I had a bad attitude I was told. I was a barrack-room lawyer, a trouble-maker, who thought he was clever.

Slumping next to a nearby tree stump, I watched as our patrol leader tried in vain to contact our headquarters. This was day one, and already you could hear the frustration and uncertainty in his voice. This was not the parade ground where screaming and shouting were the order of the day and he reigned supreme. This was nature at its rawest – strong, unforgiving and relentless, where knowledge, strength and skill were required to survive. Unfortunately for us, time would prove that our patrol leader did not have the necessary attributes required to survive or guide others in such extreme conditions.

It was getting dark. The sunset was magnificent, the ridges and surrounding mountains glowed red and orange and the leafless trees seemed like fiery quills on the back of some kind of mystical porcupine. With drooping heads, dragging feet and bent backs, we were moving in single file, at a snail's pace, along the game trail we had been following the whole day. It gets dark quickly in Africa. We were making one last attempt to find water before it got too dark to continue. It was a silent camp. Nobody was saying much. We were exhausted. The heat and the unforgiving terrain were bad enough – they would have sapped anybody's strength – but the deciding factor between just being tired and exhausted was the stupid practising of patrol formations over such rugged country.

Lying on my blanket, staring up at the stars, listening to our patrol commander frantically trying to contact headquarters, I started to feel uneasy. Rolling over onto my side, I tried to get a look at my friends. It was too dark to see the expressions on their faces. The fact that they sat unmoving, faces turned, staring silently at the radio operator, spoke volumes. Rolling back onto my raw, skinless, throbbing back, I reached for my two water bottles. One was empty, the other three-quarters full. We were lost in some of the hottest, driest country in Rhodesia. It was uninhabited, apart from a few isolated villages of Batonka tribesmen. We had no radio communication with headquarters. And, worse, we had no water. No water, no life. A feeling of impending doom settled on me.

It had just started to get light and we were on the move. The night had been long, hot and sleepless, the stifling silence broken only by the opening and closing of water bottles and the occasional muffled groan of pain. My skin felt like it was on fire, my hands hung limply by my sides, my weapon too hot to hold was stuck in the front of my webbing. Staring unseeingly at my feet, I shuffled along. My head felt as if it was going to burst, my eyes were burning and dry and seemed set to pop out of my head. I was no longer sweating. My skin was cool and clammy. I was starting to dehydrate. I was no better or worse off than anybody else in the patrol. We were in big trouble. Without water we would all be dead in thirty-six hours.

I stumbled on. My ears were being battered by the ever-increasing screeching of the cicada beetles. To my tormented mind they sounded like the orchestra of death, playing the closing score to the final scene of a tragedy that was being played out in the grey shimmering theatre of death that was the Zambezi Valley.

Green trees! It could not be, I thought to myself. It must be a mirage.

The patrol ground to a halt as we stared in amazement. There, a hundred metres in front of us, through the shimmering heat haze, was a clump of green trees. God, everybody knew green trees meant water. Morale went through the sky and smiles were a dime a dozen. We were going to make it after all.

Thirty minutes later, with trembling hands, I slowly lifted my tin cup and sipped the urine mixed with lemonade powder. I had exchanged urine with my friend Vance Meyers. I had read somewhere that if you drank your own urine you would puke, but if you drank urine belonging to somebody else you had a better chance of keeping it down.

We had spent the last half an hour running up and down like headless chickens. We had arrived at the trees en masse, like a bunch of drunks, staggering and weaving all over the place, hope written over our blistered faces. Hope soon turned to dismay, the river was dry, there was no surface water, nothing, not a drop, and the sand was as dry as a bone. Some of the hardier members of the patrol tried digging, using their mess tins, but soon gave up, as no matter where they tried or how deep they dug, the sand remained dry.

The liquid concoction tasted awful and smelled even worse. My throat was dry and swollen. Swallowing was difficult – more of the mixture ran down onto my clothes than went down my throat. Did it help? I do not know. It was boiling hot, but my skin was dry, I was no longer sweating as there was no more fluid in my body to sweat out. The exposed skin on my arms, legs, face and neck was covered in a thin layer of salt, the last of my body's reserves, and black ash from the burnt grass and trees. The deep cuts on my legs and hands had stopped bleeding as had the many grazes. I was on my last legs – another twenty-four hours without water and I would be dead, cooked in my own skin by my over-heating body. My brain was sluggish, tired and confused and I was having difficulty in making sense of what I was seeing and hearing. I had lost all sense of time and feeling. I did not know how long we had been wandering around lost and dying of thirst in this hell on earth.

We were on the move again. The heat was terrifying as it reflected off the surrounding ridges into our small valley, turning it into an oven. Using my weapon as a crutch, I managed to haul myself to my feet. One fall followed the next, getting to my feet took longer and longer. I felt nothing, I heard nothing. My head hung limply on my chest and my eyes stared blackly at the ground in front of me. I was no longer a thinking, caring human being; I was just an animal trying to survive.

Several hours later, after having split up into small groups to search for water, I was squatting under a tree, my shirt piled on top of my webbing, rifle and pack. I stared around. My whole being was concentrated on survival; anything else, even the thought of dying, brought no reaction from my boiling brain. It was all about survival. All I could think about was getting out alive. How much longer I could last I did not know. I could still stand up, maybe a bit unsteadily on my feet, but I could stand, my walk was more of shuffle, but I could still move. I was in fact a lot better off than many of my comrades, several of whom had lapsed into a semi-coma.

Sitting under the trees, my head on my knees, I waited for it to get dark and cool down a bit. What I was going to do after the darkness descended and it cooled down I did not know. It just seemed to be the right thing to do.

2

Chewore Wilderness Area, Zambezi Valley, 1972

After two days of travelling by Land Rover and Ford F250 trucks over some of the worst roads in Africa, we finally arrived at our destination: the Chewore Wilderness Area. Situated between the Zambezi River that marked the border between Zambia and Rhodesia, and the Zambezi escarpment, it was famous for its vast herds of buffalo, abundant rhino, lion, leopard, elephant and most forms of African wildlife. Basically untouched, except for the odd hunting camp and game ranger's house, it was how Africa had been before the arrival of the white man with his guns and his lust for blood. I had been looking forward to this trip for weeks. The fishing, the game-viewing, the hot springs, the fresh meat and with a bit of crocodile hunting thrown in on the side, it made this one of my favourite areas in which to base up. As I sat in the warm sun waiting for our troop sergeant to select an area to set up a camp, I remembered only the good: the fishing, the shooting, the bathing in the hot springs. I had conveniently pushed to the back of my mind the downside of the area.

The sound of tearing grass caught my attention. There, not twenty metres away, was a group of four rhino. Suddenly, in my mind's eye, in all its glory and splendour, the downside came screeching back. I remembered the 'Chewore buzzard', the tsetse fly, with its long protruding proboscis that could bore through several layers of clothing and deliver an extremely painful sting, as well as the cigarette seller's favourite: the mopane fly. These are small, irritating creatures, and given half the chance they would disappear down your throat, eyes, nose and ears. Controllable only by smoke, they convinced more young Rhodesian men to smoke than any advert ever did. Those drinkers of insect repellent, the mosquitoes, would descend in their thousands at night from the swamps bordering the nearby Zambezi. They were unstoppable, capable of penetrating any mosquito net. They made sure a good night's sleep was a thing of the past.

Then along came the heavies, led by the elephants and rhino. Most animals, including elephants, associate the smell of man with danger and try to avoid contact – not so the rhino, which is half blind and stupid beyond belief, but also utterly fearless. Glancing at the nearby group of four, I remembered my last encounter with a rhino. The Chewore Wilderness covers a huge area and this was not my first visit to this particular spot. I had been here several times. It was on one of my previous visits that I realized how utterly fearless, stupid and dangerous a rhino really is.

Our task had been simple: check for signs of terrorist crossings from Zambia. We had left our base early in the morning. The air, clear and fresh, was alive with the sounds of the African bush. The sun painted the sky in brilliant streaks of red, yellow and orange as it rose to be greeted by a barrage of sound: the bark of the baboon on sentry duty, the screech of feeding birds, the echoing grunts of the yawning hippo and the haunting cry of the fish eagle, all welcoming back the sun, the giver of life.

It was like a steam bath, extremely hot and humid. The paths were narrow, the bush very thick, in some cases forming a solid wall, giving the impression that you were walking down a tunnel as you followed the path that was the only way through. This was elephant and rhino country. Walking in single file about two metres apart, we cautiously followed the path. We were relying on our senses of smell and hearing to keep us in one piece. Elephant were not the problem; big, noisy feeders were normally easy to avoid. Rhino, on the other hand, were completely different. The first you knew about a rhino was when it burst through the bush like a battle tank heading straight for you.

We were near the end of our patrol, heading back to our base. It was mid-afternoon. It was still very hot but nowhere as bad as it had been at midday. Each of us walked in our own little world of misery, brought about by our constant companions, the heat, the mopane flies and the Chewore buzzards. We had just come through a particularly thick section of bush and I was looking for a place to have a rest up. All I could hear from the patrol following me was "for fuck's sake", as the mopane flies disappeared up noses, down ears and into eyes, followed by the sound of a striking match as the tormented individual tried to light a cigarette, the smoke of which would at least drive them away, even temporarily. The occasional slap and moan indicated that the Chewore buzzards were still hard at work. Suddenly, out of nowhere, a large clearing appeared. It was a godsend, the open ground was like heaven on earth compared to the dark, narrow game trails we had been following. A small clump of trees stood in the middle. This appeared to be an ideal place for a rest, and a chance to cool down.

We were about three metres short of the trees when I heard a thumping sound. There, ready to charge and not more than twenty metres away, stood a rhino, pawing the ground, with his head lowered and his beady red eyes staring vacantly into the distance. Blowing up great clouds of dust as he snorted through his nostrils, he reminded me of an old steam locomotive. "The trees!" I shouted, as I turned to face the oncoming rhino. He was fifteen metres away when my first two shots hit the ground a metre in front of him. He did not even bother to look up. The next two rounds hit mere inches in front of his lowered head, bringing him to a shuddering halt. As he stood there pawing the ground, uncertain of what to do next, I hauled myself up a tree. After running about aimlessly for a minute or two, he ambled off to a nearby tree about four metres away and stood there staring at us.

I was deciding on what to do next when I heard a loud snoring-like sound coming from the tree under which the rhino was standing. I could not believe my eyes. The stupid rhino had fallen asleep. Stupid was the best word to describe a rhino as far as I was concerned.

"Come guys, time is flying; let's set up base before it gets dark," the words from our troop sergeant brought me back to the present.

✂

How the hell do you mistake a man for a rhino? Jesus, what a shit way to die, shot dead because some arsehole thought you were a rhino.

It was our first night in our newly set-up base camp. On this trip we had several members from the quartermaster's stores with us. It was the policy of the Rhodesian Light Infantry that everybody in the battalion should go to the bush every so often so they knew what it was like to go on ops, do their own washing and cooking, plus lose the odd kilo in defence of their country. It was about nine or ten o'clock at night. Everybody had been in their bivvies trying to get some sleep as it had been a long, hard day. Setting up the headquarters and the kitchen, digging the refuse pit, plus our own shell scrapes in the unreal heat, had left us all exhausted.

Sleep had been slow in coming. The mosquitoes were out in their thousands. Mosquito net or no mosquito net, it made no difference at all: you got eaten alive regardless. Insect repellent was like the nectar of the gods to them – the more you put on the more they attacked you. Even though it was ten at night, all you could hear was bitching, slaps and moans and groans. In the distance, above the moans and groans, I had heard a rhino grazing. It is difficult to describe the sound; it is like someone taking a sheet of paper and tearing it into strips, very similar to the sound a rhino makes as he tears chunks of grass while feeding. Most of us had heard the sound many times before and were quite familiar with rhino and their behaviour.

The problem was the guys from headquarters. So to put everybody's minds at ease, our troop sergeant decided to warn the new members of the presence of the rhino. This act of kindness was to cost him his life.

When the shot had first gone off I had thought it was one of the quartermaster types having an accidental discharge. Now, crouched by the dead body, I realized I could not have been more wrong. In shock, I struggled to get my brain working. This was the first body I had seen of a person who had died from a gunshot. The sight of the gaping hole and the blood was all new, and all frightening. The fact that the dead person was my troop sergeant did not help. This was the person who had continued my instruction in the art of warfare after the basic training I had received as a recruit. He had taught me things you do not find in a training manual. Above all, he had been my friend. As I knelt beside his body, I felt a great sense of loss and at the same time a great anger at the man who had shot him. I could feel the tears welling up behind my eyes; I wanted to sit down and cry. Fighting back the tears, I brought myself under control. Crying would not help. On closer inspection, with the aid of the light now shining from the fully lit-up HQ tent, I could see powder burns around the entry wound in his chest, which meant he had been almost on top of the man who had shot him when the trigger was pulled. He had had no chance. The 7.62mm round had gone through his body like a hot knife through butter and the force of the bullet hitting him threw his body back at least three or four feet, shattering bone and turning meat into jelly. For the first time, I smelled the heavy, sweet, cloying smell of blood and flesh boiled and burned by gunpowder. Unfortunately, it was not to be the last time I would witness this.

My attention was now drawn to the man who had fired the fatal shot. He was lying down on his side and crying as great big, heart-wrenching, soul-destroying sobs wracked his body. By this time, his rifle had been taken away from him, for his own protection and to prevent any attempted suicide. What had been anger now turned to pity and understanding. It was one of his first trips to the bush, he was not used to the strange sounds and the thought of a rhino grazing a couple of metres away from where he was trying to sleep must have been extremely frightening. I could imagine him crouched in the corner of his shelter, imagination running wild, weapon held in sweaty, shaking hands, listening with straining ears to the sound of the grazing rhino, a sound which seemed to be getting ever louder and ever closer. A shadow, a shot, and it was all over. I was wrong: it could happen and it did happen – and under the right circumstances it would happen again.

The hours of darkness passed slowly. A deep heavy silence fell over the camp, broken only by the sobbing of the man involved in the accidental shooting. As the night progressed, the shooter became more and more difficult to control, wanting to kill himself one minute and the next crying and asking his God for forgiveness. In the end, the medic, out of sheer desperation, gave him an injection of morphine to put him to sleep.

Gradually the sky started to lighten, the dark blue giving way to streaks of bright reds, oranges and yellows, marking the return of the sun. The bush was alive with sound as the animals, large and small, welcomed back their fiery god.

We had been promised a helicopter at first light to remove the body and the shooter. A clearing had been made in the thick bush for the helicopter to land. On one side of the clearing was the body of the dead sergeant on the other sat the shooter and the medic. It had been a long night – nobody had slept and everybody was tired and irritable. It was important that the body and the shooter be removed as quickly as possible so things could get back to normal.

The helicopter landed, kicking up a large cloud of dust and leaves, before settling on the ground. I watched as the helicopter technician jumped out, black body bag in hand. Barely three minutes later, with engines screaming, the helicopter lifted off. Thank God, I thought, things could only get better. Dead bodies are not good for morale. As I stood there watching, a strong gust of wind blew the helicopter into some large trees bordering the landing zone. Amidst flying pieces of shattered rotor blades and broken branches, the helicopter landed with a loud thud.

Things had just gone from bad to worse.

3

Shamva, Operation Hurricane, 1972

The incident that seemed to set the pattern for my career in the Rhodesian army happened in Shamva in 1972, while I was serving with Support Group RLI. Shamva was a large Rhodesian army training area situated on the banks of the Mazoe River. It was hot, rocky, semi-arid and ideal for various types of training, including live firing of mortars.

The explosion was incredibly loud. I was thrown to the ground by the force of the blast. My God, what was happening, I thought, as I lay there trying to see through the thick black cloud of dust that was thrown up by the explosion. Were we under attack? No, we could not be. We were in a safe training area miles from any terrorist activity. Running my hand over my face, trying to steady myself, I could feel that my eyebrows and lashes had been burnt off by the heat of the blast – that's how close I had been.

Struggling, I managed to sit up. I quickly ran my hands over my body, checking for any damage, but found nothing. As the ringing in my ears subsided, I began to hear moaning and cries for help. Turning towards where the cries were coming from, I still could see nothing due to the thick dust. Getting to my feet, I staggered towards the cries. Slowly, oh so slowly, the cloud of black dust started to clear and I began to take in the scene in front of me. What greeted my eyes was a scene of utter carnage, a scene straight out of hell.

I could not drag my eyes off the arm – the muscles were still twitching, the fingers still moving, but it was not attached to anybody – it was lying all by itself, at least a metre from the nearest body. It was no longer bleeding, the severed end black and burned from the heat of the blast. It was as if my eyes had zoom lenses – I could see the shattered upper arm bone sticking out, the burnt meat and skin, the hairs on the arm, the dirty finger nails. I could hear the cries and moans in the background but still I stared at the arm. It took the movement of one of the injured trying to stand to get me to drag my eyes away from the arm. Turning slowly, I took in the carnage. The 81mm mortar was still in position, upright and ready to fire. From where I was standing there appeared to be nothing wrong with it. To the right of the mortar lay the owner of the severed arm. Clutching the stump of his missing arm with his remaining good arm, he was writhing in agony, his eyes wide and staring. His face and hair were black and burnt from the heat of the blast. The only colour in his face was the white of his eyes and his wet pink mouth, from which issued a low continuous moan of agony.

As I moved forward to help, I tripped and fell. Getting to my hands and knees, I looked behind me to see what I had fallen over. There, lying still and unmoving was the body of another member of the mortar crew. His shirt was in tatters and soaked in blood. His face and arms were burned and blackened by the explosion. A quick check confirmed he was dead.

I shook my head in confusion. What the hell was going on? The shock was slowly wearing off. My brain was beginning to register what my eyes were seeing. My nose was again picking up that rich, nauseating smell – of human blood being boiled and burnt in gunpowder, a smell I was to encounter many times in the future but never got used to. Talking to myself in an effort to calm down, I looked around, trying to locate the source of the devastation. When I did I could not believe my eyes. Glancing again at the upright mortar, I stared in disbelief: halfway down the barrel was a huge hole that could only have been caused by a high-explosive bomb exploding in the barrel. I had found the cause of the death and destruction that I was standing in the middle of.

✄

"FIRE!" I screamed at the mortar line. An hour and a half later, the training was back in full swing. The dead and wounded had been uplifted to the nearest hospital and we were back with the remaining mortars, firing live ammunition as if nothing had happened. Our boss, Ron Reid-Daly, was a hard man.

4
Tete Province, Mozambique, 1972

I was back in Support Group of the Rhodesian Light Infantry. I was a corporal. Three other members and I made up the patrol, one of several in the area. We were north of the Zambezi River in Tete Province, Mozambique, searching for a Rhodesian aircraft that had been shot down by Frelimo.[1]

The aircraft had been on a reconnaissance mission, trying to locate a Rhodesian terrorist base, when it had come under fire. Fortunately, the pilot had managed to send his position before crashing. The bush was extremely thick, with large rocky outcrops, some the size of small mountains. Each of these rocky outcrops was thickly wooded with massive trees and thick undergrowth, an ideal place for a base for terrorists wanting to infiltrate the northern part of Rhodesia. The area was completely untouched with no roads and no sign of civilization. The only people in the area were Frelimo, and a scattering of locals, who were firm supporters of the movement. I doubt if any Portuguese had ever set foot in the area.

Dressed in the normal shorts, T-shirt, and takkies (tennis shoes), carrying five days' food on our backs, armed with our 7.62 FN rifles and several high-explosive and smoke grenades, we started the search for the missing aircraft and its pilots. As the area was completely undeveloped, the only way of moving around to check for the missing plane and crew was along paths made by wild animals, the locals and Frelimo.

Due to the size of the patrol, the thickness of the bush and limited routes, we proceeded very cautiously, stopping often to listen. The last thing I needed to do was walk into an ambush. After several hours of moving along the path at a snail's pace, taking turns walking at the front, and slightly ahead of the following patrol to avoid being ambushed, the tension began to mount.

The countryside we were moving through was breathtakingly beautiful, with massive trees, huge rocks and thick undergrowth. Every now and again the path would lead us into a clearing devoid of undergrowth, circular in shape,

---

1 *Frente de Libertação de Moçambique*, Front for the Liberation of Mozambique

surrounded by large rocks with the gigantic trees forming the roof. It was like entering an ancient cathedral – the silence was eerie yet at the same time menacing. It was the sort of place where at night you might expect to see old men dressed in long white robes, complete with white beards, dancing around a fire chanting, carrying out strange and mysterious rituals. The grandeur, the imposing size, the silence, all reminded me of Stonehenge in England.

We had been on the move for several hours, during which time we had neither seen nor heard anything to indicate the presence of locals or Frelimo. All the tracks on the path, both animal and human, were several days old. The silence was becoming unbearable and walking in front of the patrol to avoid being ambushed was starting to take its toll. The occasional bird's call sounded alarmingly loud in the awful nerve-wracking silence. It was amazing, the countryside was untouched, sparsely populated with plenty of water, yet we had not seen or heard any wild animals. It was as if everything had gone into hiding, and worst of all was the feeling of being watched.

To stop the bitching that had now started, brought on by the strange, alien conditions that we were working in, plus to try and shake the feeling of being watched, I decided to leave the path we were following. Looking at my map during one of our many listening stops, I noticed a river running parallel to the path that we were following, heading basically in the direction I wanted to go. I also needed to get out from under the huge trees. I needed to try and pinpoint my position, but following the path under the huge trees where I could only see about ten metres in front of me I had no chance.

The map indicated that the river I intended to follow was about four hundred metres to the west of the path we were on. Calling the patrol together, I explained my new plan to them. The plan was greeted with "Thank fuck", "Let's get off this fucking path", "This place gives me the creeps – it's so damn quiet it reminds me of a cemetery!"

Twenty minutes later I was not so sure my decision had been a good one. Now that we were no longer protected from the fierce sun by the trees, the sweating had started, accompanied by the dreaded mopane flies, and all manner of biting and stinging insects. The bush was unbelievably thick and the going was very slow. To make matters worse, there were large patches of stinging nettles and buffalo beans. Dressed only in shorts and T-shirts, we had no protection against either. The pain inflicted by the stinging nettles was intense. The sting inflicted more of a burn than anything else and the resulting blisters were extremely painful and itchy. Once you started scratching, it was difficult to stop. I have seen guys turn their legs into a bleeding, soggy mess by the continuous scratching. On top of this deteriorating situation, throw in the king of itch: the buffalo bean. The small brown buffalo bean looks completely harmless, but the itch and the tiny blisters are anything but! Once covered in the tiny hairs that cover the pod, you are doomed to hours of extreme agony.

We sounded like a herd of elephants as we made our way through the thick bush towards the river. What had previously been a few words of discontent by the members of the patrol had now turned into a full-scale bitching parade.

The "For fuck's sake, corp, where are we going? We should have stayed on the path" was slowly dying away and being replaced by moans and groans of pain as the stinging nettles and buffalo beans made their presence felt. Stumbling forward, blinded by the pain inflicted on us, harassed on every foot of our journey by the dreaded mopane flies, we headed towards the nearby river. What should have been an easy half hour's walk turned into a torturous, pain-filled hour-plus marathon. Throwing caution to the wind and giving up all pretence of trying to move quietly, cursing every inch of the way, we stumbled forward.

The going was difficult as our rifle barrels and webbing were continually being caught up in the thick undergrowth. Tripping and falling over vines and creepers was commonplace, as was the cursing and swearing that followed. After what seemed a lifetime, we arrived at a clearing and there before us was the river. The relief was immense as we collapsed on the ground, all the pain and frustration of the last hour temporarily forgotten. It wasn't long before the pain of the stinging nettles and the agonizing itch of the buffalo beans reinstated themselves and the moans and groans began again.

We all looked the worse for wear. The large, red, burning, itchy welts on our legs and arms caused by the stinging nettles had now become patches of raw bleeding meat due to the non-stop scratching. The tiny blisters inflicted by the buffalo beans, mainly on our faces and necks, were dealt with in the same way: scratched until our faces and necks also had large areas of missing skin from which blood slowly oozed.

We had a medic pack which contained a drip, one ampoule of morphine, a syringe, some headache tablets, a lot of bandages and one tube of antiseptic cream. Nothing that could ease the agonizing discomfort we were now suffering. Looking at the pain etched faces of the members of the patrol, I racked my brains trying to come up with a solution, a method, a plan, call it what you will, to end or at least ease our suffering.

The burning and itch caused by the stinging nettles, I knew from experience, would fade away after a couple of hours. The buffalo beans, however, were a different story. I also knew from experience that the painful itch could last up to eighteen hours.

Then I remembered when I had walked into buffalo beans before, and had spent a whole day and night scratching open the little blisters and rubbing salt water into my raw flesh, trying to get rid of the itch. Whether the salt water worked or not, who knows, but it seemed to help. A couple of days later while on patrol I met an old black man who, upon looking at my face, legs and arms, asked what happened.

"Buffalo beans," I explained. I could see he was trying very hard to keep a straight face, but he suggested the next time I had an encounter with the dreaded bean I should head for the nearest water, completely remove my clothing and scrub my entire body with either sand or mud. This, he assured me, was the only foolproof way of dealing with the tiny hairs. I looked at my fellow sufferers who had large areas of missing skin on their legs and arms from which oozed a pink watery blood, swollen faces, some so bad that the eyes appeared closed. God, we looked like survivors of a phosphorus attack.

Getting to my feet, I walked to where the other three men of our four-man patrol were sitting, to tell them what the old black man had told me about handling buffalo beans. The closer I got, the worse they looked. A line from the Bible came to mind: "And the Lord smote Job with boils" – for basically pissing him off! What had we done wrong that he hit us with buffalo beans, stinging nettles, mopane flies and brain-boiling heat all at the same time? Squatting down in front of my patrol, I explained to them the advice the old man had given me. My suggestion that we all took turns in scrubbing ourselves down in the nearby river with sand and mud was greeted with wide smiles and plenty of enthusiasm. At worst, we would at least get some relief from the soaring heat.

One by one we stripped down and scrubbed ourselves as best we could with sand and mud. I was taking a hell of a chance, bathing in the middle of the day in a river in a Frelimo-controlled area of Mozambique. The risk was worth it. I had considered all the facts at my disposal very carefully. The overriding fact was that if I did not solve the problem I would have to request helicopter uplift. The chances of our HQ sending out a helicopter to uplift a patrol because they were bitching about buffalo beans, stinging nettles and mopane flies were not good. On a scale of one to ten, I would say minus one! I could imagine all the laughter my request would bring, plus hundreds of comments, ranging from

"Shame, poor guy, is mommy's little boy sore?" to "Get a grip; how the hell can you ask for uplift because you are itchy?" So I had no choice. There were three men on guard, while one bathed. It was a slow, time-consuming exercise, but well worth the effort.

A couple of hours later, all shiny and new, dripping with water from our freshly washed shirts and shorts, we started our patrol again. We were still a bit itchy and the welts on our bleeding legs and arms still burned, but the swelling in our faces had subsided a bit. Overall, we were feeling a hundred-per cent better than we were three hours ago.

Sticking to the river in single file, at least ten metres apart in case of ambush, we continued our search for the missing aircraft and the two pilots. Never deviating more than a metre or two, I religiously followed the river. I would rather take on a Frelimo ambush than have another encounter with the stinging nettles and buffalo beans.

Time passed ever so slowly – walking up a slimy, boulder-strewn river was not the easiest of tasks. You had to try to look where you were walking without tripping and falling, as well as keeping an eye out for the Frelimo and their ZANLA[2] comrades. We also had to look for any signs of an aircraft crash, which was impossible with only one set of eyes. It wasn't long before the clang of rifle barrels against the rocks, the splash of bodies falling and the accompanying swearing broke the silence. "Please God," I thought, "no broken bones … please." New cuts and bruises were added to the already painful ones.

The scenery was beautiful – the massive trees and rocks, the crystal-clear streams, the outcrops of pure coal jutting out into the river, sure signs that we were miles from the nearest so-called civilized outpost. Beautiful and clean as it was, among all the swearing and clanging of rifles, you still had the feeling you were being watched. The whole area had a strange medieval feel to it, a deep brooding silence. We had seen no animals, only heard the occasional bird and all the tracks were several days old.

Towards evening, we finally came across a path crossing the river. It was what I had been looking for: to leave the river without having to face the stinging nettles and buffalo beans again. It was getting dark and the mosquitoes were starting to take over from the mopane flies, eager to do their bit in making our stay as miserable as possible. The last thing I wanted was to spend the night perched on some rocks in the river, fighting off the hordes of mosquitoes.

Leaving the river, we made our way along the path, spread as far apart as before in case of ambush. I was looking for a break in the thick undergrowth that I could use to leave the path to look for a suitable place to base up for the night.

Once again, I had that strange feeling of being watched, as the orange light from the setting sun filtered through the leaves and branches of the trees and that same brooding, sullen silence that I had felt before seemed to settle over the area. As we moved along the path, I could see by the body language of the rest of the patrol that I was not the only one affected by the eerie silence that had descended. Our stiff, taut bodies, jerky head movements and constant flexing of hands holding the weapons, all told their own story.

As mentioned, in Africa the sun sets quickly and there are no long periods of twilight. I needed to find a way to leave the path, and quickly. The other members of the patrol were already bitching; not that I could blame them, as it had been a long hard day. Taking my turn at walking up front, nervous and sweaty, with my imagination running wild, I was seeing things where there was nothing. Several times I nearly opened fire on what I thought were terrorists. The strange filtered orange light, together with the silence was having an effect. I needed to get off the path as quickly as possible otherwise a shooting match was going to break out between us and the shadows. And then there it was – just what I had been looking for – a slight break in the undergrowth.

Stopping and signalling to the rest of the patrol to close up, I just hoped that the break I had spotted did not end in a solid wall of bush after the first couple of metres. Leading the way, I moved forward with a sense of urgency: it was getting dark and I needed to find a safe place to base up as far as possible from the path. It was going to be a long night. We were still suffering from the stinging nettles and buffalo beans, and to add to our misery we were now being attacked by thousands of mosquitoes. The *yyyyynnn* being raised by the beating of countless wings would have drowned out the sound of a jumbo jet flying twenty thousand feet above us. "Shit!" I said. "We must have really pissed off the gods." After all we had suffered during the day, I figured we were due a break, but no – now the mosquitoes had arrived to torment us.

Half an hour later it was dark and we could no longer see ten feet in front of us, so I decided to call a halt to the proceedings. Enough was enough. We were going to sleep exactly where we were standing. It was dangerous walking at night and was something I only did when I had no other option. Collapsing in a pile of aching, bruised, burning muscles, I tried to relax. It was not to be – the mosquitoes descended on us like a pack of starving wild dogs. Some patrol members had brought along insect repellent, which they now applied in vast amounts, commenting at the same time how smart they were in bringing the stuff in the first place and that they would be rewarded with a good night's sleep. Pleas from me and the other patrol member who had also failed to bring any repellent fell on deaf ears. Covering myself as best I could with my sleeping bag, I got ready for a long night. There was no need to post a guard as we were not going to sleep, not with the hordes of mosquitoes attacking us, not to mention the hundreds of other biting, stinging insects that considered human flesh a delicacy.

It was not long before the two members of the patrol who had covered themselves in insect repellent started muttering about how useless the product was. According to them, applying the repellent to their already raw legs and arms, courtesy of the stinging nettles and buffalo beans, was like holding a burning match to the affected areas and, to make matters worse, it had no effect on the marauding mosquitoes.

It was a long night. Our only protection against the attacking insects was our sleeping bags. However, this too had its down side. Due to the heat, the time spent in the sleeping bag was limited to fifteen or twenty minutes before your body screamed for the fresh and relatively cooler air outside. The night was endless. The paltry light put out by the stars seemed to add a silvery sheen to the huge trees and their branches. It would have made an ideal setting for a horror movie. Apart from the swearing and slapping to remind me where I was, I could I have been on another planet, in another universe.

Slowly but surely it started getting light, and with the light came the departure of the mosquitoes and many of their creeping, crawling, biting comrades. I felt terrible and looked even worse, as did the rest of the patrol. The swelling around our eyes had subsided but all the raw flesh on our legs and arms, now more black than red, was still wet and still oozing a watery red fluid.

Crouching over our small gas stoves, we started cooking our breakfast. There was no set menu; it was every man for himself. I settled on a cup of hot sweet tea and a couple of mouthfuls of bully beef. Thirty minutes later were on the move. The oldest member of the patrol had just turned twenty but, from a distance, anybody observing would have thought that we were a group of old-age pensioners as we hobbled along trying to get the stiffness out of our muscles, with our arms waving around in a futile attempt to keep the mopane flies at bay.

We eventually found the plane. Not on the ground where we thought it would be but hanging, high off the ground, in some massive trees. The green painted aircraft was perfectly camouflaged and impossible to see from the air. Looking up at the aircraft, it was impossible to tell whether the two pilots were still inside or not. Once again I was struck by the size of trees in the area, the biggest I have ever seen. The aircraft looked like a model, small and insignificant. On closer inspection, I realized it was a Trojan, the Rhodesian name for the Italian Aermacchi AL-60. It was slow, clumsy and noisy and a death trap for the pilot if used in the combat role. Every time I saw one attempt a take-off and succeed, I shook my head in wonder. The age of miracles was still with us. In my opinion, the only thing they should have been used for was relaying messages: anything else was a no go. I would always wonder what had actually caused the aircraft to crash. It would not have been difficult to shoot down, as it could be heard miles away. Flying fairly low because of the thick bush or doing a re-run of the area to confirm something they had seen, it had flown into a hail of bullets, resulting in the aircraft hitting the trees. The only other reasons I could think of were engine failure or pilot error. But the reason for the crash was no longer important: locating the two pilots was.

There seemed to be no bodies in the aircraft. Maybe they had survived the crash and had been taken captive by the Frelimo. The other possibility was that they had been thrown clear on impact and were lying nearby in the thick undergrowth, dead or perhaps alive but injured. Checking the area, no fresh tracks were found but what appeared to be a grave was discovered. It had been dug in the soft ground next to a small slow-flowing steam, no more than ten metres from the base of the gigantic trees where the aircraft was hanging.

Sentries posted, we hoped against hope that it did not contain the bodies of the missing pilots, but we decided to investigate. With shaking hands, the trials and tribulations of the previous day and night forgotten, we slowly and carefully started clearing away the soil from the top of the mound. The silence was frightening: you could have heard a pin drop. The only sound I could hear was that of the sand being gently scraped off the top of the mound. It sounded incredibly loud, like waves breaking on the shore during a storm out at sea, blocking out all other sounds.

Gently, oh so gently, with dirty hands still shaking, sweaty brows and straining eyes, we continued to shift the soil. Nobody said a word. All eyes were firmly fixed on the mound of sand in front of us.

It seemed as if hours had passed but I am sure it was no more than fifteen minutes before the first piece of clothing was uncovered. It was buried thirty centimetres below the surface and appeared to be the sleeve of a flying suit. All digging stopped as we stared in fascination at the protruding piece of clothing, unable to tear our eyes away. We all knew what it meant but nobody said a word.

"For fuck's sake!" said as only a soldier can say it, full of anger, fear, love, hate, compassion, sorrow and respect, broke the silence. The spell was broken. Before informing our HQ of our gruesome discovery, we had to confirm that both bodies were, in fact, in the grave. After a short break, we returned to the graveside and continued with our task of uncovering the bodies. The heat was intense and there was no breeze of any kind. It was like working in a steam bath, with the sweat pouring off in buckets as we pressed on with our grim task. Slowly but surely, as more and more soil was removed from the grave, the two bodies started to take shape. As we dug deeper, the sand slowly turned to mud. I do not know if the wet soil had helped preserve the bodies or speeded up the decaying process. The bodies had been buried no more than two to three days and were already starting to decay.

Barely detectable at the outset but now in the hot still air, the smell of rotting flesh was becoming overpowering. The decaying bodies were difficult to remove from the shallow grave. The skin had already started to rot and was extremely slippery. Every time you tried to use an exposed arm or leg to try and lever the bodies from the grave, you ended up with a handful of rotten, evil-smelling skin. Luckily for us, the flesh under the rotting skin was still firm as the maggots had not yet arrived. If we had found the bodies a week later we would have had to use shovels to put them in a body bag.

It was slow, back-breaking work and the smell, combined with the heat, did not help. Volunteers were hard to find. One look at the bodies, the smell and the peeling skin was enough to make most of the search party puke. As I continued to help with the disinterment, I could not help but wonder about who had buried these bodies, or why, and that they had not been left in the open to rot or get eaten by wild animals. Had the locals found and buried the bodies? Why? Because they feared reprisals from the Rhodesian security forces if the bodies were found? Or was it Frelimo, burying the bodies for the same reason as the locals? Or was it done out of respect for the dead, the Christian thing to do? I hoped it was the latter.

Several hours later, after much swearing and cursing, both bodies were ready to be transported back to Rhodesia. It had taken much longer to get the corpses into the bags than I thought. The slippery, rotten skin, the rubbery flesh that seemed to have a will of its own, the smell, the dead weight, had all contributed to making what should have been a simple job into a nightmare.

The helicopter used to uplift the bodies also dropped a quantity of plastic explosive. This was then used to blow up the aircraft so that it could not be used for propaganda purposes or to prove that the Rhodesian army was operating in Mozambique. Later in the war, nobody worried about things like that but this was still early days and politicians will be politicians.

During the entire rescue mission we had not seen or heard any Frelimo. The same applied to their Rhodesian comrades, ZANLA. That they were there is no doubt but why they did not attack us? Who knows.

I was to return to the same area many months later and be hunted by Frelimo using dogs.

5

Mukumbura, Mozambican border, 1973

It was about four o'clock in the afternoon, and we were waiting for a helicopter to come and uplift Captain Reid-Daly. It seemed as if we had been running forever. Taking great gulps of warm air, I tried to supply my lungs with the oxygen they demanded, my heart thudding loud in my ears; it had been a very long, hot, strenuous morning. Leaning back against a mopane tree with a cigarette in my mouth in a futile attempt to chase away the mopane flies, I took stock of myself.

Missing large areas of skin on my legs, arms and face, into which poured a never-ending burning stream of salty sweat, it was painful to say the least. Added to this the raw weeping rings of fire around my calves and ankles courtesy of the stinging nettles, and you could say I had definitely seen better days. Dressed in shorts, T-shirt and vellies,[1] armed with a 7.62 FN rifle and five full magazines, wearing full webbing and carrying five days' rations, we were cumbersome and slow compared to the Frelimo we were trying to chase down, who, at the best of times, carried no more than an AK-47 and a magazine or two.

We had crossed into Mozambique six or seven hours earlier, led by Captain Ron Reid-Daly, complete with a black briefcase. Why he carried a black briefcase, who knows. I never asked but it was something I would never forget. An ex-RSM, the Regimental Sergeant-Major of the RLI, and no fan of Rambo, he was dressed like he was going on parade. He wore camouflage trousers and a beautifully ironed shirt, complete with creases, his boots gleamed in the early morning sun, his bush hat had been starched and pressed so many times it appeared to be made of cardboard. There would be no shorts, T-shirt and vellies for him. If he was going to get his arse shot off, he was going to look smart while it was happening.

A village in the area had been attacked by Frelimo and the Portuguese

---

1   *Veldskoene* (Afrik), lit. bush shoes

authorities had asked for assistance. Our task was simple: locate the perpetrators and eliminate them. The area where we were operating was flat, crisscrossed by numerous, mainly dry rivers. It was thickly wooded in places with extremely thick undergrowth along the rivers. It was also the home of the mopane fly and the stinging nettle. The whole area was sparsely populated due to the lack of water. Paths were few and far between, generally running from one village to the next. Finding the tracks was not difficult.

Having little or no respect for the Portuguese as a fighting man, the group of Frelimo, after burning the village to the ground, had headed north on the same path they had used to get to their target. The heat was energy-sapping and the danger of heat fatigue was ever present, the undergrowth thick and alive with stinging nettles. Sticking to the book, we deployed in extended line with the trackers in the centre on the tracks, followed by Captain Reid-Daly, weapon in one hand, briefcase in the other. Hampered by the thick undergrowth, progress was slow: the trackers, who needed the protection of the following troops, could only move along the tracks at a speed that enabled the following troops to keep up. We were new at follow-ups; in years to come we would line up in single file behind the trackers and run on the tracks, only deploying into extended line when coming under fire.

Making enough noise to wake the dead and ignoring the burning, stinging nettles, the continual rivers of sweat pouring into our eyes and having to compete for space with the ever-present mopane flies, we cursed, kicked and fought our way through the thick undergrowth trying to keep up with the tracking team. We were about to have a smoke break when several shots cracked over our heads. We all froze. We did not know what to do. For most of us, this was the first time we had been fired at in anger. Doing what comes naturally, we hit the ground and waited. Nothing happened. There were no more shots, just an expectant silence, as if nature itself was holding its breath, waiting to see what was going to happen next. Getting up cautiously, we continued following the tracks.

The change was amazing. Ten minutes before we were walking with our heads down, eyes fixed to the ground, rifles over our shoulders, completely 'switched off' as we fought our way through the undergrowth. Now, our heads were up, our eyes as big as saucers as we darted from one clump of bushes to the next. Our weapons were held firmly, ready to return fire.

Crack, crack. Two more shots streaked over our heads. This time we did not take cover; instead, we broke out into a lurching, lumbering run. The noise was horrendous, Gas stoves clanging against gas cylinders, rifle barrels hitting magazines, tripping and falling, we must have sounded like a Russian T-54 battle tank. Glancing towards the path after one fall, I noticed that Captain Reid-Daly was now carrying the briefcase stuck out in the front of his webbing. This was the beginning of a long, hot, hard day. Frelimo were now warming to their new game. After letting us advance a few hundred metres, they would fire a couple of shots at us, and we would break into a lumbering run in an attempt to get close enough to shoot, or at least see whom we were dealing with. I can safely say we failed miserably in both. About six hours later, exhausted, bleeding from countless bruises and cuts, mopane flies driving me crazy, I still had not fired a shot.

Fascinated by Captain Reid-Daly and his briefcase, I kept an eye on him. The briefcase was constantly on the move – left hand, right hand, stuck in front of the webbing, under the shirt, never in one place for long. He looked awkward, uncomfortable and out of place. I don't know why I remember this incident so well, other than the fact that it gave me an insight into the man I was to spend most of my military career working under. Proud, wilful, unwilling to change, constantly demanding his own way, wanting to lead but only on his own terms, he was kept on a leash by the Rhodesian army hierarchy. Once free of their control, as in the case of the Transkei, with nobody to answer to, he ran amok. Maybe the shiny boots, starched trousers, shirt and bush hat say it all.

6

Operation Hurricane, Mount Darwin area, 1973

I t was hot, dark and clammy. In the distance was the sound of thunder and the occasional flash of lightning, the air alive with the sound of millions of mosquitoes, all looking for a meal. The ground was covered by an equally large amount of biting ants, dung beetles and various other unpleasant insects, all attracted to the cattle dung surrounding the cattle dip we were ambushing. According to the information we had received, two groups of terrorists were going to meet that night at the dip.

In an effort to escape both the ants and mosquitoes, we doused ourselves in strong-smelling insect repellent and used our groundsheets to cover ourselves. The night passed slowly, the silence occasionally broken by the sound of thunder in the distance, and continually by the sound of groundsheets and slapping by the members of the patrol as they fought a losing battle against the mosquitoes and ants.

Today, when I think about the noise we made, and the fact that we smelled like Salisbury's red-light district ladies of the night, I cringe. No wonder no terrorists came near the place: they could smell and hear us a mile away. We were lucky we did not get our arses shot off. But, like I said, I was young and stupid.

Around 04h00 in the morning, the rain arrived in bucket loads, accompanied by strong winds, vicious, eye-searing lightning and ground-shaking thunder. Cowering under my groundsheet trying to keep dry, I thought I heard gunshots. It was difficult to hear or see anything in what seemed like a world gone mad. The lightning struck continuously, lighting up the sky in a strange blue-white light, turning night into day. The thunder no longer rumbled, it exploded in a roar of anger as it shook the ground; the wind, determined not to be outdone, howled like a demented animal as it uprooted trees, broke branches and flattened maize fields.

After the storm abated, the silence was awesome, clean, fresh, beautiful, broken only by the distant sound of thunder. As I stood there, sopping-wet rifle in my hands, taking in the reds, yellows and oranges of an African sunrise, the silence was destroyed by a burst of automatic rifle fire. Man indulging in his favourite sport: war.

Lying on my belly in the mud and cattle dung, weapon firmly clutched in my shaking hands, I tried to determine from which direction the firing had come. Having patrolled in the area before, I knew there was a small trading store nearby. Apart from killing and raping, terrorists loved robbing and burning down trading stores, definitely one of their favourite pastimes: a real must-do for all up-and-coming terrorists.

Glancing in the direction of where I thought the store was situated, I could see a large cloud of dark smoke just above the tree line. Calling everybody together, we headed for the burning store. Headed is the right word. Like a herd of gut-shot buffalo, with no formation and no control, we huffed, puffed, tripped, fell, squished and squashed our way towards the store.

We arrived in dribs and drabs, breathing hard after our headlong rush through the bush and rain-flattened maize fields. We were lucky no terrorists were lying in ambush for us. Things could have turned very nasty if they had. The store was gutted and the terrorists long gone. After reporting the incident over the radio to my HQ, I was told to check the roads for landmines, as they were going to send in a tracking team by vehicle.

The normal terrorist tactic at that time was to mine all the roads in the immediate area of the incident, be it burning a store, killing a headman or a good old-fashioned mutilation like cutting the lips off of a so-called sell-out. They knew the Rhodesian security forces would react to the incident and, due to the shortage of helicopters, would most likely arrive by vehicle.

Standing there, smelling to high heaven in my dung-covered, mud-splattered, insect-repellent-soaked, wet uniform, I tried to recall what I had been taught about landmines. A brain-draining, mind-boggling thirty seconds later, I gave up. The only thing I could remember, and as far as I was concerned the only thing worth remembering, was that it required a couple of hundred kilograms of pressure to set it off: I was safe.

Taking one trooper with me for protection, I proceeded nervously up the road in the direction from which I knew the vehicles would be coming. It was a lovely clear morning, strangely silent, as if nature itself was in shock, still trying to recover from the fury of the earlier storm. Moving slowly, weapon at the ready, I checked the road carefully, at the same time keeping a wary eye on the flattened maize fields bordering it. Whatever signs there might have been to indicate where a landmine had been planted had been washed away by the rain, or covered by the large amount of leaves and maize plants deposited on the road by the storm. A long kilometre later, I stopped. I needed a break. My head throbbed, my eyes burned, my shoulder muscles ached and my legs were refusing to bend at the knees: all the tension and the concentration were starting to take their toll. Crouching at the side of the road, I tried to relax, get the blood to flow and the brain to work.

Two hours later, the warm sun beating down on my back, I watched the two army trucks coming down the road towards me. Old and well past their sell-by date, the old Bedford trucks made hard going of the dirt road. With engines screaming and wheels spinning, they lurched from one pothole to the next, the poor troops on the back hanging on for dear life.

"God," I thought as I watched, "some of those potholes must be at least two feet deep." Immediately, my brain started screaming: "The potholes, arsehole, the potholes – you did not check the potholes!"

On the one-kilometre road-clearing exercise, I had come across numerous potholes, some big, some small, some deep, some shallow. Being a white man I did not want to get my already soaking wet shoes wet: how stupid is that? So I walked around them. "What are you going to do?" I asked myself. "It is decision time – come, big mouth, time is running out!"

Skirting round the problem, I came to a compromise: I would walk in front, with the two vehicles following about ten or so metres behind, and I would re-check the road on our way to the burnt-out store. So, moving along at a snail's pace, with the two vehicles following, I re-checked the road, paying special attention to the potholes, checking carefully for any signs that might indicate a landmine was hidden under the water. Still, I did not get my feet wet. Talk about a half job! I have no excuses, only to say I was tired, young and stupid, none of which gave me the right to take shortcuts and put other people's lives at risk.

The closer I got to the store the more confident I became that the road had not been mined. Suddenly, my head felt like it was going to burst, I screamed in pain as I tried to cover my ears with my hands, my chest felt as if a great weight had been placed on it, as the force of the blast sucked all the oxygen from my lungs and threatened to rupture my eardrums.

As I lay there in the mud with pieces of metal, rubber and rocks falling around me, all I could think of was my weapon. It may have been shock, or refusal to face the consequences of my failure to clear the road properly, I do not know, but my whole world now revolved around finding my weapon. Crawling about on my hands and knees, among the bits of tyre and metal, searching for my weapon, I looked up, and there in front of me lying on its side, half in and half out of the now-huge pothole was the vehicle I had guided on to a landmine.

Struggling to my feet, I stared in horror at the result of my half-hearted effort to clear the road. I was lucky nobody had been killed or injured. It was an expensive way to learn, but learn I did. Never again would I take shortcuts or do a half job.

⚔

The sun struggled to burn through. The dark grey cloud reeked of gunpowder, flashes of red and yellow piercing its darkness as mortar bombs exploded with ear-shattering cracks, sending up clouds of dust and stones. Flashes from the rifle barrels indicated the whereabouts of the combatants in this game of death.

I was nineteen years old, a corporal in Support Group, the Rhodesian Light Infantry. We were operating in the Mount Darwin area in the north of the country, up towards the Mozambican border. I had spent the first two weeks of my stint in total mind-boggling, morale-destroying boredom. Apart from an early-morning run, we were left alone to stew in our own juices. With nothing to do we played volleyball, and we talked and we talked some more – all in an effort to keep our minds occupied. No matter how the conversation started, we always ended up talking about somebody who had been killed. We were together but we were also very much alone, each of us living in a world created by our own imaginations.

Night time was by far the worst, and we were restricted to two beers a night. Sleep was impossible, causing many of us to use *dagga* (marijuana) in an effort to keep control of our emotions and to help us relax. Emotionally, I was a disaster. The ten days of so-called rest and refit after every six weeks in the bush was too short to achieve anything and turned into a ten-day orgy of violence, booze and women. I did not know if I was Arthur or Martha. I was doing something that I had been taught from childhood was wrong: killing people. When I was in town I wanted to be in the bush, when in the bush I wanted to be in town. I loved the super-charged feeling of being alive, brought on by the adrenalin rush that accompanied each and every Fire Force deployment, and when I was in town I missed it more than I cared to mention.

Loaded down with five days' rations and armed with our customary FN rifles, wearing our normal shorts, T-shirts and takkies, we were patrolling by day and ambushing by night – but we had no luck. This was not surprising, considering every local in the area was a terrorist supporter, and that we had not a clue on what we were supposed to be doing. It was hit or miss: we were still learning. The ground itself was very sandy, the type found on the beach or on sand dunes, which made it difficult to tell the difference between animal and human tracks, let alone their age.

On the morning of the fourth day, we came across what appeared to be the tracks of eight to ten terrorists, crossing a road and heading towards some villages we could see in the distance. In a rush of overconfidence, they had failed to remove their shoes. The tracks were very fresh, no more than one hour old according to the tracker. With the patrol in extended line, the tracker leading, we followed the tracks. I could already feel the tension mounting and the adrenalin starting to flow; my body began to tense up and my legs became stiff and uncoordinated and I seemed to trip over the smallest of things. I could not keep my head still, my eyes were darting from one bush to the next, my rifle held in a death grip and a cold, strange-smelling sweat covered my body as I walked in to my first contact.

We had been following the tracks for about half an hour when the tracker stopped and indicated that I should join him. As I ran forward, I indicated to the troops on my left and right to lie down. We had stopped in a newly ploughed mealie (maize) field, out in the open, sticking out like dog's balls. How we had not already been seen, either by the locals or the terrorists, I will never know. Upon reaching the tracker, he pointed to small, thickly wooded river, fifty metres to our front, as the spot where the terrorists were based. Just on the other side of the river was a village that would supply the group with everything they needed from food to young girls for sex. The fifty metres between us and the terrorist base was open, ploughed ground. Decision time had arrived: how to cover the last fifty metres without alerting the terrorists or the locals to our presence.

We were about five metres from the trees when we heard somebody in the terrorist camp shouting. I couldn't understand what he was saying; maybe it was the sentry alerting his fellow terrorists to our presence. Suddenly, there were bullets everywhere, some going over our heads, some hitting the ground in front of us.

With my body pressed pancake-thin against the ground, with branches and leaves raining down, staring through the grey dust cloud with burning eyes, I no longer thought I was bulletproof. This was completely different to what I had expected. This was nothing like we had talked and bragged about when drunk in the nightclubs back in Salisbury. I always had visions of firing from the hip, jumping effortlessly over cover and mowing down the enemy by the hundreds – a bulletproof hero.

We sprinted forward to the trees, took cover, and started returning fire. As I lay there firing, peering through the dust, shooting into positions where I thought the terrorists were hiding, I felt no emotion whatsoever. The training had taken over. I did what I had been trained to do. I had practised this a thousand times before, now it came naturally and easily, no need to think. Suddenly the crack of bullets passing overhead was drowned out by the sharp thump of exploding 60mm mortar rounds.

Out of the corner of my eye I saw a member of my patrol kneeling behind a large tree. He was firing into the terrorist camp when a mortar bomb exploded no more than five metres to the left of him. As he fell, I thought that he had to be dead. The explosion was so close that he surely could not have survived.

"Medic!" I screamed.

The noise was unreal: the sharp crack of the AK-47 rifles used by the terrorists, the answering solid thump of our FN rifles, the ear-shattering bursts of fire from the machine gun and the deadly thumps of exploding mortar bombs. The contact area was enveloped in a cloud of dust caused mainly by the exploding mortar bombs. Visibility was down to a few metres.

"Medic!" I screamed again, and out of the dust appeared Lance-Corporal van der Walt, our troop medic, combat cap missing, glasses all cockeyed, rifle in one hand, medic bag in the other, sprinting like a bat out hell towards the injured patrol member. How he made it, I do not know, but he did. A few minutes later he gave me the thumbs-up, indicating all was well.

Gradually everything quietened down. A strange silence settled over the area. Shafts of sunlight from the early morning sun pierced the grey canopy of dust, lighting up the interior. The strange yellow-blue light reflecting from tree to tree, twisting and turning on the still, slowly rising dust, created a beautiful, almost mystical scene, turning a place of death into a place of beauty.

Through the thick dust I could see the guys to my left and right not more than two metres away. Shouting as loud as I could, I managed to get out a 'Prepare to advance' command. Slowly, everybody got to their feet and moved forward, weapons at the ready, towards the terrorist camp. My throat was dry, my eyes, red and burning, feeling as if they were going to pop out of my throbbing head. Still in extended line, we swept forward through the camp. It was well used, I noted, no more than 400 metres from the main road. Plenty of overhead cover made it difficult to spot from the air. Only one path led in and there was nothing at all to indicate the presence of a terrorist camp.

The adrenalin was wearing off: I felt very tired and light-headed and my entire body ached. I felt as if I had just run a marathon. I looked around, trying to figure out what to do next. Somewhere in the back of my mind I knew I should send a search party back into the terrorist camp to search for bodies and documents, but at that point I felt it was far more important to check on the welfare of my own men.

Dragging myself to my feet, I went along the skirmish line, checking to see if everybody was in one piece. I did not get far before the radio came alive: "Hello Eight One [my call sign], "give us a situation report. Did you copy, over?" I knew if I did not respond I would get no peace. Sitting down, I leaned my weapon against a tree, took off my backpack and pulled out the map that I carried in the front of my shirt. It was wet from my sweat and dirty from all the dust. Calling my radio operator across, I detailed a search party to check the area. One of the first things my HQ would want to know was the number of terrorists killed. In the Rhodesian Light Infantry, as in most units in the Rhodesian army, there was fierce competition between the different companies, or in the case of the Rhodesian Light Infantry, Commandos, as to who had killed the most terrorists.

Gathering the required information, I sent a situation report to my HQ, after which I continued my walk around, checking to see if everyone was alright. I ended up at the thin tree I had taken cover behind. God, it was so thin I might as well have lain in the open with no cover at all! Three to four metres in front of the position where I had been lying was a large tree, at the base of which were many bullet holes, most of which, I am sure, were mine. I can remember seeing the barrel of a weapon sticking out the side of the tree when I took cover. I was already firing at the base of the tree before I hit the ground, hence all the bullet holes. I took a walk across to the tree to see if I had managed to do any damage to whoever had been hiding behind it. Nothing – no body, no blood – whoever had been lying there had escaped unharmed.

Walking over to where the terrorist bodies were lying, I could not help but notice the smell. It was a smell I would never forget. The combination of unwashed bodies, drying blood, wood smoke and body fluids, all baking in the hot sun, put out a smell that was sweet but nauseating, very similar to the smell around abattoirs.

Taking a closer look at the bodies, I noticed that the faces were of youngsters similar in age to mine: nineteen. I wondered what promises had been made to them when they were convinced to join the ranks of ZANLA. In the distance, I could hear the beat of the approaching helicopter coming to remove the bodies and take the trooper wounded by the mortar bomb back to base for further treatment.

7
Fire Force: Mount Darwin, 1973

Ignoring the high-pitched scream of the engine, the sand blown up from the rotor blades blasting painfully into my face, I concentrated on the helicopter pilot, awaiting the boarding signal which was normally a simple thumbs-up. Barely thirty seconds later, we were lifting off – one of four helicopters. Sitting half in and half out of the helicopter, directly behind the pilot, I tried not to think. With a stupid, sickly grin on my face, I stared with watering eyes, unseeingly at the countryside as it flashed past barely metres below my feet.

The sound of the engine, the buffeting wind and my churning stomach all brought a sense of reality to the otherwise, unreal, detached feeling I was experiencing. Glancing at the other three members of my stick, it was like looking in a mirror: they all had the same sickly grin and the same faraway look in their eyes.

I hit the ground crouched and running, ignoring the clouds of red dust and flying debris thrown up by the huge main rotor blades of the helicopter, and headed for a nearby hollow in the ground. There was not much cover available. Apart from the odd clump of trees and a small anthill, there was nothing. Overgrazed and over-farmed, what few trees there once were had been cut down for firewood, and the area now resembled a red-earthed, grassless football field.

The contact was like the jungle lane we practised time and time again, only this time, the pop-up and moving targets were live human beings. Ten minutes later it was all over. Lying in the hollow with the rest of my four-man stick, I stared at the dead bodies twenty metres in front of me. I felt absolutely nothing. No sorrow at having killed another human being, no pride and no happiness in having killed an enemy of my country, nothing, just emptiness. The feelings of guilt, anger, loneliness, the outbursts of violence, the bouts of depression, would come many years later, when my mind, no longer able to handle the pressure and uncertainty, would start to tear itself apart.

A strange motionless silence descended on the contact area. There was no breeze, no birds, and no movement; even with the helicopter circling overhead it was strangely still and silent. Already the flies were arriving in their thousands. Trying hard to stop my hands from shaking, and breathing through my mouth, I helped search the bodies of the terrorists we had killed. The rich, sweet, cloying smell of fresh blood, mixed with the smell of unwashed bodies, urine, sweat and faeces, was all-pervasive. Thick and heavy, it was impossible to breathe without retching.

The grass was waist-high. In extended line, we were doing one last sweep of the contact area before returning to the terrorist base for uplift back to Mount Darwin. The adrenalin rush was a thing of the past, my body stiff and uncoordinated. My legs refused to bend at the knees as I kept stumbling over the smallest of obstacles. I was nervous and sweating, my eyes never still. My hands clasped my weapon like a vice, with fingers opening and closing in an effort to stimulate the blood flow.

I stopped. I stared. I froze. No more than ten metres in front of me was a terrorist. Like a jack-in-the-box, he had popped up from the long grass. My FN seemed to weigh a ton and it took me forever to get the butt into my shoulder.

Staring down the barrel, both eyes open, I was about to pull the trigger when the terrorist took a shuddering step backwards. The dirty white of his shirt turned dark brown and he disappeared back into the grass. A split second later the sound of two shots split the silence, echoing in the surrounding hills. I had been tense, my nerves stretched to breaking point before the sudden appearance of the terrorist. Now I was one raw, sweating nerve end. I could not stop the jerky movement of my head as my eyes tried to see everywhere at once. My trembling hands gripped my weapon so tightly that my knuckles were white, my whole body taut, my muscles stiff and unresponsive, making it difficult to keep up with the advancing patrol.

It was like flushing pheasant. The first terrorist had caught us by surprise but the next two never stood a chance. Twisting and turning under the impact of numerous rounds, they were dead before they even had a chance to stand upright or fire a shot. God, they were so young. Their bullet-riddled bodies were piled one on top of the other, like dead animals. Sixteen, seventeen years old, most of them were young boys. There was also the occasional young girl – civilians, unarmed and caught in the terrorist camp, they never stood a chance. Innocent civilians caught in the crossfire? Innocent? You decide.

Off to one side were the bodies of the dead terrorists. Slightly older, but dressed in similar clothes to their civilian counterparts, they blended in, just like fish in water, as the little red book puts it. In the heat of battle, it would be impossible to distinguish between terrorist and civilian, thereby ensuring both would die.

With eyes fixed on the feet of the man running in front of me, still unable to get over how young the dead had been, I began another day on Fire Force.

✂

I was bleeding like a stuck pig. I had left a good portion of my skin and a pound or two of flesh plus a gallon or so of blood behind in the ravine that I had just climbed out of. Resting under a stunted, leafless thorn tree, dressed in my normal shorts, T-shirt and takkies, armed with an FN and wearing my webbing with five extra magazines, I looked around me.

The entire area, as far as I could see, was covered in a shimmering blanket of heat. It was overgrazed by thousands of goats, the flat, red ground devoid of any vegetation: apart from the occasional stunted thorn tree, it resembled a football field. How the locals from the nearby village survived in this waterless wasteland was beyond me, never mind supplying a group of terrorists based in the area with food and water.

Waiting for instructions from the over-flying helicopter, I dug into my soaking wet shirt pocket and found a somewhat damp, crumpled packet of smokes and lit up.

He was close enough to touch, stuck half way up the thorn bush, young, clothes dirty and torn, eyes wide, mouth agape, breathing heavily as he tried to untangle his weapon from the numerous branches and get it pointing in my direction. This was my second call-out in two days. My nerves were stretched to breaking point, the slightest sound enough to make me take cover. My rifle lifted, I stuck the barrel in his face – all I had to do was pull the trigger.

Thirty minutes before, I had been about to light up another cigarette when the radio on my back had come to life. It was time to move on. There was no breeze. The blinding white heat was a physical force, battering your senses, draining your strength and destroying your willpower. Standing up was a mission, never mind walking. Standing on the edge of the hollow to which the helicopter had guided us, nervous as a sixteen-year-old on her first date, in extended line, sweaty hands holding our weapons at the ready, ears straining to pick up the faintest of sounds, eyes straining to penetrate the grey mass of stunted thorn bush, we had slowly moved forward.

Cursing, heads down, sounding like a herd of drunken elephants, we had fought our way through the thorn trees. It had been the sun glinting off the barrel of his AK-47 that had caught my attention. Now looking into his wide, bleeding eyes, noting the tautness of his body braced for the impact of the bullet, I hesitated. It was one thing killing a person shooting at you from a distance, another to kill someone face to face. A prisoner is always useful: information wins wars, I muttered, trying to justify not killing him.

Part II
Selous Scouts, 1975–80

8

Selection course: Kariba, 1975

The Selous Scouts' selection was run in an extremely isolated area on the shores of Lake Kariba, with no other human beings for miles around. The selection course was broken down into two phases. The first phase was the actual selection of likely future leaders of pseudo groups, which was much needed in the ever-expanding Rhodesian bush war. The second phase dealt with terrorist tactics and personalities that were covered in great detail, from how to set up a terrorist base camp to the name of the nurse in charge of the hospital in the training camp in Mozambique where you were supposedly trained. Great importance was attached to the names of various terrorist detachment commanders and their politically trained second-in-commands, the all-powerful political commissars. Attention to detail was what it was all about. Letter-writing was the chosen medium by terrorist groups to make contact with each other. What was written in the letter sealed your fate: you were either accepted as a real terrorist or rejected as a sell-out, depending on the contents of the letter. The majority of the 'dark phase' training was conducted by ex-terrorists who were vital to the success of Selous Scouts as a whole, be it in the training or operational sectors.

The selection course run for the Transkei Special Forces, on the other hand, was conducted in a heavily populated area, where there is nowhere with little or no population. Every square inch of ground capable of supporting life is ploughed and planted with maize. The thicker, isolated areas of bush unsuitable for maize are planted with *dagga*, or 'Transkei gold'. It was extremely difficult to run a selection course of any kind in these circumstances, especially for a Special Forces unit.

The Kariba climate is extreme, with temperatures reaching the high forties in summer and barely less in winter. The array of biting, stinging insects is mind-boggling, never mind the lions, hippos, leopards, crocodiles and elephants that occupy the area. Throw in several instructors with unlimited power and you have a selection course designed in hell.

To pass this type of no-holds-barred selection you had to be very strong, both mentally and physically; you also needed to be a good all-round soldier.

The aim of the exercise was to weed out the weak and the unsuitable. If you could not work alongside black soldiers, no matter how fit you were or how good a soldier you were, you would fail. The fact that eighty per cent of Selous Scouts was black speaks for itself.

*

It was extremely hot sitting in the back of the old truck. We had left Salisbury, the capital of Rhodesia, several hours earlier, on our way to Lake Kariba and the Selous Scouts' selection-course camp situated on its shores. On the way down there had been a lot of nervous laughter, poor jokes and statements along the lines of "It can't be that bad: so and so made it – and he's a complete arsehole!", "After our recruit course, this will be a piece of piss", "Who cares if there's no food – the lake is full of fish" and "I brought plenty of fishing line and hooks. Yeah, we can always steal food from the instructors".

However, as we turned off the main tar road onto a narrow dirt road, all horseplay stopped. The moment of truth had arrived. Due to all the potholes in the road that we were now on, the trucks were reduced to a crawl. We no longer had the speed of the truck to create a breeze to cool us down. The new, slower speed was, in fact, causing suction at the back of the truck and vacuuming up all the dust churned up by the huge tyres. It was not long before we were all covered by a thick layer of red dust. Along with the dust came the inevitable mopane flies, Chewore buzzards and the heat.

With no breeze whatsoever to cool us down, covered in thick, red dust and travelling at a snail's pace, it was not long before the intense heat had us all sweating. The drive seemed to last forever, from one pothole to the next, the mopane flies constantly harassing us, getting into our eyes and ears, and, if you took a deep breath, down your throat. This was complemented by a sharp, burning sensation every time a Chewore buzzard paid you a visit. I figured if I could survive the ride I had a chance of surviving the selection course. Looking around at my travelling companions, I saw in some faces doubt, in others anger and, in a few, a quiet confidence and a determination to handle whatever came their way, no matter what. It was nearing midday and we were still bouncing along at a steady five kilometres an hour. The driver seemed determined not to miss any potholes whatsoever. We were sweating buckets: we looked like we had been standing in a shower. After what seemed forever, the truck in front ground to a halt.

Peering through the dust with swollen, bloodshot eyes, I could dimly make out the shape of an open Land Rover. As the dust cleared, I could see six people, dressed in camouflage shorts and T-shirts, each holding an AK-47 assault rifle. These were obviously the instructors. Wasting no time, they shouted for us to debus and fall in, in one straight line, complete with all our kit. All one hundred and eight of us debussed. About fifteen of us were whites from the various white units, mainly the RLI, the remainder black troops from the Rhodesian African Rifles.

We had heard rumours about the run from the drop-off point to the actual course camp, and that whatever you had brought with you from base had to be carried on your back. This would be a run of maybe ten to fifteen kilometres. The run itself would be bad enough in the extreme heat, what with carrying all your kit but add a log and it would become a killer. Some of us listened to the stories, others did not. Some of us decided to bring minimum kit, only what we could fit into our packs, others brought two packs and some even brought their steel trunks packed to the top with food and cigarettes.

A friend and I, sharing a fairly large log between us, had started near the back of the one hundred and eight hopefuls. We had brought only the bare essentials, so we managed to move along at a steady jog. After a mere twenty minutes, we had already passed many of the Selous Scouts hopefuls who had started in front of us. The intense heat, coupled with the mopane flies, Chewore buzzards, and complete lack of any breeze whatsoever, was already taking its toll. It was like running in a steam bath, only worse as the road was full of potholes and loose stones, making it difficult to run at a steady pace but very easy to trip and fall.

After a while, the road began to look like the Arab retreat during the Six-Day War: kit lying all over the place and bodies in various stages of exhaustion crouching under trees that offered little or no shade, with mouths agape in an attempt to get oxygen into burning lungs. Forgotten were the mopane flies that disappeared down our gaping mouths, bringing on fits of coughing. Numbed bodies no longer felt the burning bites of the Chewore buzzards. With eyes wide and staring, our mouths so dry that our tongues had swollen, the little water we had brought with us long since drunk and with skin cold and clammy, there was no further thought of passing the selection course and bragging in the Round Bar about how tough it had been.

Now it was all about survival, water and rest. To hell with what everybody else thought about you: if you failed you failed, enough was enough! Why the hell you had volunteered in the first place you did not know; all you wanted was to get out of this hell on earth you found yourself in. Several hours later, the last of us dragged our weary bodies into the base camp, harassed all the way by the instructors whose only words of encouragement were:

"Give up; you aren't going to make it."

"You are too fat!"

"You run slower than my mother."

"Give up now and by tomorrow night you can be having a cold beer in the Round Bar."

On and on and on – non-stop.

Closely following us was an empty truck picking up all those candidates who had taken the advice from the instructors and gave up. As the last of us stumbled into camp, closely followed by the no-longer-empty truck, we were ordered to fall in, at which time we were each issued with a twenty-four-hour ration pack. The Rhodesian army twenty-four-hour ration pack normally contained a tin of meat or fish, a vegetable, sometimes a tin of pasta and rice, tea, milk, sugar and salt: plenty of food for a day under normal conditions. With the rations, all thoughts of giving up disappeared.

A large clearing was pointed out as the place where we were to set up our shelters for the first phase of the selection. At the time nobody seemed to notice that the nearest trees offering any shade were at least twenty metres away. Picking up our kit, we slowly made our way towards what was to be our home for the next couple of weeks. The run in the extreme heat had taken its toll: we were covered in blisters and knees to elbows had been rubbed raw of skin, caused by the constant pounding of the logs. It was the damage not visible to the naked eye that was far more dangerous: the dehydration inflicted by the harsh African sun was the main enemy. Sure, we were camped by a huge lake and water was freely available – a mere fifty metres away. Dehydration not only robbed you of your strength but also your willpower and the ability to think clearly. Some of the guys who had managed to survive the run were not looking too strong. Their big eyes and pale skin told their own story. For somebody suffering from dehydration fifty metres is fifty metres too far.

I was part of a group that had survived the run without too many problems; we started to set up our shelters for the night. It was difficult not to notice others doing nothing – just sitting on their kit staring into the distance. What they were thinking is anyone's guess. They paid no attention, nor did they take any notice of what was going on around them. When they moved it was like watching old men, all bent over and shuffling. Even drinking water seemed to be a mission, never mind trying to erect a shelter and cook a meal. It did not take a rocket scientist to figure out that they were not going to make it.

It was now decision time for me. Our shelters were up. It was time to eat. What to eat and how much was the question. Once again, I had heard many stories about how much food you got and how often you got it. After much thinking, I decided to throw caution to the wind and eat as much I needed to feel comfortable and save the rest for the next day.

The night was hot and clammy and, no matter what you did, you could not stop yourself from sweating. To make matters worse, the mosquitoes arrived in their countless thousands, the buzzing sound created by the myriads of tiny wings enough to drive anybody crazy. Nothing seemed to have any effect on them. Insect repellent failed, smoking was equally ineffective, and it seemed the only way to escape the onslaught was to cover yourself with your blanket or sleeping bag – a non-starter in the unbelievable heat. The night dragged as the mosquitoes, the heat and countless other biting, stinging insects made sleep impossible.

The next morning started off with a bang. The sun had barely started to show its presence and we were already hard at work running along the same road that we had run yesterday carrying logs, but this time they were much bigger and heavier – there were at least four people per log. Due to the large potholes and the thousands of loose stones, it was difficult to get into a rhythm and with no rhythm the log bounced up and down, removing what was left of the skin on your shoulders and badly bruising your muscles, and into this bleeding mass of pain ran all the sweat. The pain was intense, which resulted in the run turning into a shuffle as we moved the log from one shoulder to the other trying to ease the pain. All the while, the instructor was telling us how useless we were and that we should give up. This continual harassment was starting to have an effect, as they not only told us how useless we were but also pointed out the lazy members in our group. "Look at him, the log is not even touching his shoulder; he's having it easy while the rest of you arseholes carry his share of the log." Human nature being what it is, it was not long before the rest of the team turned on the culprit; whether he was guilty or innocent was beside the point, as all that was needed was someone on which to vent the anger and resentment.

It was still early morning and as cool as it was ever going to get. Already we were sweating like pigs as we shuffled along, backs bent under the weight of the log, cursing and muttering as we bickered and fought among ourselves, much to the delight of the instructors. With the sweat came the inevitable mopane flies and their comrades in arms, the dreaded Chewore buzzards. While some of them enjoyed feasting on the salt from our sweat, others demanded fresh blood – on the hoof, as it were. The instructors gave us no rest, continually swearing shouting, taunting, pushing and pulling. No encouragement: just how useless we were and always urging us to give up.

The road run was followed by log drills then the assault course. Hour after hour of extreme physical and mental torture with no rest, just the never-ending "Give up, you aren't going to make it". The hours passed in a pain-filled haze. My body ached in places I didn't even know I had and muscles screamed their objection to the torture. By lunchtime, we had been on the go for six hours or so and we desperately needed a break. As we dragged our bruised and battered bodies back to our shelters, I realized why our campsite was where it was, out in the open. Even though we were on our so-called lunch break we would get no respite from the merciless sun. We were not allowed to leave the immediate area of our shelters, and so the break was spent in the hot sun with our friends the mopane flies and Chewore buzzards. All the food that we had saved from our ration packs was gone. While we had been sweating our guts out, the instructors had searched our shelters and removed all the food, cigarettes and anything else they thought might help us survive in the coming days.

Morale was low, to say the least, and it only got lower as the day progressed. There was no let-up in the pressure and the rest of the day ended as it had begun, in a haze of pain and exhaustion. The sun was setting and it was starting to get dark before a halt was called to the day's torture. We all assembled under a large tree and, looking up, we could see a bell hanging from one of the branches. It was at least fifteen metres off the ground, and leading up to the bell was a rope, about 30mm in diameter. It was to be rung every day at the beginning of the day, and again in the afternoon at the end of the day. It sounded so easy – and under normal circumstances it would be – but we were not operating under normal circumstances. That bell would cause more pain and misery than the road runs, log drills and assault courses combined.

Our torture was not restricted to land, as we also had many 'fun' hours in the lake. Running in the hot sun over rough terrain carrying heavy logs was not easy, especially when suffering from lack of sleep and on an empty stomach, but it was a walk in the park compared to our exploits in the water. On the third day, after our so-called lunch break, we were called down to the water's edge. In front of us was a large bay. Our task, according to our instructors, was to ferry ammunition from our side of the bay to the opposite side, where it was needed by our comrades. In fact, the bay we saw in front of us was actually a river that we had to cross at its widest point.

Representing the ammunition were some old empty ammunition boxes filled with sand and stones, weighing roughly twenty-five kilograms. To ferry the ammunition across the bay/river, we had to build a raft from a pile of nearby logs. Sounds simple enough, but we had gone without food for three days and you could count on one hand the hours of sleep we had managed to get. Our bodies had taken a beating, never mind the mental damage done by the instructors. Slowly, we made our way across to the pile of logs. We had to make a raft big enough to carry four boxes of ammunition – about a hundred kilograms in weight – without sinking the raft. Selecting the logs we intended to use for the raft, we dragged them to one side and used whatever we could find, including our shirts and shoelaces and bound them together to form the raft. We only used four average-sized logs, yet it took us well over half an hour to strap them together. The heat, combined with the lack of food and sleep, tired aching bodies and raw, bleeding hands all contributed to making what should have been a simple task into a mission.

That was the easy part. When the time came to drag the raft down to the water, a good ten or twelve metres away, we wondered why we had assembled the raft so far from the water. We were just too tired to think about the finer details. Huffing and puffing, swearing and bitching, we managed to get it down to the water's edge and gave it a final heave into the river. Wonder of wonders: it floated! We even managed a bit of a cheer. Loading the ammunition boxes slowly and carefully, we were now ready to attempt the crossing. Half way across the bay was a small island and we figured if we could get to it without mishap we could have a rest before being able to complete the crossing without too many problems. Pushing the raft out into deeper water, we made our way towards the island. Swimming alongside us were several instructors offering their usual words of 'encouragement' and advice as to how we should give up and go home.

For the first couple of metres everything looked good but as we progressed, the raft started to come apart – the binding we had used was not holding. Frantically we tried to hold the logs together and retighten the shirts and shoelaces. We were doomed to failure. The water was too deep to stand in and the majority of our team were black soldiers from the RAR, most of whom could not swim. From the shore it must have appeared hilarious: a few white men trying to hold the raft together and prevent the ammunition boxes from falling into the water and a dozen black men who could not swim and did not give a shit whether the ammunition boxes fell into the water or not. The dozen prevailed and the raft broke apart, the logs being used by the non-swimmers to get to dry land. We white guys knew that this was not the end of it. It was far too easy. You were told to build a raft and move ammunition from A to B. You fucked up and that was the end of it? Never, not in this lifetime!

Sure enough, we had no sooner dragged our weary bodies onto dry land than the instructors descended on us like a flock of vultures on a dying animal. Offering words of 'encouragement', we were informed that we, the swimmers, the whites that is, were going to recover those ammunition boxes, if it was last thing we ever did. Wearily, we returned to the water. We were dead tired. Swimming is far more demanding than most, if not all, athletic activities carried out on land. Here we were, barely able to walk and about to swim out into deep water to try and recover four ammunition boxes filled with sand, each weighing twenty-five kilograms, if not more.

By the time we had located them, we were so exhausted that we had to swim back to shallower water where we could stand and rest before attempting to relocate them back to dry land. Working in teams of two, we began to move the ammunition boxes towards the shore. The procedure was like a never-ending nightmare: dive, grab the handle on your side of the ammunition box and then try to walk it towards the shoreline. The bottom of the bay was covered in a thick layer of black, vile-smelling mud that did not make things any easier. With burning eyes, screaming muscles and bursting lungs, we dived again and again, slowly inching shoreward. How long it took to drag the boxes to shallow water so the rest of the group could take over and carry them to dry land, I do not know. Staggering onto the bank, I started puking up the evil-smelling black water I had swallowed. My stomach was empty and the whole process was extremely painful. Never in my life before, or after, have I felt so tired.

Standing up, I prepared to make my way back to my shelter. I did everything slowly and methodically. I had learned that in my weakened state, anything done quickly could have detrimental effects. Moving more like a zombie than a human, I made my way to my shelter. "Sleep," my brain screamed, "sleep – to hell with the food – sleep first." It was not to be.

Before we could sleep we had to entertain the instructors. Later that evening as we dragged our weary bodies up the hill on which the instructors' camp was situated, an unbelievable smell greeted us. It was the smell of meat cooking over an open fire. Hope flared: was the meat for us? Was this the end of the enforced starvation? With a spring in our step, hope in our hearts, mouths watering, we came to a halt in front of the fire. There, in front of us, on a large grill, cooking slowly was the source of the unbelievable smell that had greeted us. Meat of all kinds – beef, pork, and lamb – it was all there, sizzling away over the fire. Sitting on either side of the fire were two instructors, grinning like cats who had stolen the cream. One look at their faces told me that no way was the meat for us. So there we stood in the flickering firelight, eyes firmly fixed on the gently sizzling meat. Looking around at the faces of my fellow soldiers, both black and white, the toll of the previous four days of mental and physical hardship were clear to see. We all had sunken, bloodshot eyes, dirty matted hair, tattered clothing, protruding ribs and numerous cuts and bruises sustained in our efforts to keep up with the unrelenting physical challenges presented by our instructors. The glazed looks on our faces were similar to those seen on the faces of concentration camp inmates.

How many were left of the one hundred and eight who had started, I had no idea, and I am sure nobody else had a clue either. We were all in our own little worlds, just trying to survive as best we could.

"Who would like a steak and an ice-cold beer?"

And it came to pass, as it says in the bible, that temptation was once again sent to try us. Nobody answered. There had to be a catch. It could not be so easy. What price would be demanded by the instructors from anyone who took them up on their offer? We stood there in stunned silence, undecided on what to do, not believing what we had heard. Our tormentors' laughter broke the silence. According to the guardians of the fire, we were obviously not hungry enough to appreciate their grand offer and, so to improve our appetites, we were to sing and dance. Blacks are natural singers and dancers, while whites, on the other hand are terrible singers and even worse dancers. Combine the two and the sound produced is similar to a gut-shot buffalo breathing his last; our dancing resembled a bunch of zombies, half on steroids and the other half drunk.

As one day blurred into the next we got weaker and weaker. By day four, with no food, most of us were on our last legs. Sure, we had been taught how to make traps and snares to capture small animals for food but the problem was, you never got time to set your traps, and due to the activity in the area most, if not all, the small mammals had moved on to greener pastures. The only source of food in the camp was what was in the instructors' kitchen and the rubbish pit, where the leftovers were thrown.

The kitchen itself was a non-starter, as the cook slept in the tent with his rations, leaving only the rubbish pit. Several guys raided the pit but the pickings were small: a few pieces of bread or a couple of potato peels and nothing much else. Due to the heat, which turned food rotten very quickly and attracted millions of flies, the cook had been covering the day's waste with a layer of dirt every evening, which did not help. I had seen pictures of prisoners of war taken during the Second World War: we were not that thin but we were not far off. Our bodies were full of sores, cuts and bruises. Most of us had bad rope burns on our hands from our efforts to ring the dreaded bell. The instructors maintained the physical and mental pressure non-stop, day and night. At night our camp resembled a hospital ward with bodies lying all over the place. Everyone had given up sleeping in their shelters; it was slightly cooler in the open.

The first phase of our selection finally came to an end after what seemed to be a lifetime, and we were presented with the first food we had seen for over a week: a rotten baboon. The smell was beyond belief. It had been shot the previous week and hung from a tree in the hot sun. Now as it lay on the hot, dry ground in front of us, with liquid running out of its eyes and mouth, it appeared to move as the millions of maggots went about their business. The skin was expanding and contracting as the maggots moved from one place to the next, which gave the impression the baboon was alive. I am sure if we had listened hard enough we would have heard them munching at its flesh. This, we were informed, was our food for the next couple of days. I stared in dumb disbelief: they could not be serious, a rotten baboon! It was quite safe to eat rotten meat, we were informed, as long as we boiled it and ate it in one sitting while it was still hot. If we let it get cold and tried to reheat it and eat it later, we would endure a very bad case of food poisoning.

The air came out of the swollen baboon's stomach with a rush. The smell brought tears to my eyes; a burst sewage pipe was child's play compared to the smell that exited the rotten baboon's stomach. I watched in fascination as the wielder of the knife proceeded to remove the guts of the baboon, which consisted of mainly maggots, millions of them, and then butcher the rest of carcass into pot-sized pieces. To me, it was a body I could not tear my eyes away from, with the hands so very like those of a human. While the butcher continued merrily on his way with his gruesome task, covered from head to foot in flies that had arrived in their thousands, several other members started a fire, on which a large pot filled with water was placed. Once the water had boiled the baboon would be put in the pot and cooked.

I sat as close as I could to the fire, trying to use the heat to dispel the flies and to discourage the mopane flies from attacking my eyes and disappearing down my throat and nose. Looking around at my fellow survivors – their dirty battered bodies, long unwashed hair, matted beards, torn clothes, crouched over the rotten baboon helping to cut it up, others like me, unable to stand the smell or the sight of our upcoming meal, helping around the fire – made me wonder how much longer we could last. The more I looked the more I was reminded of a picture I had once seen in a book of cavemen grouped around an animal with a fire in the background. I now saw the same thing in the faces of my comrades that I had seen in that picture. We humans have not changed much over the last few thousand years, and our will to survive, regardless, is just as strong now as it ever was.

There was no need to try and skin the baboon: it was so rotten that the skin fell off on its own accord. Piece by piece, the rotten meat was placed into the pot of boiling water. As each piece was added, the maggots floated to the top until eventually the water was no longer visible, covered as it was by a thick layer of maggots.

We had buried the guts so the foul smell of rotting meat was replaced by what I can only describe as a beautiful, awesome, mouth-watering smell of the cooking baboon, An hour ago, I would have sworn on a bible that there was no way I was going to eat the human-like baboon; now I could not wait to get my share.

Thus ended the first phase of our selection, with all of us quite happily eating rotten baboon, and with all the trappings of so-called civilization discarded.

The next stage, commonly known as the 'dark phase', was about to begin, but first we were given a night on the town. After being informed by our instructors that we had passed the first phase of selection, the few of us that remained were told to go down to the lake, clean ourselves as best we could, change into our cleanest clothes and prepare for a night on the town. The feelings of relief, happiness, joy and pride were all evident on our faces. What a few minutes before had been a group of men desperate to survive, sullen and untalkative, was transformed into a bunch of young guys ready to paint the town red.

The chosen site for this upcoming party to end all parties was the Mahombekombe township football field in Kariba town itself. Unfortunately, or perhaps fortunately, I remember little or nothing about the party, apart from a deep-rooted feeling that I danced too much, drank too much, sang too much and generally made a fool of myself.

The next morning we prepared to start the dark phase, complete with hangover. A hangover in the heat of Kariba is an awesome thing: it robs you of your strength and your ability to think straight. You are convinced you are going to die. All you want to do is find a cool, dark place and do just that. As we stood there in the boiling hot sun, sweating like pigs, bitching and complaining, a message arrived: a large group of terrorists had crossed over from Zambia and we were given the task of locating the landing point and tracking them down. This was surely a message from the gods – we were saved! Anything was better than trying to work in the heat of Kariba with a hangover. Morale began to climb. We would not have to build the mock terrorist base camp that was required of us to start the second phase of our selection, the dark phase. I am pretty sure that had the life-saving message not arrived, most of us would have passed out in the heat as we tried to build the mock camp.

And things only got better. We were going on operations which meant that we had to be supplied with food: no more dieting. Yes, indeed, this was a message from the gods. The fact that we might get killed in the next couple of days was irrelevant. We were young and stupid and, as young people do, we were living for the moment. Tomorrow was a lifetime away.

Several hours later, armed to the teeth and with full stomachs, we were lounging about on the deck of the ferry, being cooled by the slight breeze it generated as it slowly made its way to Binga, a small fishing camp situated at the western end of Lake Kariba. Talk about paradise lost and paradise regained. This was it. All we needed was a bit of the old wine, women and song and things would be perfect.

I thought Kariba was hot but compared to Binga it paled into insignificance. After disembarking from the ferry we had been split into groups of five or six and given different stretches of shoreline to patrol. The aim was to try and locate the tracks of the group of terrorists that had supposedly crossed over from Zambia.

It was eight o'clock at night and extremely hot and humid. My soaking wet T-shirt clung to my body, and the mosquitoes were out in their thousands, attacking any piece of unprotected skin they could find. We had spent the day patrolling an allocated section of the Kariba shoreline. The heat was intense, the reflection of the sun off the water blinding, the assault by the mopane flies and other biting, stinging insects never-ending. The temptation to have a swim in the tepid waters of the lake was ever-present, as were some of the largest crocodiles I have ever seen.

We had just finished our evening meal. After the food of the selection course, the tinned bully beef tasted like manna from heaven. On a full stomach, with a cigarette in my hand, I took in the beauty of my surroundings. Like accusing fingers, the grey, dead trees rose out of the molten-red waters of the lake. The silence was occasionally broken by the splash of an unseen fish, the distant grunt of a hippo and the plaintive cry of a fish eagle. I would gladly suffer the heat, the mopane flies and everything else nature could throw at me, if at the end of each day I could relax and enjoy the beauty of an African sunset.

Night four, ambush four. The moon was full. The long-dead trees with their leafless branches and twisted trunks took on strange bizarre shapes under its silvery light. The air was alive with the distant roar of lions and the wild laugh of hyenas. As I lay behind some old tree trunks on the still-hot red soil, in ambush, being constantly harassed by mosquitoes, I found it difficult to keep still. Morale was low. We seemed to be getting nowhere fast. We had spent the last four days patrolling ever farther away from the lakeshore, trying to locate the tracks of the group from Zambia. Among us were some of the best trackers in the Rhodesian army but nobody had come across any sign whatsoever, let alone tracks, that a group had moved through the area.

As I listened to the sounds of the African bush, I started to second-guess myself. It is funny how the human mind works: there I was with a full stomach, having a reasonably easy time of things and wishing I was back on selection! Like the saying goes, be careful what you wish for, it might just come true.

※

I decided one more squat with my weapon above my head and I was going to call it a day. I was confused, abused and battered. I had heard that the dark phase of the selection was a lot less strenuous than the initial stage. Standing there in the dark, my thigh muscles felt as if they were on fire, my throat was raw from singing terrorist freedom songs, my eyes were two lumps of unseeing pain and my arm muscles shrieked in agony as they tried to hold the AK-47 above my head. I started to have my doubts. As far as I could ascertain, the second phase was as bad as the first.

This was day three since our return from Binga. My body was covered in lumps and bumps, cuts and bruises, from which a never-ending stream of foul-smelling yellow liquid ran. Nothing got a chance to heal. Your body and clothes never got a chance to dry, being constantly wet, either from sweat or midnight jumps into the lake. Clothes were rotting, skin was peeling off in great sheets, dead from the lack of sun and air and being permanently covered in black camouflage cream. To say I smelled bad was the understatement of the year. The sweat, the pus from the sores, the smell of unwashed bodies and decaying flesh was enough to bring tears to your eyes. Even the instructors kept their distance. Sleep was non-existent and food was something you dreamed about. Hunger, exhaustion, heat and pain, were your constant companions.

"Weapons down. The logs, four to a log!" screamed the instructor. "Come on, come on, what's the matter with you people? You're running like a bunch of pregnant fairies. My grandmother can run faster. What's the matter? Are you tired? Hungry? Want to go home to mommy? God, this is the worst selection course I have ever run; so many poofs on the same course, it's unbelievable."

Day and night the torrent of abuse continued.

It was dark, hot and humid. What little light the stars produced failed to penetrate the thick canopy of trees under which we had established our camp, making moving around at night dangerous. Swearing at the instructor under my breath, I broke into a stiff-legged, ungainly shuffle to where I knew the logs were.

"Get them up, get them up!"

No longer sweating, my body cold and clammy, head sunk between my shoulders, I barely had the strength to hold the log up against my chest, never mind get my thighs parallel to the ground as the bellowing instructor demanded. Running on the spot holding a log to your chest is never easy at the best of times, but being exhausted, hungry and on the verge of collapse, it was a nightmare.

"Up, up, get them up!"

The leering face of the instructor was inches from mine, so close that I could smell the toothpaste on his breath. I dropped the log and my fist went back …

"Hey, wake up Andy, time to fall in."

God, I had been dreaming again.

There were about twenty of us left of the original hundred and eight. We all had matted hair and beards, our faces and arms were a patchwork of black and white with sunken eyes and slumped shoulders. A group of unwashed bodies covered in sores, ribs sticking out like rungs on a stepladder, we looked like survivors of a failed attempt to break out of a Soviet gulag.

The sun was hot, very hot, so was the big fire we had built. Happy and smiling, we stared at the large pot in the middle of the roaring fire. An hour ago I had been ready to call it a day. I had a boil on my knee and another on my calf muscle, both on the same leg, but after a pep talk from one of the instructors and the appearance of a bit of rice, beans and a few strips of rotten meat, I was ready to continue. Luckily for me, the tempo of the course had slowed dramatically. Muscles were out, brainpower was in.

For the next couple of days we concentrated on terrorist tactics, the layout of the major training bases in Mozambique and elsewhere in Africa. Great emphasis was placed on names, and we spent many hours learning the who's who in the terrorist hierarchy. Food was being supplied on a more regular basis and we were slowly getting a bit of our strength back. For some it was too little too late and they quit. Several other candidates came down with malaria and had to be admitted to Kariba hospital.

It was a small, sorry group of survivors that assembled outside the instructor's tent ready to start the endurance march. Looking down at my badly swollen leg, I knew my chances of completing the march were not good. But I was going to try. With the end in sight, I was buggered if I was going to quit now.

The one-hundred-kilometre march started from where we were standing on the shores of Lake Kariba and ended up high in the Zambezi escarpment, just below the Makuti hotel. It was not only the distance to be covered that was frightening but also the fact that you had to complete it in three days, finishing with a ten-kilometre speed march.

Passing through some of the driest, hottest countryside in Rhodesia, with little or no food, sharing a sealed, sand-filled ammunitions box weighing forty kilograms between two of you, wearing full webbing, carrying your personnel weapon plus five full magazines, this was no walk in the park; this was a walk designed to push you to the limits.

I did not know what to do or say. Standing in the semi-darkness of the instructor's tent, I was speechless. I had been thrown a lifeline. It was the last thing I had expected, especially not from a group of men who had spent the last five weeks trying to break me. I was told not to start the march because of my leg. There was no problem – I had passed as far as they were concerned – but if I started the march and failed to finish because of my leg, they would have to fail me, rules were rules. They wanted to keep it simple and uncomplicated. Feeling very guilty, I accepted the offer.

The first beer cold beer in the Sahara Bar back in Salisbury tasted like heaven.

9

Ruya River, Mozambican border, 1975

It was early evening. A full moon covered everything in a ghostly, silver light. Sitting on the top of a small hill was a group of eight of us, two black and six white Selous Scouts, dressed in a combination of Frelimo uniform and civilian clothing, blackened up in the case of the whites, some wearing balaclavas, others hats. Armed with AK-47s, we each carried an extra two hundred rounds over and above the five thirty-round magazines we normally carried. For my sins I was also carrying a 60mm mortar, with the twelve bombs we might need distributed among the remainder of the patrol.

We had been in our present position for the whole day, taking turns in watching our intended crossing point into Mozambique. The border between the two countries was represented on the ground by three rusted strands of barbed wire, strung from one rotten wooden post to the next.

It had been a long day, the heat, as usual, a killer. Our long-sleeved shirts and trousers, coupled with the foul-smelling camouflage cream, hat or balaclava, turned us into mobile steam baths. And as ever, the mopane flies were driving everybody crazy. The area was very dry and water was hard to come by, so our sweat was like an oasis in the desert as far as the mopane flies were concerned, as was our blood to numerous blood-sucking, flying, crawling insects.

We each passed the time in our own way. Some carried a book to read, others cleaned their weapons time and again until they gleamed. I passed the time sleeping. The heat did not bother me too much, nor did the bright sunshine. Finding whatever shade I could and using a large rock as pillow, I could normally sleep for a couple of hours, no matter what the conditions. Rocks were used by most of the operators as pillows while in the bush: they supplied support for the neck but were too uncomfortable to allow you to get into a deep sleep – ideal, especially if you were operating alone.

Now, lucky blanket clutched in my one hand – I never went on operations without my lucky blanket – and AK-47 in the other, I lay down in the little shade I could find, ignoring the mopane flies and their wingless, blood-sucking friends and tried to get a couple of hours of rest or sleep – either was fine.

This time I had no luck: sleep just would not come, lucky blanket or no lucky blanket. My body was tired but not so my mind.

※

I had been in this general area two months previously, on, for the want of a better word, a harassment operation. I still carried pieces of shrapnel in my legs, courtesy of a Russian 82mm mortar bomb, and in my hands courtesy of a French-made 60mm mortar bomb, coupled with a healthy dose of my own stupidity. Some of the shrapnel in my legs would go septic and I would have to have them cut out. The smaller pieces in my hands I would remove myself.

There were four of us in the group, each dressed in Frelimo uniform, blackened up and carrying our normal AK-47s, with four thirty-round magazines in our chest webbing. In addition, we all had small packs on our backs containing four 60mm mortar bombs each. I was carrying a 60mm mortar barrel. Our task was to attack the Frelimo base situated on the Ruya River, about ten to twelve kilometres into Mozambique's Tete Province.

Six months prior, we had crossed the border into Mozambique and had laid landmines on all the main roads leading into the base. In the subsequent explosions, the commander and his second-in-command had been killed, with the result that the whole area had quietened down. Now with a new commander, the base was up and running and the crossing of ZANLA terrorist groups into Rhodesia had started up again. The aim of our little attack was to remind Frelimo of what happened last time when they had continued to assist Rhodesian terrorists, even though they had been warned not to do so.

Sitting on the highest piece of ground in the area, I studied the lie of the land between us and the Frelimo base we intended to attack. Swearing at the mopane flies that refused to give me any respite, wiping away the perspiration that poured down my face into my eyes, turning them into two red burning holes, I tried to select a route for the approach to our target. The base itself was surrounded by small ploughed fields, each with its own little village of five or six huts, all of which acted as early-warning posts for the Frelimo camp. The occasional clump of bushes would offer no cover at all and were probably used as toilets by the locals. The only cover of any kind was along the Ruya River itself, which was also the main water supply for the area and was constantly visited by the locals. This was therefore a no-go area.

I had been sitting in my present position for two days, trying to come up with a plan. My original idea had been to attack the camp at last light so as not to allow Frelimo to react until the following morning, by which time I would have been back in Rhodesia. I had planned the whole approach and selected a firing position all off a map, and now I was to realize, not for the first time, how different things were on the ground compared to a map. The plans of mice and men!

By late afternoon, I had come to realize that there was no way I was going to get close enough to the base to attack it by moving during daylight hours. I would have to move during the night and attack at first light, the complete opposite of what I wanted to do. After the attack, there would be no darkness to provide cover, only bright sunlight and open fields. This was not my idea of fun. What should have been a walk in the park was starting to turn into something totally different.

Making my way between the large rocks that were scattered across the hill, I went down to join the rest of my patrol to tell them the good news of having to do a first-light attack on the camp. The news was greeted with little or no optimism. Not that I could blame them; it was my plan and I was not very fired up about its chances of success myself. After answering the questions that they threw at me, I settled down and tried to answer a couple of questions that had been troubling me, the main one being: how would I know where I was at any given time?

I could not use the river as the route in: it twisted and turned too much, the banks were very steep and the bush too thick. It was altogether too dangerous to move along it at night. All I needed was for someone to fall down the steep banks on to the rocks below and break a limb. I quickly pushed that thought, and the route, to the back of my mind. There was only one way and that was across the open fields, trying to use whatever paths were available to cover the ground as quickly as possible. Walking across ploughed fields was extremely difficult: apart from tripping and falling every few minutes, it buggered up your breathing and turned an intended silent approach into a noisy, clanging, huffing, puffing, bitching disaster.

As recruits, we had been taught to march on a compass bearing and to count your steps as a way of moving at night, ending up more or less where you wanted to be. I had tried this method before and had always got lost, due mainly to the fact that I did not trust the compass. A smile spread across my face as I tried to imagine the four of us walking in a single line, stumbling, falling, bitching and complaining, over the uneven ground of the ploughed fields, making enough noise to wake the dead, never mind all the dogs in the area. On top of all this we had to try and count how many paces we had taken: it was just not going to happen. There is a big difference between getting lost on a training exercise and getting lost on operations in hostile Mozambique. In the first instance, the instructor shits all over you; in the second, you stand a good chance of losing your life, which is one thing – that it might cause the people under your command to lose theirs because you didn't know what you were doing, is quite another. After much thought, I decided to play it by ear and rely on my experience. In the Scouts, due to the nature of our work, we moved mainly at night. I had been doing it for years and had never got seriously lost – a bit off course, yes, lost never.

My second problem was slightly more complicated: the maximum range of the 60mm mortar is about two thousand metres when fired on charge four. To fire on charge four it is safer for the mortar be correctly set up using the baseplate and tripod. I had only the barrel. The safest charge to use would therefore be charge two, at a push charge three. That meant I had to get within a thousand metres of the base. This all sounds easy but on the flat ground it is extremely difficult. There were no landmarks to use as a guide and at night everything looked the same. The only thing I had going for me was the river – it, at least, would stop me from stumbling head-on into the Frelimo camp.

My main problem still remained: how would I know how far I was from my target?

Getting up, I took my binoculars and, followed by a huge cloud of excited mopane flies, I headed back to the top of the hill. I had to find some feature on the ground that would indicate that I was more or less a thousand metres from the target. The sun was going down. Time was running out.

Twenty minutes later I found what I was looking for. A piece of high ground right next to the river and, from what I could see, it was about eight hundred to a thousand metres from the Frelimo base – ideal! To make it easy to locate, it had a burned-out hut plus a wooden tower-type structure on it, probably used as a look-out post for the baboons that raided the maize as soon as a cob formed on the plant. The damage caused by a troop of raiding baboons has to be seen to be believed. I felt we were now in with a chance.

We crossed over into Mozambique at about 19h00 that evening, trying to leave no footprints to indicate where we had crossed. We lay at the edge of a ploughed field and waited to see if our crossing produced any reaction. I was already sweating and, after a mere five-metre sprint, the pounding of my heart sounded like a bongo drum in my ears. As I lay there in the dark trying to get my breathing back under control, I went through all the landmarks I intended using to guide me to the position that I wanted to use as the firing point for the mortar. In the back of my mind was the thought that if I messed this up, and come daylight I was still wandering around the open lands, lost, unable to find my selected firing point, I would be in serious trouble, to say the least.

Five minutes passed and all was quiet. Tapping the person next to me, I whispered, "Let's go, single file." Standing up slowly, trying to make as little noise as possible, I waited until the rest of the patrol fell in behind me.

It was a hot, still night with a full moon; everything was bathed in a strange silvery light. Every sound made by the patrol as they moved into single file behind me seemed to be magnified ten times over. A slight clearing of the throat or cough sounded like a clap of thunder. The attacking mosquitoes sounded like a cruising jumbo jet. Every time a twig snapped, I had to force myself not to take cover. After what seemed a lifetime, we were ready to move out.

I had planned to open fire on the base at first light the following morning. It started getting light at about 04h30. I had given myself around ten hours to cover the ten kilometres to the firing point which I thought would be ample. Little did I know!

After the first ten minutes, I knew I was in trouble. From the top of the hill that I had used to observe the area, I had noticed that the fields had just been ploughed. The locals were now waiting for the first rains before planting. What I had failed to notice was how deep they had been ploughed. What should have been a reasonably easy walk turned into a slow, noisy grind. Unable to get into a rhythm because of the ridges thrown up by the plough, our pace slowed to a crawl, stumbling commonplace. I was worried: all I needed was for someone to twist or break an ankle.

About two hours later, I came across a path that seemed to be heading in the direction I wanted to go. We were exhausted. The stumbling and falling caused by the ridges had drained our strength. We were well behind time. At the rate we were going we would be lucky if we got to our firing point by midday.

Decision time had arrived. If I stuck with my selected route across the ploughed fields, I was not going achieve anything, apart from getting us all killed. My choices were simple: change route and try to make up for lost time or abort the attack and try again the next day. The thought of going back and trying again was a no-no. Apart from all the questions that were bound to be asked, the thought of having to go back across the ploughed field we had just crossed sealed the matter for me. We would change our route.

Once we had got our breath back, we started down the path. I was in front and the remainder of the patrol in single file ten metres behind me. This was now a completely new ball game. We were no longer walking across open fields where, although progress was slow, we had been relatively safe. We were now following a path that went from village to village and each village had its own dog.

Walking in front, I was tensed up like a coiled spring. My eyes darted from one shadow to the next, my ears straining to pick up the slightest sound. Bathed in the silvery light of the moon, the trees and scrub bordering the path took on shapes of their own. To my wildly darting eyes, they all looked like terrorists about to attack us.

About a kilometre later, the first village began to take shape in the moonlight. Luckily, all the trees in the immediate vicinity had been cut down, allowing me ample time to see the village and stop the patrol before any dogs heard or smelled us and started barking. Skirting around the village, we continued on our way. Things were going very well, we were making up for the time lost in the field and the path was still heading in the right direction. I began to relax, even the death grip on my AK-47 eased as I took the opportunity to flex my fingers to get the blood flowing again.

And there it was: a hut – no more than seven to eight metres in front of me. In the moonlight it looked even closer. I felt I could reach out and touch it. I froze. My heart was pounding, the hairs on the back of my neck stood up, my grip re-tightened on my AK-47. How I had missed seeing it in the first place, I will never know. Too relaxed, overconfident or maybe a mixture of both, I do not know. All I knew for certain was that I was in big trouble. Careful to make no sound, I eased my body down into a crouch and took a slow, careful look around.

The smell was the first thing that hit me: a combination of wood smoke and human waste, strong in the still evening. I should have picked it up. I failed. I had been so busy worrying about how I was going to cross the fields on my way back after the attack without getting my arse shot off that I had lost a bit of concentration.

Continuing my slow scan of the area, I noticed nothing unusual. The coals in the fire were still glowing, even though they were covered by a thick layer of grey ash, indicating that the locals had gone to bed several hours earlier. Checking all the doorways of the four huts in the village, I searched for any indication of a dog but did not spot anything. I began to breathe a bit easier. Maybe, just maybe, I would get away with my screw-up.

Standing up carefully, I started to ease my way back to the rest of the patrol. My legs felt as if they were made of lead. I was straining to see in the dark and was sweating profusely, partly from the heat and partly from excitement, or was it from fear? On top of all this, my brain was screaming, "Get out here, get out of here!"

Moving slowly backward I concentrated hard on putting one foot behind the other. My legs appeared to have a will of their own as I continually tripped over my own feet. To my patrol, I must have appeared drunk as I staggered along the path to re-join them.

Twenty minutes later, we were back in the ploughed fields, trying to skirt around the village we had almost walked into. The going was slow, even with the help of the light from the full moon. It was difficult to keep your balance and not fall. Huffing and puffing, picking our way carefully, we eventually managed to get around the village.

After what seemed a lifetime, the trees bordering the path that we had been following came into view. Home high and dry, I thought: get back on the path and try to make up for lost time. I was starting to get worried as I was losing a lot of time and expending a lot of energy bypassing the villages. Time I could ill afford to lose. "Ask of me anything but time," Napoleon had said to his generals.

My train of thought was interrupted by a loud clanging noise. Instantly freezing, heart pounding, ears straining, brain racing, I tried to put a picture to the sound. I looked to my rear though the haze of red dust thrown up by our movement across the open field. I saw that one of the patrol members had tripped and was lying face down in the red soil. He made no attempt to stand up but lay perfectly still. Behind him, the rest of the patrol had frozen just as I had done.

The dogs were already barking. Everything was now in the hands of the gods. We were no more than twenty metres from the village. Although unable to see the huts themselves because of the trees bordering the path, we could hear quite clearly: it was a hot, still night and sound travels long distances at night. The barking continued for what seemed an eternity. Many thoughts raced through my mind as I crouched there in the open field, the main one being: was this village occupied by off-duty Frelimo soldiers and, if so, were they armed? Would they check to see what was causing the dogs to bark? So many questions but I had no answers; only time could tell.

I was getting desperate. Time was running out. I had a headache from hell, my eyes felt like they were on fire, thanks to a combination of sweat, red dust and blackening cream. My muscles ached I was so tense. I was about to throw caution to the wind and move out, barking dogs or no barking dogs. As I was about to stand up, I heard what seemed to be a door opening. This was it, I thought, all my questions were about to be answered.

A loud yelp, followed by a couple of unpronounceable words, followed by complete silence said it all. The gods were smiling upon us. It was starting to get light. We were back on the path and things had gone remarkably well. After the barking-dog-village, we came across several other villages that we managed to skirt around without wakening the inhabitants, but we had lost time and we still had a way to go.

I was walking up front and to say I was nervous would be the understatement of the decade. It was broad daylight, I was in Mozambique and heading for a large Frelimo base that I intended to attack with a 60mm mortar, ably assisted by my three comrades. I was shit-scared, to say the least. My body was so tense that my legs would not bend at the knees. I walked as if I had a carrot up my arse. My head moved in short, jerky, movements. My hands gripped my AK-47 so tightly they throbbed. My eyes darted from one clump of bush to the next. My brain was working overtime. What should I do? Turn around and get out or continue on and complete my task? We had already passed groups of locals working in the fields; they waved and we waved back. Dressed as we were in Frelimo uniform, we were accepted as the real deal. Compromise was not my problem: as long as we avoided meeting any of the locals face to face, we were relatively safe. Getting back to safety across the open fields without getting shot was a different story.

My brain was like my legs: it refused to function. I was still debating the problem when my darting eyes picked up the broken wood scaffolding that I had been searching for since it had become light enough to see. My firing point! The sense of relief was immense, as if the steel band that had enveloped my body had been removed. The jitters left and my brain relaxed, no longer burdened with the stay-or-go question.

Leaving the path, I headed across the open fields to the scaffolding. There was a spring in my step. I was feeling a lot more confident. Maybe, just maybe, we would get away with what we were trying to do. The closer I got the better it looked. There were several fairly large trees and even some undergrowth that would afford us cover from view if nothing else.

Up popped the question – totally unwelcome – now that I had reached the firing point, which provided a certain amount of cover, would it not be better to revert to the original plan and attack the Frelimo base at last light instead of now, at nine o'clock in the morning, and use the cover of darkness to make good our escape? This sounded good but one thing bothered me: sure, we had been seen, but only from a distance, and dressed the way we were I was pretty sure the locals took us for members of the local Frelimo garrison. The locals were not the problem, Frelimo was. They had taken to doing clearance patrols around the base at odd times, to ensure that no enemy was lying in wait to ambush them or attack the base. All I needed was for one such clearance patrol to stumble into me or locate my tracks and decide to check them out, and I would be dead meat. Caught in the open, I would not last long.

Pushing all doubts to the back of my mind, five minutes later I was ready to fire my first mortar bomb. I had only the mortar tube: the baseplate and bipods were not needed on an operation of this sort, apart from the fact that they were heavy and difficult to carry. I was relying on the recoil of the first bomb to drive the barrel into the ground, thereby eliminating the need for the baseplate and bipods. With something to occupy my mind, I relaxed. If there was one thing I was good with, it was mortars – big ones, small ones, French, Russian, Chinese, it made no difference.

Getting on the radio, I made contact with the relay station that was situated on the highest hill in the area, and that was going to act as my fire controller. Grabbing the mortar barrel in both hands, I slammed the rear portion into the ground as hard as I could. I needed to make sure that it did not jump out on firing. The thud as it sunk into ground seemed to be extremely loud. I looked around, my eyes darting, my hands shaking, the sound of my rapidly beating heart filling my ears. How I ever let myself get talked into this job, Lord only knows. Looking at the other members of the patrol, I could see that they were just as anxious as me. The darting eyes, the trembling hands and fleeting smiles, all told a story. The longer I waited the more dangerous it would get. God, I thought, let's get this over with and get the hell out of here.

Recalling all the information I had worked out from the map, I held the barrel at what I thought was the correct angle and checked the charge on the bomb. Heart in mouth, I ordered the first bomb to be fired.

"Shot time of flight – eighteen seconds," I reported over the radio to the relay station.

The sound of the charges exploding and sending the bomb on its way were nerve-shatteringly loud and would have been heard for kilometres around. With shaking hands, singing ears and semi-blind eyes, courtesy of the flash at the mouth of the barrel as the bomb exited, I waited for corrections from the relay station.

The silence was unnerving, heavy, sullen and brooding. It was mid-morning, the sun was shining, there was not a cloud in the sky, yet something did not feel right. It was as if everything was holding its breath to see what was going to happen next. Even the dreaded mopane flies were keeping away. The tension, the pressure, the fear, call it what you will, was like a live enemy draining you of your confidence and your will, something that you had to constantly fight against, especially when doing this type of operation. It would have been a lot easier and safer to fire all the bombs at the same time and take pot luck, instead of firing one and waiting for corrections to ensure the rest of the bombs would hit the target, thus making the whole exercise worthwhile.

Something was bothering me and I could not put my finger on it, but I knew I had missed a trick along the way. I could not keep still. My ears were still ringing from the blast but that little warning bell in the back of my mind gave me no rest. I rechecked the charges on the bombs and checked the angle of the barrel again. The first bomb had driven the barrel about four inches into the fairly soft ground. When we started firing again it would not be necessary to hold the barrel: we would be able to fire as fast as we could put the bombs down the tube.

After what seemed a lifetime, the radio came to life: "On target," a voice reported.

On target! I could not believe it! "FIRE!" I screamed.

There was no need for silence, all hell was about to break loose. The bombs were all laid out in front of the firer; all he had to do was to pick them up, one at a time, and drop them down the barrel.

Things were going a bit slowly, so, relieving the firer, I started putting the bombs down the barrel myself. I wanted to finish and get out before the base knew what had hit it. Having had to wait the eighteen seconds for the first bomb to land to find out whether or not it was on target was bad enough; I had no intention of worsening the situation by firing slowly.

One second I was putting mortar bombs down the barrel and the next there was a blindingly bright flash of light. I found myself lying on my back, winded. Struggling into a sitting position, the first thing I noticed was the thick cloud of dust and the unmistakable smell of an exploded mortar bomb, a smell I would never forget after one had exploded in the barrel, killing and wounding several of my friends while on a training exercise. I tried to get my brain working and figure out what had happened. Had we come under attack ourselves? All I could remember was the blinding flash of light and being thrown to the ground by a shockwave, yet I had not heard any sound of an explosion. Running my hand over my face, it came away wet and sticky. Checking, I could see traces of blood among the grass, leaves and sand that stuck to my blackened skin yet I could feel no cuts on my face.

As I sat there in shock, struggling to get my brain to work, I looked at my friends. They too were covered in debris from the blast and, like me, seemed to be at a loss as to what had happened. Lurching to my feet, I knew that now was not the time for deep thinking; now was the time to get the hell out of there as fast as possible.

Glancing up at the sky to see where the sun was, to get an indication of the time, I could not help but notice that the tree under which we had been firing was missing several large branches, all of which were now lying on the ground around the mortar barrel that was still stuck firmly in the ground. By this time, the shock was beginning to wear off and I was thinking more clearly. I knew what had happened: as we had fired more and more bombs, the barrel embedded deeper and deeper into the ground, shifting the angle with each round until it was eventually pointing at the branches directly overhead that, when the mortar bomb hit and detonated, caused the tree to become a deadly weapon and to rain shrapnel down on us below.

My hand automatically went to my head and there, sure enough, I could feel lots of little pieces of metal sticking out of my skull, the cause of the bleeding I had discovered earlier. Before I could congratulate myself and my comrades on our lucky escape, the ground a hundred to a hundred fifty metres to our rear, that happened to be open ploughed land, erupted into two columns of sand, stone and flying metal shards as two 82mm mortar bombs exploded on contact. Now I knew what the little alarm bell at the back of my mind had been trying to tell me. I knew what trick I had missed. If two minutes had passed it was a long time and yet, here I was, coming under fire and pretty accurate fire at that, from Frelimo 82mm mortars. The spot I had chosen as a firing point was one of the few pieces of high ground along the Ruya River and had been recorded as a target by the Frelimo mortars. Now, as I lay flat on the ground, I tried to steady myself, forcing my uncooperative brain to come up with a way out of the predicament we now faced. I had been in bad situations before but nothing like this.

Panic is contagious and spreads like wildfire. I was in charge and it was my responsibility to get us out alive. Ignoring my instinct for survival that was screaming, "Run, get out of here", I tried to come up with a plan. Time was running out. The longer we stayed where we were the better the chances of getting killed. I heard the second salvo of mortar bombs explode about four hundred metres to our left. I absently wondered why they had switched targets. It took a few seconds and then it dawned on me: they, the Frelimo mortar teams, were not sure of where we were. They had a series of targets that they were firing on, hoping to get a response. Once they had fired on the last target, they would start again from the beginning, either increasing or decreasing the range and going either left or right of the initial salvo. This would continue until they were happy the threat no longer existed or they ran out of ammunition, whichever came first.

My plan was simple: hit the open fields at speed and spread out. The way I figured it, the ploughed earth would work in our favour: the mortar bombs would penetrate the soft topsoil and only explode on hitting the harder ground underneath, with the softer soil above then absorbing most of the blast and shrapnel, And, as important, it was the shortest route back to safety.

God, we were a pitiful bunch, covered in grass, leaves and dust. Some were bleeding, some not, all still partly in shock, all having the same lopsided grin and wildly darting eyes, all equally determined to survive. Looking across the field that was our intended escape route, a strange sense of detachment descended on me. I was there, but only in body, as if I was floating and looking down as a spectator on the unfolding drama.

We hit the field at a steady trot, five to ten metres apart. It was slow going. It was now about ten o'clock in the morning and the heat was already unbearable. Dressed as we were in long trousers and long-sleeved shirts, covered in the foul-smelling black camouflage cream, we did not have to do much to build up a sweat, now jogging – up, down, up, down – and it was not long before it was pouring off by the gallon. How long we would last under these conditions only time would tell.

In the distance I could hear mortar bombs exploding, salvo after salvo, seemingly farther and farther away. So far so good, I thought. Five minutes into the crossing we had slowed to a crawl: the adrenalin had worn off, we were tired, hungry, on our last reserves of energy, stumbling every few metres, yet somehow we managed to pull ourselves up and continue. There was no training on earth that could prepare you for this: you either had it in you or you did not.

As we lurched from one ploughed ridge to the next, we began discarding unwanted items of clothing. The first to go were the jackets, followed by the balaclavas and the now-empty packs we had used to carry the mortar bombs. Every bit helped and improved our chances of survival. We had our shirts unbuttoned in an attempt to cool our bodies down. It was all about survival, the hell with who we were or where we were going.

We were now falling more frequently, some of us face first into the soft red soil and staying down on our hands and knees longer. Things were going from bad to worse. We were barely four hundred metres from our starting point and we were down to a crawl, a very slow and painful crawl. The terrible heat was starting to take its toll. Dehydration, heat fatigue, call it what you will, was a deadly enemy, just as effective in putting a man out of action as a bullet. Looking at the faces around me, I could see the sweating had stopped, as was the case with me. What skin I could see in the places where the camouflage had rubbed off looked pale and, most importantly, everybody's eyes were large and staring.

We were twenty metres, at the most, from the closest trees but we just could not make it. We had to stop. Crouched together in the open – the ten metres apart had long since gone by the wayside – we needed each other's help if we were going to get out of this in one piece. Chests heaving, shirts open, bleeding hands, clutching our AKs, we sat in the blazing sun waiting for our breathing to slow, our bodies to cool down and for some strength to return to our limbs.

In the back of my mind I had been following the progress of the Frelimo mortars. Had my brain not been so sluggish from exhaustion, I would have picked it up sooner. The salvos were getting closer and closer. It appeared as if they had increased the range of each target and were firing again to see if they could get any reaction on the new ranges. Forcing my brain to work faster, I tried to come up with a rough idea where the bombs would land when they fired into our vicinity. We had covered about five hundred metres since we had left our firing point. The bombs then were about a hundred to a hundred and fifty metres to our rear, in the open field that we were now crossing in our effort to escape.

"Think, think!" I screamed at my brain. "Where are the bombs going to land?" The answer came back all most immediately: "WHERE YOU'RE SITTING, ARSEHOLE!" Using what little strength I had left, I struggled to my feet. I was swaying all over the place like a drunk; my misadventure with the 60mm mortar had given me a dry throat and a pounding head.

"The trees!" I screamed. "The trees!" However, due to my dry throat, it came out as a low meaningless croak.

The rest of the patrol stared at me as if I was mad, not that I could blame them. I must have been a sight to behold. Long, filthy hair, covered in a mixture of red soil, grass, leaves, black camouflage cream, with a bloody shirt hanging open, my white chest and stomach clashing with the black of my face and arms. Add to this my croaking voice, my staggering and wildly gesticulating hands and you had a picture of a lunatic.

Falling to my hands and knees in front of the patrol, fighting to control my voice, I managed to get my message across: "The mortar bombs," I said deliberately, "are going to land where we are sitting. We need to get to the trees and take cover." Looking up I realised that the patrol now consisted of me plus one other, the rest were scattered far and wide.

It took a couple of seconds for the message to get through. Tentatively, the rest of the patrol, being me and the other person, stood up and we stumbled our way to the trees. We had no strength left. Our legs, already weak, seemed to be made of rubber. Any thought of running was out of the question: the best we could manage was a slow, lurching walk. We were on our last legs but we were also young, very fit, both mentally and physically: all we needed was a half-hour rest and a good drink of water and we would be good again for the next challenge.

We were a few metres short of the trees when my straining ears picked up the whistle of the incoming mortar bombs. I was brain-dead by the time I had figured out what the sound meant and what I should do about it. The bombs exploded about thirty metres behind us. I felt a sharp, burning pain in my calves that dissipated as fast as it came and in no way caused me any discomfort. Nobody even tried to take cover. Like rusting old robots, we lurched, stumbled and staggered our way to the relative safety of the trees. Looking behind me as we finally reached the trees, I could see the red dust hanging in the hot, still air. If we had not moved we would have been dead, of that I was sure.

The next salvo landed way to our left. We were safe for the time being. Their mortars were still searching; they had no idea where we were. Sitting in the sparse shade of the trees, we tried to relax, drink what little water we had left and regain our strength. The border was still ten kilometres away, a good six- to seven-hour walk that would not be fun in our condition

❧

"Wake up Andy, time to get ready. We're moving out in ten minutes."

Sitting up, I stuffed my lucky blanket into the small terrorist pack I was carrying. I hoped the blanket would deaden the sound that the 60mm mortar bombs made when they knocked against each other. I had thought of wrapping them individually in cloth to help eliminate the sound problem but the thought of having to unwrap each bomb before firing, especially while under fire, gave me grey hairs.

The next thing I did automatically. Reaching for the bottle of disgusting, foul-smelling black camouflage cream, I applied a thick coat to my face, neck, ears, arms and hands, after which I spent my remaining time on getting my mind right. This was not my favourite part of Mozambique: I still carried the odd bit of shrapnel in my legs and hands from my last visit and, lucky blanket or no lucky blanket, I was very tense. Time is a soldier's worst enemy. It provides him with a chance to think of all the 'buts' and 'what ifs'. The human memory is a strange thing: you never seem able to remember the good things, like getting out in one piece after surviving incredible obstacles – only the bad things, like getting hurt, lost, almost dying of thirst or having to eat rotten meat. The list provided by your memory is endless.

Jerking myself out of my pit of self-pity, I started thinking about our up-and-coming operation, which was to attack and destroy a terrorist transit base situated twelve or so kilometres into Mozambique. The aerial photographs I had seen of the area where the camp was supposed to be situated, showed a small river, its banks crisscrossed by hundreds of game trails and covered in what appeared to be fairly thick bush, and even though it was the latter part of summer, it still had what appeared to be flowing water in it. This is a rare sight in that part of Mozambique, no matter what time of year. It was a big draw card for every terrorist and what wildlife still survived in the area, including the occasional elephant.

As I sat there waiting for the sun to set and the order to move out, I knew from experience that we were in for a long hard night. What the photographs did not show were the countless gullies caused by rain and erosion, all running into the river, ranging in depth from a couple of centimetres to a metre or more and all capable of breaking legs or twisting ankles. The obstacle course on selection would be like a walk in the park compared to this.

As the sun set, the moon took over and everything took on a silvery hue. A calming silence settled on the area. The mopane flies and ants retired to be replaced by the mosquitoes and the other biting, stinging insects on the night shift.

Even though it was cooling down, I was sweating. The camouflage cream was running into my eyes, causing them to burn. I knew rubbing would not help: they would continue to burn for however long this operation took to complete. The longer I sat there waiting for the order to move out the more uneasy I began to feel. My imagination started to run wild, all the 'ifs' and 'buts' coming back to haunt me. The tension of waiting caused my shoulders to throb and my hands to clench my AK so hard it hurt. The mortar barrel slung over my shoulder and the bombs in my pack seemed to weigh a ton. My whole body was taut, like a spring under pressure, and the dreaded headache was starting up in the background. The silence that I had previously found calming now seemed heavy and forbidding.

"God", I thought, "let's get this show on the road."

An hour later, I wished I was back on the hill overlooking our crossing point, complete with all my doubts, wild imagination and the mosquitoes. I had known it would be tough going but not this tough. Crossing the three strands of rusty barbed wire into Mozambique had gone off without a hitch. Walking in single file, we headed for the river that we intended to use to guide us to the terrorist transit camp. The going was easy to start with, trees were few and far between and the light from the full moon enabled us to avoid any obstacles in our path and cover the ground at a rapid rate. Walking at the back of the patrol, I began to relax, my feelings of impending doom somewhat lifted – maybe I had been overreacting.

My newfound feeling of wellbeing did not stop my straining ears from bringing me to a dead stop every time I heard a strange noise, or my burning, red eyes from darting nervously from one bunch of isolated trees to the next. The headache was still there as were the throbbing shoulders and deathlike grip on my AK. I was now as relaxed as I was ever going to be. The closer we got to the river the thicker the bush became. Our pace slowed to a crawl.

The full moon that had at one time been our ally was now our enemy, causing the trees to cast long, dark shadows that hid numerous obstacles. Tripping, falling, bitching and complaining became the order of the day. In desperation, our patrol leader decided to move away from the river. The bush was too thick and the continual climbing in and out of the thousands of gullies was both tiring and noisy. We soon came across a fairly large, well-used path running parallel to the river and so, with the full moon shining down on us, we quickly made up for lost time.

Red and green tracer lit up the sky, cracking as it flashed over our heads. In our effort to make up for the time we had lost in trying to follow the river, we had put our heads down, stuck our fingers up our arses and had walked straight into an ambush. Caught in the open, silhouetted against the moonlight, surrounded by grass *bashas* – the thatched bivouacs that terrorists used in their temporary bases – and getting the shit shot out of us, we were in big trouble. If we stayed where we were we were dead meat.

Running doubled over, returning fire as best we could, with mortar bombs exploding all around us and bullets coming in from all sides, we made a dash for a nearby mealie field. The smell of burning animal skins and rotting meat was overpowering. Crackling flames leaped high into the sky, with thick black smoke from burning blankets, clothing and shoes blocking out the moon, as collapsing *bashas* sent streams of red and yellow sparks into the air. It looked and smelled like hell.

Just before first light we slipped back across the border into Rhodesia.

10

The snatch: Eastern Highlands, Operation Thrasher, early 1976

To snatch or capture a person whom it is necessary to keep alive is a very difficult operation to accomplish, more so at night.

It was hot, sticky and uncomfortable sitting around the smoking fire, but it was a necessary evil. We had to make sure all traces of the smell of washing powder on our clothing, toothpaste in our mouths, shampoo in our hair and our own body odour were eradicated and replaced by the smell of smoke and sweat, the aim being to smell the same as the locals. This was done to try and fool the many dogs that each village was home to, into believing we were locals, hence obviating their need to bark. Two hours later, smelling like mobile meat-smokers, we were ready to move out.

We were operating in the Chimanimani Mountains, our base an old deserted farmhouse about three or four kilometres from the Mozambican border. Our task was to capture alive a certain Mozambican local responsible for the movement of Rhodesian terrorists groups crossing the border into Rhodesia.

That evening, eight of us crossed over into Mozambique: four white and four black Scouts. As usual, the black Scouts were walking in front in case we bumped into any locals or terrorists on our way to the target. The reason was simple: they could speak the language. Our cover story was that we were a group of freedom fighters wanting to cross into Rhodesia but we needed to speak to Mr X, our target, to find out where it was safe to cross.

Dressed as we were in a mixture of Frelimo uniform and civilian clothes, carrying AK-47s, wearing chest webbing and completely blackened up with the foul-smelling camouflage cream, the chances of us being recognized as whites were very slim.

As we approached the first village, the tension started to mount. Would the dogs bark? Would the locals run away? Would we be accepted as real terrorists? Would we be ambushed? The same questions always hovered in the back of my mind. I had been on such operations in the past and would go on more in the future. The feeling of impending doom, the stiff-legged gait, the aching shoulders, the pounding head, the staring, glazed, red eyes, the straining ears that always seemed filled with the sound of crashing waves and the vice-like grip on the AK-47, were to be my companions on each and every border crossing I did.

Progress was slow but steady. We were well received by all the locals we met and our cover story was accepted without question. Yes, they knew the man we wanted to talk to. Yes, he was the contact man for the area and all freedom fighters reported to him before crossing into Rhodesia. We approached each village carefully, stopping often to listen and check the ground to our front for anything suspicious. It was a full moon; every shadow looked like a terrorist, every sound sounded like an AK-47 safety catch being switched to automatic.

The information we had received on the whereabouts of our intended victim led us deeper and deeper into Mozambique. What should have been a simple 'locate and remove' was turning into a slog. Village after village, kilometre after kilometre, still we found nothing concrete on the whereabouts of Mr X. Time was running out and we were thinking of turning back when our luck changed.

We were in village number nine or ten asking the same questions and getting the same answers when an old man who had just been sitting there listening joined in the conversation. Yes, he knew Mr X; in fact he knew where Mr X was sleeping that night. According to the old man, Mr X was extremely worried about his personal safety and did not sleep in a hut but rather in the middle of a cattle kraal, surrounded by sheep, goats and cows that acted as his early-warning system. And, furthermore, according to the old man, he did not like to meet groups like ours at night. That was a minor problem as far as we were concerned: once we had located him, the rest would be easy. Or so we thought – the plans of mice and men.

After receiving what can only be described as vague directions from the old man, we headed off in the direction of where we thought the kraal was situated. The spring was back in our step, morale was on the up and I even noticed the odd smile in the bright moonlight. Several cattle kraals later, the feet were dragging, the smiles were gone and the complaints were on the way up.

Time was running out, we were deep into Mozambique and it was touch and go. When it seemed as if failure was inevitable, our luck again changed. There, standing upright in a kraal, surrounded by sheep, goats and cattle, was the man who could only be Mr X. We all stared at him in disbelief: we had just about given up and there he was.

Now came the difficult part. If our job was to kill him there would have been no problem, but we needed him alive. He would know the whereabouts of all the terrorists in the area, how many had crossed into Rhodesia, where they had crossed and when they were due back for resupply: the man was a gold mine of information. We needed to get him back to Rhodesia in one piece as quickly as possible. Looking at him bathed in moonlight, surrounded by animals, you knew this was not going to be easy: he was over six foot and built like a tank.

Phase one was to get him to leave the protection of the animals and the kraal of his own volition. There was no way we were going to get him out by the use of force, short of killing him. Two of the black Scouts strolled up to the kraal and, leaning against the wooden poles, started talking to him. I have no idea what they said but he kept shaking his head, gesturing to the rest of us sitting in extended line, ten metres or so behind the black Scouts. That he was not happy about something was obvious. The moon was very bright and visibility was good, so I wondered what he had seen that had made him suspicious. It had been a long, hot, tiring night. Looking around at the rest of the group, everything appeared fine. But the way we whites were dressed – long trousers, long-sleeved shirts, jackets and, in some cases, balaclavas – in our attempts to blend in had led us to sweat profusely. I was hoping the sweat had not removed the camouflage paint from our faces.

A couple of minutes later, after much talking, gesturing and pointing, Mr X finally moved. He still looked unhappy. He would walk forward a couple of metres shuffling the livestock out of his way, stop and look around. Progress was painfully slow but after what seemed forever, he finally left the protection of the kraal.

Phase two now swung into action. The plan was to take Mr X to meet our leader, who happened to be an ex-Rhodesian boxer. When Mr X was close enough, our patrol leader, the ex-boxer, would hit him in the stomach and hopefully wind him, thus giving the rest of us a chance to get a set of handcuffs on him. The operative word here is 'hopefully'.

Looking at Mr X as he walked by, I began to have my doubts: the man was huge, he appeared to be all muscle and it was going to take one hell of a punch to wind him. Talk about David and Goliath! This time I figured David had bitten off more than he could chew. It was like an old silent black and white movie. There was not a sound; even the livestock in the kraal had fallen silent as if they could sense something dramatic was about to take place. We all watched in numb fascination. Everything was bathed in the pale yellow light of the moon – no colours, only black and white. The tension was palpable. No one moved, as if we were props on a stage, unable to influence the outcome in any way.

The boxer then punched him in the stomach, but nothing happened; Mr X seemed unaffected. I could not believe my eyes. I had seen the boxer hand out some quite serious hidings to some pretty big guys in the Salisbury nightclubs. Failure was not an option as we had no plan B, so we reverted to the old standby of brute force and ignorance. All eight of us jumped on him, but we could not wrestle him to the ground, never mind subdue him. He was tossing us around as if we were children, the adrenalin and a healthy dose of fear giving him amazing strength. He had been hit very hard several times on the head with rifle butts but to no avail: he simply would not go down. Standing on his own, chest heaving, covered in dust, blood gushing from the deep cuts inflicted by the rifle butts, he showed no sign of surrender. You had to admire the man. Like a leopard surrounded by a pack of hunting dogs, he was going to fight to the death.

Everything ground to a halt. We were exhausted and most of us were carrying bruises and cuts from our attempts to subdue him. In the entire five-minute fight, not a single word had been uttered; apart from the sound of shuffling feet, the thump of landing bodies, the sound of heaving chests trying to get oxygen into burning lungs, the whole struggle had been strangely quiet.

Time was not on our side and we had to end this quickly, one way or another. As we stood there staring at each other, the contest took a turn which sealed Mr X's fate. Darting forward, he grabbed a large piece of wood and attacked one of the black Scouts. The gloves were off and the time for playing was over. There was no way we were prepared to let him injure any of us. What had been admiration quickly turned to anger as bayonets flashed in the moonlight and Mr X collapsed. Whether he died or not I do not know. I like to think he did not and is still living in his village, occasionally telling his grandchildren the story of the fight he had with the white men dressed as black men.

He was a brave man and deserved to live.

11

Attack on Mapai: Mozambique, June 1976

Mapai sounds like an exotic seaside town in an exotic country. It is neither: it is a small, one-horse town, situated in Mozambique's Gaza Province, about a hundred kilometres inland from the border with Rhodesia. It was used as an ammunition depot by ZANLA terrorists and provided support to a nearby transit camp known as Chicualacuala. The aim of the raid, as far as I understood, was to destroy Mapai and its large ammunitions cache and, at the same time, show Frelimo that it was not a good idea to support ZANLA. I had been on raids before into Mozambique and would go on several more after the Mapai raid, but none would haunt me or appear in my dreams as did the raid on Mapai.

One of the secondary tasks allocated to us was burning down all the buildings in Mapai, hence the search for the perfect petrol bomb. Pete Mac and I had been using different combinations of petrol, diesel and oil, trying to come up with the right mix for the perfect petrol bomb. After days of experimenting, we were close – all we needed now was to sort out a method to ignite the fuel combination when the bottle shattered against the target.

�֎

Prior to the actual raid on Mapai, a reconnaissance team was sent into the area of Malvernia, the Mozambican border town across from Vila Salazar in Rhodesia, to capture a member of either Frelimo or ZANLA, and hopefully update the intelligence we had on the whereabouts of the transit camp supposedly in the area and which was our second target, time permitting. Although Malvernia and Mapai were about hundred kilometres apart, they were connected by both rail and road and maintained regular communication with each other. So the chances were good that the Frelimo and ZANLA in Malvernia would know just as much about what was happening around Mapai as the Mapai residents themselves, hence the decision to try and snatch a body

100

from Malvernia instead of from Mapai a hundred kilometres down the road. It would be almost impossible, with the limited time available, to get in and out of Mapai with a capture.

The reconnaissance team, of which I was a member, was led by Sergeant-Major Jannie Nel, a Selous Scout legend and a brilliant, unconventional soldier. Among many other things, he was well known, whenever he got drunk, for his attempts to shoot the cats that abounded at Inkomo Barracks near Salisbury with his hand gun, much to the disgust of Ron Reid-Daly who had a soft spot for the cats.

We crossed the fence into Mozambique just as it was getting dark, led by a black Selous Scout just in case we bumped into a Frelimo patrol. We were all dressed exactly the same as the ZANLA operating in the area, right down to the shoes on our feet. Attention to detail was crucial: it could save your life. The white members were blackened up as usual with the foul-smelling, so-called 'black is beautiful' camouflage cream, and sweating like pigs due to the extra clothes we were wearing in an attempt to disguise the fact that we were white. The extra clothing included balaclavas to hide our hair and distort the outline of our faces, long-sleeved jackets and shirts to cover our white skin and the hair on our arms, and long trousers to do the same for our legs. As a white operator, sweating became an accepted part of the bush war.

As we moved cautiously through the thick bush towards Malvernia, I thought back to the last time I was involved in a snatch, in the Chimanimani Mountains in the east of Rhodesia, where we ended up likely killing the guy we had been trying to snatch. I hoped things would go better this time round. We had no real plan as such; the idea was to hang around the road that linked Mapai and Malvernia and take advantage of any opportunity that presented itself: it was pure hit or miss.

After about three hours of walking, the lights of Malvernia appeared through the trees about a kilometre to our front. After a quick discussion, it was decided to skirt around Malvernia itself and head for the road as we had planned. We would only try to snatch somebody from Malvernia if all else failed. We had been sitting on the side of the Mapai–Malvernia road for a mere fifteen minutes or so when we heard the sound of a vehicle approaching from the direction of Malvernia. Our plan had to be simple, there was no time for anything fancy as the vehicle would be on us in a matter of minutes. It was decided that one of the black Selous Scouts would flag down the vehicle and the rest of us would hide on the side of the road and play it by ear, depending on whether the vehicle stopped or not.

Crouching on the verge, listening to the noise of the approaching vehicle, I could feel the adrenalin starting to pump and the sweat beginning to run, even though it was the middle of winter. We were only a kilometre or two from the centre of Malvernia: if anything went wrong all hell would break loose. The Frelimo in Malvernia were armed with 82mm and 60mm mortars, among other things. Our present position put us well within range. On the flat, hard, open ground, with a lethal area of twenty metres and a danger zone of a hundred, they would be devastating. We were taking a big chance: we did not know the type of vehicle, the number of passengers, whether they were Frelimo or ZANLA, armed or unarmed. One minute the vehicle lights shone into the sky, the next they disappeared as the driver carefully picked his way through the large potholes littering the road. When the vehicle was about three hundred metres away, the black Selous Scout stepped out into the road and started to flag down the oncoming vehicle. At first it seemed as if the driver had not seen the waving figure standing at the side of the road. Not that anyone could blame him, as he tried to dodge what potholes he could and navigate the ones he could not. He was only a few metres away from the now frantically waving Selous Scout before he appeared to notice and hit the brakes. The vehicle came to halt in a small cloud of dust, with the driver leaning out the window, pointing and shouting at the lone Scout. He seemed to be very upset about something – but we could not make out what he was saying.

With that, Jannie Nel jumped into the passenger seat of what turned out to be a dirty, brown-coloured Land Rover and stuck his AK-47 into the ribs of the gesticulating, shouting driver. The silence was immediate and before he could recover, the driver was dragged out of his seat and handcuffed. So far so good: the gods were smiling on us, and they continued to smile as our prisoner turned out to be some sort of ZANLA liaison officer. When it was explained to him that he had been captured by the dreaded Selous Scout he would not stop talking.

We had been very lucky indeed that things had worked out so well for us, or so I thought as I clung to whatever I could in the back of the bouncing Land Rover to stop myself from falling out as we made our way home. Our escape route required us to turn the dirty brown Land Rover around and head back in the direction of Malvernia.

As we bounced along at a steady ten to fifteen kilometres an hour, hanging on for dear life along the pothole called a road, heading for Malvernia, the tension started to mount again. The road split just before it entered Malvernia, one fork going straight on into Malvernia, the other turning sharply right and running parallel with the border, our escape route. If we could reach the turning without alerting the Frelimo garrison at Malvernia of our presence we would be home and dry. However, 'if' is a small word with a big meaning. The closer we got the more the tension increased, the adrenalin flowed, the muscles strained, the eyes burned and the head pounded. I gripped my AK-47 so tightly that my hands actually throbbed in pain. It seemed as if we would never reach the fork in the road: we kept on getting closer and closer to Malvernia and still there was no sign of it. How we had not been seen, the Lord only knows. We were so close to the town that we could see the individual houses, their windows glinting in the streetlights and, off to one side, the huge storage sheds at the railway station. Doubt entered my mind: had we already passed the turning? In our excitement at the capture of the ZANLA officer, had we failed to notice it and driven straight past? Winter or no winter, we were all sweating. The tension was palpable; you could actually feel the uncertainty, the indecision.

We had two options: one, to carry on believing that there was no way all of us could have missed the turning or, two, believing we had missed it, turn around and retrace our steps. Jannie Nel chose the first option. He was correct. We had progressed no more than a dozen metres after the topic had come up for discussion when there, in front of us, was the turning to the right, our escape route.

Morale went through the roof and we even managed a smile or two. The tension flowed from my body and the death grip on my AK-47 eased. I stopped sweating, not completely, for the layers of clothing would not allow that, but yes, for the first time since we had crossed into Mozambique, I felt confident we were going to succeed in our mission. Sure, I was still a bit nervous as we were pretty close to Malvernia and why we had not been seen, who knows. It was late at night and cold, so maybe the sentries had found a warm place out of the wind and had fallen asleep. I knew that in a couple of days' time they had a big holiday coming up, and these guys knew how to party; maybe they were starting early. Whatever the reason, I was not complaining, just extremely grateful.

As we turned off the main road, the front passenger door suddenly opened and out jumped our captive, screaming at the top of his voice, legs pumping like pistons as he started off down the road for Malvernia with a burst of speed that rivalled a Formula One car. We were caught completely off guard. It was the last thing we expected. We had all been too busy looking for the fork in the road to pay much attention to our prisoner. He, on the other hand, had been watching our every move and probably understood every word we said. Seeing the writing on the wall, he had decided that discretion was the better part of valour and hit the road running. We were all caught by surprise, that is, everyone except Jannie Nel. Jumping out the vehicle, he fired one short burst and down went our captive. A quick check confirmed he was dead.

Now all eyes swung towards Malvernia. The shots had sounded extremely loud in the still night air, like a clap of thunder in a cloudless sky. "For fuck's sake, why now?" my brain screamed. "Everything was going so smoothly." The adrenalin began to flow again and the death grip on my weapon returned, as did the sweating. It was so quiet that you could have heard a pin drop but, unbelievably, there was no reaction from Malvernia, no movement, nothing.

As the seconds passed I gradually relaxed; maybe the gods were smiling on us after all. Slowly, oh so slowly, we got back into the vehicle and proceeded down the road on our return to safety, taking the Land Rover with us.

About four kilometres from Malvernia, well out of Frelimo mortar range, we left the road and headed through the thick bush for the border. After several hours of hard work and much swearing, we reached the border fence and cut it to cross back into Rhodesia.

Thus began the worst week of my life, and probably the worst in Selous Scout history. The gods of war would turn their backs on us and we would suffer accordingly.

※

Several nights later we were back on the same road where the failed snatch had taken place, only this time we were heading deeper into Mozambique, not trying to get out. Our target was the small town of Mapai that was being used by Rhodesian freedom fighters, ZANLA, as a transit, resupply and storage depot. Situated about a hundred kilometres, as the crow flies, from the border with Rhodesia, with the main road and rail links between Malvernia and Maputo nearby, it was ideally suited for this purpose.

Our armed column consisted of six Unimogs, the first one being a Pig, a Unimog converted to an armoured personnel carrier. I was travelling in the last Unimog with a section of two 60mm mortars and all the petrol bombs that

Pete Mac and I had made. A lot of care, attention and time had been put in to make the vehicles look exactly the same as those used by Frelimo, right down to the number plates. The same amount of care taken to make the vehicles look authentic was also put in to make ourselves, the raiding party, appear as Frelimo-like as possible.

We had crossed into Mozambique earlier that evening and, using a series of cut lines, had joined up with the main road–rail link between Malvernia and Maputo, just before Mapai. The idea was that we would hole up just short of Mapai and attack at first light the next morning. As we moved slowly up the road to our laagering area, I could feel the tension mounting. Through my mind shot the details of the attempted snatch and all the consequences that that failure might bring. Had we left behind a clue to indicate that Mapai was our intended target and, if so, was there an ambush waiting for us? Had the roads been mined? The questions were endless and the more I thought about it the more worried I became. At least the armoured vehicle was travelling at the head of the column, better suited to handle an ambush than us in the soft-skinned Unimogs. About the landmines, I was not so sure. Bouncing along at the rear of the column, covered from head to foot in the dust of the vehicles in front, I tried to think positive thoughts. With me on this venture were some of the finest fighting men in the world: Jannie Nel, Dale Collett, Pete Mac, Tim Bax, to name but a few.

After we had passed through several small villages without mishap, I relaxed a bit. The tension, however, was incredible; nobody said much as we stared out into the darkness with burning, bloodshot eyes. What we hoped to see, Lord only knows. All the excitement we had felt when the operation was first announced had disappeared, swallowed up by the thick dust thrown up by the vehicles. Going on a raid into Mozambique was one thing, dying was another.

I had been on the first exploratory raid into Mozambique several weeks earlier. It had been an altogether lighter affair in which we were given no particular target, just an area in which several ZANLA camps were supposed to exist. The aim of the exercise was to see if it was possible to cross into Mozambique and, using existing roads therein, ride around without arousing the suspicion of the locals and Frelimo alike. It had gone off like a dream. We rode up and down the roads, shooting anything that moved, stopping only to mark our route with maize meal. It was basically a drive-by shooting and, being constantly on the move, the chances of being ambushed or pinned down were slim.

The attack on Mapai, however, was a totally different kettle of fish, in that we would have to leave our vehicles and fight on foot, losing our main advantage, mobility. Once static we would be open to counter-attack. The longer we stayed in Mapai the greater the chances of being ambushed on our way out.

After a stressful but uneventful night in the holding area, we refuelled and continued on to our target. At first light we arrived at Mapai. The booms were open and unmanned. Great! Everything was going to plan. The fact that the boom was unmanned was an added bonus. We moved into our pre-selected positions as we had practised back at base in Salisbury. It was deathly quiet, no movement, no sound. The buildings appeared deserted; not even a barking dog. Was this the dreaded ambush I had feared? My mouth was suddenly dry and the sweating started, even though it was early morning and still cold.

Our vehicle came to a stop. With a croaking voice, I ordered the mortars into action.

Within a matter of seconds, the crews had the mortars set up, ready to fire. The task given to me and the mortar crews was to inflict as much damage as possible on the retreating enemy once the attack started. Crouching behind the crews, I had a look around my immediate vicinity: a metre or two to my front were several trenches. Thank God they were deserted: had they been occupied we would not have stood a chance. The only sign to indicate that they were still active was a scattering of empty beer and wine bottles. Beyond the trenches, about twenty to thirty metres, was a double-storey building. It appeared to be a community centre-cum-Frelimo headquarters. To my right were several shops, behind which appeared to be a large workshop housing several trucks and buses. To my left was open bush. To take in my surroundings had taken a few seconds at the most, and still the eerie silence continued. Nobody quite knew what to do: we had expected to come under fire almost immediately on entering the town and, to make matters worse, there was nothing for us to fire at. My feeling of unease increased: this was going to be a bad day.

The silence was broken by a loud explosion coming from the area of the workshop. The task of destroying the vehicles had begun, our almost trancelike state shattered. Several guys sprinted forward to the large double-storey building to clear it of any enemy. Pete and I collected together our lovingly made petrol bombs and headed to the closest of several stores, our task being to kill any enemy therein and burn them to the ground. We were like two kids on a picnic, smiling and chatting, AK-47s in one hand, petrol bombs in the other, as we made our way to the stores. All thoughts of impending doom disappeared. A holiday-type atmosphere seemed to envelope the entire column. We had been expecting a hard fight and now, nothing. It was too good to be true.

We were busy clearing buildings and throwing petrol bombs when a burst of automatic fire shattered the silence, and with it the holiday atmosphere. Running from a store, we took cover behind a low brick wall surrounding it. Looking to the double storey where the firing appeared to be coming from, I noticed a group of Scouts carrying what appeared to be a wounded comrade. It was now obvious that the top floor of the building was occupied. Everybody was ordered to withdraw to a safe place before we opened fire on the roof and passage with everything we had, including RPG-7s.

Once things quietened down, another attempt was made to clear the top floor, but we encountered another burst of automatic fire. Back were the all the feelings of impending doom. Out the corner of my eye, I noticed two Scouts running down the steps; there appeared to be a body lying at the bottom of the stairwell leading to the top floor. A dead Frelimo soldier, I thought. It was difficult to tell the difference between us and Frelimo. We were dressed in the same uniform – shirt, trousers and cap all the same – the only difference being veldskoens, the footwear we preferred. We wore chest webbing, carried AK-47s and all the whites were blackened up. From a few metres it was extremely difficult to tell the difference. We even went as far as not wearing deodorant in our attempt to be accepted as the real deal.

The body I was staring at was twenty to thirty metres away, lying on its back, arms outflung. The hair stood up on the back of my neck. Unless Frelimo had taken to wearing wigs, the body lying on the stairs was definitely one of us. The long black hair shining in the sun, the thick black beard, the veldskoens, all pointed to a member of the raiding party, but who was it?

As the shock wore off, I put together all the facts my eyes were telling my numb brain. The thick beard, the shiny black hair, the build and a million other small things, and I knew who the dead man was. It was the man who had convinced me to join Selous Scouts: Jannie Nel. What had started out as raid on a Frelimo–ZANLA resupply and transit base now became a hate-filled vendetta.

One of the conditions imposed upon us by Army HQ was that we would not have access to any form of air support during the raid. The reason given was that the politicians did not want the rest of the world to be able to prove that we, the Rhodesians, were conducting raids into Mozambique and, according to them, the use of aircraft was a dead giveaway. This logic was frightening. Who would the rest of the world think was carrying out the attacks – Father Xmas, for fuck's sake? Who cared? The only aircraft available to help us was a helicopter, to evacuate any wounded.

The anger and frustration boiled over as everyone opened fire at the roof in a vain attempt to kill whoever was hiding in the ceiling. It was a failure. In the next half an hour, two more Scouts were seriously wounded as they tried to clear the top floor. We had used every weapon available to us, including RPG-7s and a 12.7 machine gun, in our efforts to clear the roof. We had failed. Now it was decision time. The choices were simple: request air power to destroy the building or pack up and leave. We could not afford to lose any more men: the price we had paid was already too high. As we waited on the decision from Army HQ, the feeling of isolation grew. Here we were, stuck in the middle of Mozambique, miles from the Rhodesian border, with one dead and two critically wounded – and we had to wait for a decision by men hundreds of miles away, who only had a sketchy idea of the situation on the ground and, to make matters worse, with little or no combat experience. The tension mounted as we waited for an answer.

It was vital that the wounded be uplifted as soon as possible to receive the care they needed. But before the uplift could take place we had to clear or destroy the building to make the area safe for the helicopter to land. The bus that we had commandeered from the workshop, now loaded full of ammunition, was moved away from the building to a safe place, in preparation for the hoped-for airstrike.

It was June, the middle of winter, but still very hot. The whole operation had ground to a halt. A strange, brooding silence shrouded the area. Where before there had been movement and voices, now there was nothing, each of us locked in our own little world. As I crouched there behind the wall, waiting on the Army HQ decision, I tried to relax. Yesterday had been my birthday, now, a day later, here I was knee deep in the shit, stuck in the middle of Mozambique on an operation that had gone wrong. The longer the decision took the greater the chances were of Frelimo being able to launch a counter-attack or plant landmines on the road out. Maybe an ambush or two; the possibilities were endless. We had to get out. As far as I understood it, the route we used to get in was the only way out.

My head felt as if it was going to burst, my eyes were burning and felt swollen, courtesy of the black camouflage cream that somehow always found its way into your eyes. Having to travel at the back of the column and the complete lack of sleep had not helped either. Concentrating extremely hard, I managed to get one of my hands to release its grip on my AK-47 and reach for my water bottle. My throat was so dry I could not talk, and my mouth tasted like an open sewer, not helped by the fact that in my endeavours to burn down the stores I had somehow got petrol and oil onto my clothes and into my eyes and mouth. With a hot, sweaty, blackened hand, I raised the bottle to my mouth. The water was hot, also with a hint of oil and petrol, yet it tasted like the nectar of the gods. The relief was instant: I could talk and my mouth tasted better, not good, but better.

Looking about, I tried to make sense of what had happened but no matter how hard I tried I could not get the sight of the body lying at the foot of the stairs out of my mind. It was as if my brain, my eyes, my entire thought system, were frozen in time and all I could see was the body. Silence dominated the battlefield: no one talked, there was no movement, no sound, no breeze, nothing to take your mind off the terrible situation we now found ourselves in. It was like being a prisoner on death row, wondering if today was going to be the day. Lighting a cigarette, trying to relax, my dry mouth only got drier and tasted worse than it already was. Forcing my brain to work, I took another long look around the conflict area. The 60mm mortars were still where I had set them up just in front of the empty trenches; all the column vehicles had withdrawn at least a hundred metres from the double-storey building in preparation for the airstrike that we prayed would come. The roof of the intended target had huge holes in it, caused by the RPG-7 rockets and the 12.7 machine gun. Had the Frelimo gunman survived or had he been killed? That was the question. There was only one way to find out: get onto the roof and check. The risks were too high; the casualties we had suffered were already unacceptable.

Time was a-wasting, as they say in the old cowboy movies. We needed an answer and we needed it soon. As I crouched there behind the wall smoking, all the old doubts came flooding back. I was like an old woman, nervous, fidgety, unable to sit still, huffing and puffing on a cigarette, eyes darting all over the place, trying to see everything but noticing nothing. My body was covered in a cold sweat, my breathing short and shallow. I was starting to panic. "Steady," I told myself. "Steady, get the breathing under control … what's the matter? Get a grip of yourself … you're carrying on like an arsehole … show a bit of faith in your leaders. Reid-Daley will come through. Relax, my man, relax."

Concentrating hard, I began to get my breathing under control. "Shit, that was close," I thought to myself. "Imagine breaking down and crying." The thought made me cringe. Things were not that bad: I was alive and fit, dirty and smelly maybe, but I was alive. Compared to the two wounded – one paralyzed and the other's legs attached to his body by a few bits of skin and the odd muscle – I was in paradise. The pain my two comrades were suffering, both mental and physical, morphine or no morphine, must have been incredible. Looking around at the people nearest me, I could see by the wobbly grins, the continual thumbs-ups, the jerky head movements, that they were just as unsure of the situation as me.

Lighting up another cigarette with the same dirty, now somewhat steadier, hand, I tried to think positive thoughts. Then it dawned on me that that was the problem: the THINKING! The attack had come to a grinding halt and in doing so it had given us time to think, hence all the doubts and uncertainty. The easy beginning was turning out to be more of a liability than an asset. Without a shot fired by either side during the initial capture of the town, our concentration and senses had lapsed. We had become overconfident, with the end result of one dead and two seriously injured men. If, on the other hand, we had had to fight from the town entrance and clear each building one at a time, I do not believe we would have suffered as many casualties. We would not have had time to relax, to think, to become complacent. We would not have lost that edge we had when we had first arrived at the boom.

My train of thought was broken by what sounded a like the drone of an approaching aircraft. As the seconds passed, the noise grew louder. It was definitely an aircraft. I sighed with relief. Forgotten, for the moment, were the doubts of whether we were going to get out of this mess in one piece or not. Our salvation had arrived. All that needed to happen now was for the aircraft to destroy the building and the Frelimo gunman within.

Staring up to the sky, I tried to locate the aircraft. I wanted to see what type they had sent us, hoping against hope it was not a dreaded Trojan – the flying coffin. After several minutes of gazing into the clear sky and seeing nothing, it dawned on me that I was seeing nothing because the aircraft was flying very low to avoid missile and small-arms fire. Maybe the headache and burning eyes had disappeared but the brain still seemed sluggish. Sitting where I was I had a good view of the targeted building. My mind was still trying to work out if I was too close to the target when the scream of an aircraft in a dive caused me to look at the building. Out the corner of my eye, I caught a flash of colour. It was a black person dressed in what appeared to be a Frelimo uniform, the same as us, bent over and running for the bush. The sighting lasted a second or two at the most. "For fuck's sake," I thought, "who the hell was that?" Surely it was not one of us. It was a fleeting thought but it was to come back time and again to haunt me. Who had I seen? Was it the man who had killed one of us and seriously wounded two others?

My eyes were now firmly fixed on the roof of the doomed building. The aircraft flashed into view, the undersides of its wings momentarily lit up as the rockets left their mounting, heading for the target. The roof seemed to shimmer and lift slightly before the blast of the rockets sent it in all directions, followed instantly by a loud explosion as the ammunition still in the building ignited. A low, thick cloud of black dust hung over the area, the smell of gunpowder unmistakable. As we waited for the dust to clear, a strange, morbid silence took hold: there was no cheering, no movement, nothing, just a deep sad silence.

The headache returned with a vengeance as did the burning in my eyes. My petrol-soaked clothes were now making me feel nauseous. The feelings of relief and happiness I was expecting did not materialize. I felt now exactly as I had felt before the strike, tired, physically dead tired but more so, mentally. And hovering in the back of my mind was the question that would continue to haunt me: who had I seen running from the building seconds before the airstrike?

As the dust slowly lifted, the target emerged. It was almost completely destroyed, the roof had gone and just the odd wall and a good bit of that staircase to hell had survived. Any humans in the building would surely have perished: the combination of the rockets and the exploding munitions would have seen to that.

The clear-up operation then began. Firstly, most importantly, was the uplift of the two wounded and the one dead member of our raiding team. In due course, a helicopter arrived and the casualties were taken back to Rhodesia. Or so I thought.

Time was not on our side. We had to move as quickly as possible to check the wrecked building. To my knowledge, no bodies were found. I was not involved in the search, so I do not know how thoroughly the rubble was searched. All munitions and papers that survived the blast were loaded onto the bus saved for this purpose. A sense of urgency prevailed. Our weary bodies seemed to get a new lease on life and a spring returned to our step. All my suffering was forgotten, short-lived though it was. We all knew that the longer it took to do what we had to do the more time Frelimo had of getting organized to make our return trip a nightmare.

It was on one of my trips to the bus to load up some recovered ammunition when I saw something that turned my blood cold and ignited a burning anger and a feeling of mistrust against certain individuals, something that would stay with me for the rest of my life. On previous trips to the bus I had just dumped whatever I was carrying on the step, as there had always been someone else busy inside. On this occasion, the bus was empty, so I decided I would pack my box of ammunition myself to save someone else the trouble. Climbing up the steps, I moved towards the back of the bus where most of the ammunition was being packed. I was tired. The bounce in my step had long since disappeared and my headache was back. My eyes were burning again and I had a feeling of wanting to puke. This was all forgotten in an instant to be replaced by a sense of disbelief.

There, lying on one of the seats at the back of the bus was the body of Jannie Nel.

I could not believe what I was seeing. Shaking my head, I had to sit down. No ways, I told myself, I must be seeing things. The heat, combined with exhaustion plus the never-ending tension, was causing my brain to short-circuit, and I was seeing things, surely. Taking a deep breath, I closed my eyes and counted to ten. My whole body was shaking, the sweat was pouring off, my ears were filled with a loud roaring sound and my head was throbbing, seemingly on the verge of exploding. Slowly opening my eyes, my head lowered, the first thing I saw were my filthy hands, black in places and white in others, cut and bruised from lifting ammunition boxes, but remarkably steady. A good sign: as far as I was concerned, I had not lost control of myself. I was back in charge of my emotions. As I continued to raise my head, the sight I dreaded came into focus, bit by bit, until I was staring, unblinking, at the body of Jannie Nel. I gradually let the air from my burning lungs as I fought to understand what I was seeing.

I had seen the helicopter come and go and had assumed that all the casualties had been uplifted, including the body of Jannie Nel. If the helicopter was too small to uplift all the injured and dead why had they not sent two? What difference would it have made? If you send one you might as well send a thousand. Maybe the helicopter was coming back, I thought, trying to convince myself. But in the back of my mind I knew there was no chance. The column was forming up and we were getting ready to move out.

The horizontal rope on the selection
assault course at Wafa Wafa
training camp, Kariba. The 34-
foot drop is in to thorn bush.

Selection course, Wafa Wafa. Back blisters at the end of the 90-kilometre endurance march.
The soldiers had to carry a 35kg pack filled with rocks plus webbing, rifle and ammunition.

Relief shows on the faces of these soldiers at the end of their selection course. At their feet is the hated log that they have had to lug around for days.

A simulated (and realistic) contact during training. In the foreground are the 'guerrillas'.

Aerial photograph, taken from a Canberra bomber piloted by Wing Commander Randy Durandt, of a muster parade at the Nyadzonya/Pungwe base before the raid. A count revealed over 800 guerrillas on parade.

Some of the ZANLA dead after the raid.

C

Operation Aztec – near Mapai.

Unimog with home-made mounted SNEB (white phosphorus)
and armour-piercing rocket launcher.

Flying column troops.

Padre Grant addresses the troops at a memorial service.

Operation Mardon – the Pig in action for the first time.

A Pig during Operation Mardon.

A flying column stick leader checks the route ahead.

Colour Sergeant Andy
Balaam, MLM.

Selous Scouts Medals Parade.

The Selous Scouts – a proud regiment.

View of my first home in Port St Johns and the point where the
ferry crosses the river. The ferry is an old rowing boat.

Cape Hermes Hotel used to be the upmarket drinking capital
in Port St Johns, now it is a broken-down ruin.

The main road into Port St Johns, where I was paraded after my arrest.

The training camp for the Ciskei Liberation Army was situated at the base of this hill.

The road leading to George Matanzima's house, now converted to holiday flats.

Quacha's Nek and surrounds with the mountains in the distance.

The area around Quacha's Nek – rugged and beautiful.

The main road I had to cross to get to the golf course.

In the background is the stream/water trap where I tried to clean up and shave.

Main entrance to King William's Town Golf Club.

The church in King William's Town. The house in the background
is the priest's house where I was turned away.

The main entrance to the church – and the door I could not open.

The site of the public telephone I used to call my contact in Port St Johns. The old public telephone has now been replaced by more modern telephones.

The garage in King William's Town where I was picked up after the failed Palace attack. I was sitting on the wall. In those days there was no fence.

What used to be the police station – across the road from the public telephone.

The railway bride over the Kei River where I was to cross back into
Transkei after walking the 70 kilometres from Bisho.

I understand the saying used by medical people: 'Help the living, only God can help the dead', but surely we were not going to transport the body back to Rhodesia in the back of the bus? This was the body of Jannie Nel: he was one of us, not a dead terrorist, yet we were treating his body like a side of beef. The longer I looked at his body, the more my resentment grew. This was the man who, six weeks prior, had stopped two SAS soldiers from beating the shit out of me in the Sahara Bar.

I had arrived early and the bar was empty. The bar counter in the Sahara was shaped like a horseshoe. Sitting down at the side of the U-shape farthest from the entrance, I ordered a beer. I had just returned from a long bush trip and needed to relax. An ice-cold beer in an air-conditioned bar was a good way to start. Gradually, the bar started to fill up with mainly soldiers and their girlfriends. Some I knew, some I did not. Glancing up, I noticed two guys staring at me. I had seen them before and I knew they were SAS. I knew quite a few SAS guys and was good friends with several. These two, however, were not among those I would call friends. One look told me that all they wanted to do was cause trouble. Sure enough, not five minutes later, they got up, walked all the way round the U-shaped bar and sat down next to me. Ignoring me completely, they started to discuss the Selous Scouts between themselves. Words like 'arseholes', 'fools', 'fairies', 'poofs' and the like were thrown about with gay abandon. Trying my best to ignore them, I ordered another beer. I knew the drill: they wanted to give me a couple of good slaps, not in the bar – there were too many bouncers – but rather in the toilets where they would not be disturbed. After the second beer, I had no choice but to go to the toilet and get a slap or ten or stay where I was and wet myself. As I was about to stand up, I heard a familiar voice: "Hi Andy, long time no see." And there, forcing his way between the two SAS soldiers by now almost in my lap, was Jannie Nel. A broad grin on his face, he turned to the two SAS guys and asked, "You aren't giving my friend here a hard time, are you? I thought not," he said, answering his own question.

"START UP, START UP, WE'RE MOVING OUT!" snapped me back to

reality. Getting wearily to my aching feet, I had one last look at my friend, knowing there was nothing I could do to prevent his body from being dragged across the countryside like a side of beef. The anger and mistrust that began that day were to stay with me, as did the picture of the body lying at the bottom of the stairs, as did the never-answered question: who had I seen running from the building just prior to the airstrike?

12

Attack on Nyadzonya / Pungwe base: Mozambique, August 1976

There were at least forty of us crammed into the small tin room that passed for an operations centre-cum-control room at Inkomo Barracks, our barracks just outside Salisbury. I had just returned from a couple of days off after the disaster that was Mapai. I had drunk myself stupid, wasting a chance to relax and eat some decent food. I was sorry now but at the time it had seemed like a good idea to get drunk. In hindsight, it was perhaps not the best thing to do. As I listened to the briefing, my stomach started to knot. The more I listened the bigger and tighter the knot became. The distance to be covered and the number of terrorists involved were massive. Mapai was a minor skirmish compared to this.

⚔

Rounds were bouncing off the barrels, the ground was erupting in little fountains of dust and the grass was falling in sheaths as though being cut by an invisible reaper. Lying between the two 81mm mortars I was in charge of, I was caught in the crossfire between the Selous Scout column and Frelimo. I was being pounded by the wall of sound created by the 20mm cannon, the 12.7mm Russian machine gun, the 7.62 Belgian MAG machine guns and the.30 Browning machine guns that were all opening fire simultaneously on the five thousand ZANLA terrorists gathered in front of them. I cringed in fear.

We had crossed into Mozambique just after midnight on 9 August, having spent the day laagered up on a farm just north of Umtali, a small Rhodesian town on the border with Mozambique. All our vehicles were camouflaged Frelimo style, our uniforms were a mixture of old Portuguese uniforms and civilian clothing. Travelling at night with all the whites wearing 'black is beautiful', with a Portuguese-speaking local in the front vehicle, we would pass all but the closest of inspections. The dirt roads were a lot better than I had expected and progress was good. As usual, I was the last vehicle in the column.

Sitting on an ammunition box in the back of my Unimog, with a section of 81mm mortars, it was not long before my arse was numb, my eyes were a pool of watery red liquid and I was covered in a thick layer of red dust. Trying not to think about the losses we had suffered during the raid on Mapai, I stared unblinkingly through the dust at the bouncing taillights of the Unimog in front. Time seemed to stand still. I was in a self-induced stupor. My whole world had been reduced to the smell of diesel fumes, red dust, bouncing taillights and the whine of the engine of the Unimog in front. I felt safe, warm and content in my self-made, unthinking, little cocoon.

Grasping desperately for a canopy rail to prevent myself from falling out, I wildly stared around as the Unimog skidded to a stop. There were no gunshots, no flares lighting up the dark night, just the gentle ticking-over of the Unimog's Mercedes engine. Something was wrong, but it was not an ambush as I had first thought. Standing up in the back of the Unimog, I looked down the road to see if I could spot the cause of the hold-up. Thick red dust and more thick red dust was turned into a vast, glowing, orange cloud by the lights of the column, covering everything. Visibility was down to a couple of metres – for us that is: for anyone watching the road the glowing orange cloud would have been visible for miles. Mobility was the key to our survival. After ten minutes or so, I began to get a bit panicky. I was suffering from 'Tail-end-Charlie' syndrome: shot nerves.

The dust settled. The entire area was lit up by the headlights of the fourteen vehicles in the column. To my wild imagination it was a neon sign in the sky saying, 'Here we are, we have just crossed over from Rhodesia, come and shoot the shit out of us'. The fact that the telephone lines in the area had been cut did nothing to ease the mounting tension I was beginning to feel. Jumping off the back of the Unimog, AK-47 in hand, I took a walk up to the front of the column. In the thick dust a driver had missed a narrow concrete bridge and his Ferret armoured car had plunged into the river below. Half in and half out of the river, with its engine completely submerged, there was no way we were going to get it out. God, I hated this Tail-end-Charlie bit: you always felt vulnerable, isolated and lived with the permanent fear of being left behind or getting lost.

It was in the early hours of the morning and I did not know whether to sit down or stand up, laugh or cry, as we drove through the Frelimo garrison town of Chimoio, formerly Vila de Manica in Mozambique's Manica Province, on our way to attack the ZANLA terrorist base of Nyadzonya / Pungwe. In the end, I settled for sitting huddled up in the corner, cigarette hanging out of my mouth, AK-47 between my knees and mind in neutral. With my mind lulled into a state of limbo by the gentle whine of the tyres on the tarmac, I stared blankly at the empty streets, the small, run-down houses and the deserted guardhouses. I heard, but I was not hearing. I saw, but I was not seeing. I was, as it was known in the Rhodesian army, 'switched off'.

The reds, oranges and pinks in the sky heralded the start of a new day. We had spent the last few hours laagered up on the side of the road just short of the Pungwe River Bridge. So far, so good: apart from the Ferret armoured car ending up in the river, everything had gone to plan. From here on in it was all about timing. We had to arrive at 08h30, the time of the muster parade, for our plan to succeed.

The dirt road seemed endless. The potholes were deep and countless. Covered in a thick layer of dust, I clung desperately to the canopy railings in an effort to keep on my feet and avoid falling out of the vehicle as the driver continued his losing battle to miss the numerous potholes.

My body went cold, the hair on the back of my neck stood up as, standing on the back of the Unimog with my mortars deployed below me, I watched in amazement and fear as the column, in extended line a mere twenty metres to my front and facing the parade ground, was swamped by a tide of black bodies, with four or five thousand cheering ZANLA recruits running forward to greet them.

Long yellow flames shot from the barrels, vehicles shuddering under the recoil as the entire column opened fire. Faces disintegrated, bones shattered, meat shredded, blood boiled, skin burned. I watched, fascinated by the horror unfolding before my eyes. Bullets smashed into the vehicle I was standing on, bringing me back to earth, and giving me a frightening reminder of where I was.

Then silence. Awesome, eerie in its completeness. Still lying between the two mortars, I cautiously lifted my head and looked about. Where thirty seconds ago had stood a large, cheering crowd of terrorists, there was only emptiness and silence. The column vehicles were still in extended line facing the parade ground, the occupants frozen, staring in disbelief at the death and destruction they had wreaked.

The escape routes, do not forget the escape routes, a tiny voice reminded me. One of the main reasons the mortars had been brought along was to put down fire on likely escape routes and cause as many casualties as possible to the fleeing terrorists. Fifteen, twenty seconds later, standing unsteadily and covered in a thick layer of dust, grass and leaves, I managed to croak, "FIRE!"

Sometime later, tired, hungry, dirty, eyes hanging out on my cheek bones, looking more dead than alive, I tried to concentrate on what I was supposed to be doing, which was helping Pete Mac clear huts. We worked as a team, relying on each other. One mistake, one second of not concentrating on the task at hand could get us killed.

The mud hut was small, round, dark and evil-smelling. A quick look seemed to indicate that it was empty but as we were about to leave, a hand shot out from beneath the low wooden bed and latched on to Pete Mac's ankle. The end of his AK-47 lit up and his shoulders shuddered under the recoil. The hand released its grip and we moved on to the next hut.

Standing on the back of the vehicle ready to move out back to Rhodesia, surrounded by bags of money and the odd briefcase we had taken from the burning huts, I stared transfixed at the carnage before me. This was indeed a garden of hell on earth. The landscaper was Satan, his props the dead bodies and burning buildings. The once flat, uninteresting, bland, brown parade ground had, with clever use of the corpses, been turned into a colourful, gently undulating eye-stopper of blacks and reds, with splashes of whites and browns. The mundane blue skyline had been turned into a breath-taking thing of beauty. Oranges, reds, blacks and greys now leaped high into the sky as the entire base burned, all set to the screams of agony of those caught in the inferno. Having one last look before moving out, I was sure that Satan would have been happy with the results of his work.

God, not again, I thought to myself, as the column once more came to halt. A few minutes later I heard the sound of trees being chopped down. Another bridge needed to be built or repaired. Thank God all the vehicles were carrying picks, shovels and axes. Our Portuguese guide, who had once farmed in the area, was using derelict farm roads that bypassed the numerous Frelimo outposts in the area – hence the bridge-building.

Gradually the thick bush gave way to more open countryside and the appearance of the occasional village. I was struggling to keep awake. The warm sun, the gentle rocking of the Unimog, the ever-present diesel fumes and dust clouds were slowly getting the better of me: my catnaps were getting longer.

"Hey, sir! Wake up – Frelimo."

Earlier when the vehicle had stopped I had not bothered opening my eyes, figuring it was yet another halt for our guide to get his bearings. Now with the magic word 'Frelimo' ringing in my ears, the adrenalin started flowing. Gone was the feeling of tiredness. My swollen, weeping eyes acquired the ability of a telescope, distance and clarity were not a problem, my blocked ears could hear a pin drop from a hundred metres, my tired, used and abused brain was up and running to rival any super-computer in speed and clarity of thought. I was now in survival mode.

Opening my bottle of 'black is beautiful', I spread the vile-smelling cream all over my face and hands before replacing my balaclava. I stood up, AK-47 in hand. I was ready to try and handle whatever came my way. My back was tingling, a gentle river of sweat ran down my spine, my muscles were so taut that they felt as if they were going to burst through my skin and the urge to look back was overpowering. Moving at a snail's pace at the back of the column, it had taken several lifetimes to run the gauntlet of suspicious Frelimo soldiers lining the dirt road we were using to get back to Rhodesia.

Now I was relaxed, happy and cheerful, with a cigarette hanging out my mouth. I even managed a smile or two. We were about to cross back into Rhodesia and all that stood in our way was a small but deep river. All was well. In an hour, max, we should be back in Rhodesia and safety. It appeared that the Frelimo soldiers had bought our guide's story of being on our way to the border for deployment into Rhodesia.

Thump, thump.

My hair stood up, I broke into a cold sweat. Jumping up from my bed of money and briefcases, I stared disbelievingly in the direction from whence the sound had come. It could not be, not now, not mortars; half the column was already in Rhodesia and in another thirty minutes we would all be across. Thirty seconds later the first salvo landed about a hundred to a hundred and fifty metres short of our position. So much for our cover story.

My worst fears were realized. From the sound of the exploding rounds, they appeared to be 82mm mortars. I still bore the scars of my last encounter with Frelimo mortars. Seventy-five seconds later, I listened to the first of the ten rounds I had fired back landing. Direction and distance sounded fine. Abruptly, all incoming fire ceased, which meant I was close enough to scare them. To show there were no hard feelings, plus the fact that I wanted to lighten my vehicle before crossing the border, I fired a further ten rounds. The crossing proceeded without a hitch.

Once back in Rhodesia, smelling to high heaven, my mouth tasting like a blocked septic tank, eyes looking like they had been pissed in, lying on a bag of escudos and bouncing along in the back of the Unimog, I was as happy and content as could be. Reaching under the bag of cash to find out what was digging into my back, I pulled out a black briefcase. Staring at it, the memories came flooding back.

13

Pseudo op: Operation Repulse, late 1976

"Wake up Andy, the boss wants to see you."

The toe of a boot gently nudged me in the ribs. It was hot and clammy in the cattle truck, the darkness broken by the flaring red ends of cigarettes and the whites of the black Selous Scouts' eyes. Sitting propped up in the corner, dressed in my normal long trousers, long-sleeved shirt, jacket and wearing a balaclava plus chest webbing, covered in black camouflage cream, I was hot, uncomfortable, itchy and trying by all means not to rub my burning eyes. I was the only white in the group of seventeen Selous Scouts.

It is difficult to explain how I felt: I was lonely, but I should not have been, I was among friends. I had worked as a troop commander for years with the same group of guys and I trusted them with my life. It was not so much the physical part of being alone that worried me, but more the mental part. The days and nights were endless and I had nobody to talk to, and nobody to help me make decisions. The pressure, the tension, nerves strained to breaking point, caused every sound to magnify like the clap of doom. It was enough to drive any sane person mad.

We were being deployed by train as a last resort. The area where we were going to try and operate had been completely subverted by the local terrorist groups. Every man, woman and child was a staunch enemy supporter, acting as the eyes and ears for the local terrorist groups. I had worked in areas like this before and knew from experience that, to sort out such areas, drastic measures were required, up to and including death.

Sitting in the corner of the wagon on top of my big pack, AK-47 between my knees, I tried to think up a plan that would work, concentrating on the use of brainpower and only to resort to brute force and ignorance when all else had failed. Like the saying goes, grab them by the balls and the hearts will surely follow. However, this was easier said than done.

The hot, dung-smelling, gently swaying, airless cattle truck and soothing clickety-clack of the wheels soon had me on the verge of sleep. I am slow to wake up, and so the last thing I needed was to jump off the train disoriented and half asleep, head off in the wrong direction into an unfrozen area and get my arse shot off by friendly forces. In an effort to keep awake, I used an old trick I had learned while doing guard duty back at barracks in Salisbury. Digging around in my jacket pocket, I pulled out my cigarettes and sticking one in my mouth, I lit it. I could see in the flickering light of the match that most my comrades had succumbed to the gentle swaying of the cattle truck and the soothing click-clack of the wheels and were fast asleep. Making myself comfortable, I cupped the cigarette in my hands so that if I happened to nod off, it would drop onto my hands and burn me awake, as I tried to come up with workable plan.

A packet of thirty cigarettes later, still with no workable plan and having decided to play it by ear as usual, I braced myself against the side of the wagon as the train shuddered to halt amidst much screeching of brakes and hissing of steam. "Ye gods!" I thought to myself as I stood up on unsteady legs, hitching my thirty-kilogram pack onto my back. "I hope there are no locals nearby." The screech of the brakes would definitely wake them up and they would mostly certainly wonder what was happening. Why would a train be stopping at a siding at 04h00 in the morning? And come investigating they would but, with a bit of luck, I would be long gone.

Moving slowly and carefully, my pack on my back, my AK-47 in my hands, trying not to trip over my comrades, I headed for the now-open door of the cattle truck. The pink and reds heralded the start of a new day and in the distance I could hear a cockerel screeching his welcome to the rising sun. After exiting the wagon, we broke down into three groups: two groups of eight to try and infiltrate the area and locate the resident terrorist groups for the Fire Force to sort out, and the third made up of me as the controller-cum-observation post.

As it began to get light and I could make out my surroundings, I realized that what I had thought was a reasonably sized, thickly wooded hill was not. Crisscrossed by paths and overgrazed, it provided little or no cover where I could hide. Blackening up, I grabbed my AK-47 and with my pack on my back I moved out, searching for a hiding place. The smell of faeces and urine was nauseating. It was summer and the locals were out and about early.

I had been scratching around like a headless chicken for some time looking for a place to hole up when I heard voices of approaching men. Whether they were local or terrorist, I had no idea. Either way, I needed to take cover. Crisis time had arrived. There was not a blade of grass for miles around. The overgrazed area was turning into a desert. I had no choice. A few metres from where I was crouched in the open was a small clump of bushes. I knew what it was but I had no choice. Surrounded by faeces, old and new, in what was a local roadside toilet, I paid no attention to the mopane flies, the stench or the wet feeling against my stomach. I concentrated on the voices.

Several minutes later, I was up and moving again, fighting back the urge to puke. The front of my jacket and shirt was covered in, for the want of a better word, human shit, as was the one leg of my trousers. Instead of coming nearer, the voices had faded; by the time I realized this, taking cover was unnecessary. The sun was high in the sky before I found a place to hide: nothing more than a hollow in the ground, about the size of an average bathtub and about a metre deep, it was ideal. Trying to keep the mopane flies and countless flies at bay with one hand, AK-47 and big pack safely out the way, I attempted to remove the shit from my clothes with handfuls of sand. Five minutes later I gave up: all I had succeeded in doing was to spread it deeper into my clothes. Having no extra clothes to change into, I would have to live with the smell and the thousands of flies.

It was now 23h00. I was crouched next to a small pool of water in an otherwise dry river, not far from where I had spent the day. Unable to handle the smell of faeces and the flies, I had decided to look for a place where I could strip down, clean myself and give my clothes a rinse. Crouched next to the pool, however, I was having second thoughts. "*Ja*, big mouth," I thought to myself, "what's the matter? Scared you're going to get caught with your pants down?" Leaving my pack and webbing on dry ground, I waded into the dung-filled pool, weapon held above my head.

⚜

"For fuck's sake, Corporal Clemence, do not kill him," I whispered into the radio, after being told by Corporal Clemence that a *mujiba*[1] had walked into him while he was setting up the radio and that, having no choice, had taken him prisoner.

"Ah, you know me, sir," came the silky reply. "I do not kill innocent

---

1   A local child, normally a young teenager who acted as a runner for, or the eyes and ears of, ZANLA terrorists

civilians; I'll only talk to him to see what he knows about the terrorists in the area and then I'll let him go."

"Sure," I thought to myself, "you're going to let him go after he has seen you talking to me on the radio … pigs can fly, too."

The *mujiba* was as good as dead. There was nothing I could do or say that would change that. This was one of the things that I always wondered about. Did our big bosses really know what went on in the bush and choose to ignore it, or did they seriously think all the incredible results achieved by the Selous Scouts pseudo groups came without a price tag?

Four weeks had passed since being dropped off by train and I was beginning to take strain. Cover in the area was restricted to a few lightly wooded, small hills that were constantly visited by locals in their never-ending quest for firewood. With the hills off limits, I had taken to hiding in anything from old maize fields to deserted huts. On the odd occasion, when the sun was rising and with no cover available, I just lay down in the open and hoped for the best. I had thought of joining up with one of my pseudo groups to overcome the problem but I knew from past experience that this would not work. At night, if I kept my mouth shut, I would probably get away with passing myself off as a member of the group but night time was not the problem, it was the day: my green eyes and black camouflage, which constantly needed replacing, would compromise the whole operation.

I no longer stank of human faeces, thanks to my midnight bath, but I now stank of stale sweat, rotten inch-thick black camouflage cream, urine and rotting flesh. Suffering badly from foot rot, I had taken to removing my shoes at night and urinating on my feet in an effort to get rid of it. Unable to find decent cover, I spent most of the daylight hours lying on my stomach in the baking hot sun, surrounded by thousands of mopane flies. When I needed to urinate I merely rolled onto my side. Accidents did happen which added to the vile odour surrounding my person.

Progress had been slow. The only information of any interest we had gathered was the fact that there was only one group of terrorists resident in the area, not the three or four that had been suspected. Lying hidden in a small outcrop of rocks, I waited for Corporal Clemence to come back to me with the results of his chat with the young *mujiba*.

It was early morning and the sky was slowly changing colour from a deep purple to a greyish blue, flecked with pinks, reds and oranges. Apart from the odd rooster welcoming the rising sun it was dead quiet. Sitting behind a few small bushes on an otherwise treeless hill, I was awaiting the arrival of the Fire Force from Buffalo Range, Chiredzi. Already the locals were on the move, women with buckets on their heads off to collect water and, my main worry: the herd boys driving their cattle in the never-ending search for grazing.

The news from Clemence had been good: the captured *mujiba* had voluntarily identified the terrorist camp. I very much doubted the 'voluntarily' part; nevertheless, the corporal had done a reconnaissance that confirmed the presence of the terrorists. All I needed now was for some young herd boy to stumble upon me before the arrival of the Fire Force, which would compromise the whole operation and cause four weeks' work to go down the drain.

The helicopter gunship shuddered; the ground erupted around the fleeing terrorist as he tried to outrun the 20mm cannon shells. It was no contest: one second he was alive, the next just a black blob on an otherwise brown ploughed field. It did not take long. The small group of six terrorists stood no chance. With the countryside almost a desert – bare and overgrazed with most of the trees cut down for firewood – there was no place to hide. It did not take long.

After the Fire Force had eliminated the group, I had arranged for me and my troop to be uplifted by helicopter back to the Scouts' fort at Chiredzi. It had been a long and none too successful bush trip. So I decided to drown my sorrows and, as usual, had one too many.

I was surely going to die. My hangover was going to be the death of me. My breathing was quick and shallow, my heart pounded, my head was one mass of pain and into my bleary red eyes ran a never-ending river of sweat. The heat was murderous and the sun, combined with the heat of the engine and the smell of diesel, had turned the airless armoured vehicle into a mobile, nauseous, puke-inducing steam bath. Struggling to my feet, I stuck my head out of the top of the vehicle. God, how I hated these vehicles: they were slow, clumsy, underpowered and it took forever to get from point A to point B. Travelling as we were, from Chiredzi to Salisbury, was going to take the better part of a day.

Looking at Corporal Clemence sitting propped up in the corner sweating like a stuck pig and fast asleep, I wondered what really had happened to the *mujiba* he claimed to have let go. It wasn't that I hadn't tried to find out, but all I got from him on the two occasions I had asked, was, "Don't worry, everything is all right." Time would tell. If I was asked the odd question by our security branch then I would know that Corporal Clemence had messed up on the burial of the *mujiba*. If no questions came my way, it meant the body had not been discovered. There was no doubt in my mind that the *mujiba* was dead and buried.

⚒

Rolling over onto my hands and knees, I lifted my throbbing head and opened my eyes but immediately shut them again. My eyes were swollen and red from too much alcohol and too little sleep and were in no condition to handle the glare of the bright sunlight. Keeping my eyes firmly closed, I tried to stand up. It was a failure. I managed to reach the gorilla-walk position before collapsing in a heap, much to the amusement of my audience. One failure followed the next. In one desperate last attempt, I crawled to a nearby tree, and using it as a support, I managed to get to my feet.

The tea was spilling all over the place. Over my dirty shirt and trousers, onto the carpet, onto the chair I was sitting on. Try as I might, I could not stop my hands from shaking. "God, Andy, get a grip of yourself," I murmured. "If you don't stop with the shaking, there'll be no tea left in the cup to drink.

I was sitting in Colonel Reid-Daly's office in the same dirty clothes I had been wearing for the last two days, smelling to high heaven. Covered from top to bottom in leaves and grass, I had not bathed, brushed my hair or cleaned my teeth since leaving Chiredzi the day before. As I sat there waiting for Colonel Reid-Daly to finish reading whatever it was he was reading, the events of the previous evening came flooding back.

It was late at night, maybe ten or eleven o'clock. We were hungry and tired and it had been a long bush trip. We had handed in all our weapons and equipment and were waiting at the pay office for our pay. It was one of Colonel Reid-Daly's things that, no matter what time you got back from the bush, your pay would be waiting.

"What fucking training programme?" I had screamed when told by the duty officer that neither I nor any member of my troop would get paid until I had produced a training programme for the next few days in base. I lost it – the wheels came off. All the anger and frustration that had been building up over the days, weeks, months and years, came pouring out. I told the unfortunate duty officer what I thought about him, his training programme and where it would best fit. I then gave him a detailed and colourful rundown on what I thought about all HQ staff, or cupboard *kakkers*,[2] as they were known. I spared

---

2   Lit. 'cupboard shitters' (Afrik.), aka 'jam stealers' – rear-echelon personnel

nobody. I started at the top and finished with the dishwasher in the kitchen. Sitting hunched over with the almost empty cup of tea in my shaking hands, I wondered if this time I had gone too far.

"Well, sergeant-major, what have you got to say for yourself?"

Looking into the pale, cold, blue eyes of Reid-Daly, I felt that maybe this time I had pushed a little too hard and once too often. Straitening up, I put my now-empty teacup and full saucer on the table and stared back. I was still pissed off and the headache and feeling of wanting to puke did not help. The way I figured was that, if I was going to go then I might as well go out in a blaze of glory.

The cold water from the shower was washing away the effects of a heavy night's drinking. My alcohol-soaked brain was beginning to function. I had been lucky, very lucky. I had expected to be stripped of my rank and sent back to the Rhodesian Light Infantry, my parent unit. Instead, I had got a small reminder about the rules and regulations concerning the 'dos and don'ts' when addressing an officer: "You fucking arsehole" was not acceptable, no matter what the circumstances were. Any further outbreaks of this type on my part would be dealt with severely.

14

Parachute training: Dukuduku, South Africa, 1977

After travelling nearly the whole day in the back of the slow-moving South African army trucks, we eventually arrived at our destination: an old deserted forest rangers' camp in the Dukuduku Forest on Natal's North Coast. This was to be our home for the duration of our parachute course. The scenery was stunning: massive trees with thick canopies that even the sun had difficulty penetrating, thick, damp undergrowth that I am sure never saw the sun and remained moist year in and year out, an ideal environment for birds, of which there were hundreds. And situated in this little piece of paradise was the old forester rangers' camp, our new home.

We were to be trained by the South African Special Forces, away from prying eyes, flapping ears and nosy journalists. Secrecy was of the utmost importance as the South African government did not want the rest of the world to know that it was helping train Rhodesian army personnel. Damned politicians: by the time they figured that out, everybody knew anyway and it was too late as the war was lost.

There were two reasons why we were being trained in South Africa. One was that the small Rhodesian parachute-training facility at New Sarum airbase in Salisbury was a security risk for our black members who survived on their wits and the fact that their faces were unknown. The second was that, with the war escalating so rapidly, the demand for paratroopers was increasing exponentially and New Sarum was simply unable to cope. Enter the South Africans.

I was quite happy to be trained in South Africa by South Africans. I had taken a walk around the facility at New Sarum while training was in progress and it was all very regimented, as if the instructors were trying to teach you to jump in the same manner you were taught drill on a drill square, with lots of shouting, screaming and swearing. No smiles, no encouragement and, oh so British. At that stage of my life, I was anti-British and hated drill with a vengeance. No thanks: I was quite happy to be in Dukuduku Forest enjoying the beautiful scenery and the peace and quiet. At least I was away from the ex-British parachutists who seemed to run the New Sarum training school, away from the stupid rivalry between the different units as to who should be para-trained and who should not, who should be paid for the skill and who should not. We were supposed to be fighting for our country, not acting like a bunch of school kids. Thank God for the change of environment and mind-set.

The old forestry camp consisted of two houses that were used as living quarters for the instructors and as storage for the course equipment. There were also three long wooden barrack-room structures that were to serve as our accommodation and ablutions, as well as an extremely large kitchen–dining hall.

Early the next morning we were running down a narrow tar road, towels clutched in our hands, heading for the beach. This was the life: start each day with a road run and a swim in the sea; things were looking good. The road run itself was a different experience, with no instructor screaming left-right-left-right and setting a pace that caused the less fit to struggle, just a nice slow jog to our destination. The sea was a whole new experience for our black members, with most only venturing in up to their knees and no further.

On our return to camp, the hard work began under the guidance of our South African instructors. With most of us wearing overalls and boots, some of our tougher members had opted for shorts and takkies but after meeting the thick undergrowth head on, they backed down and reverted to overalls. We built our own small but tough assault course, intermixed with the apparatus required to train a paratrooper. Once again, there was no shouting and screaming, just advice and encouragement. Little did I know at the time that this was to be one of the most enjoyable periods in my army career. It was slow, hard work, the thick undergrowth alive with a multitude of stinging insects and plants, the trees massive, difficult and dangerous to climb. The heat and humidity that made you sweat day and night regardless of what you were doing turned the work area under the trees into a vast steam bath. I figured I lost a kilogram or two in the first couple of days alone. There was plenty of swearing and bitching but there was also plenty of laughter.

The only dark cloud on the otherwise clear horizon was our early-morning run. It was day two and we had set off on our run to the beach, the white guys with their towels and cameras, the black guys with their towels and empty plastic Coke bottles that they would fill with sea water as it was supposedly very potent when used in traditional medicine. On our arrival at the beach, we were met by a delegation from the nearby town. This was no welcoming committee: one look at the faces and you could see trouble. Standing quietly to one side, we watched and waited while our instructors went forward to find out what the problem was. Barely two minutes later and after much gesticulating, our instructors returned. In their faces you could see the anger and frustration but, most of all, the shame. The chief instructor explained that the whites could use the beach but the blacks would have to swim in among the rocks off to the side as this was a 'whites only' beach. I stared at the delegation in disbelief: there they stood, arms crossed in a holier-than-thou position, with an I-am-going-to-heaven expression on their faces as if they had just made a major contribution to make the world a better place.

There was no discussion: we all swam in the rocks.

Three days later we were ready to begin training proper. All the obstacles had been tested and were found to be safe. The training was extremely physical, the obstacles strong, crude and rough, claiming many pints of blood and pounds of flesh as we crossed them. Parachute training, I was to discover, was a series of repetitions.

Our instructors had now adopted a new mantra: training was training; sitting on the beach was sitting on the beach. From early morning to late afternoon they drove us without let-up: "Knees together", "Side left", "Side right", "Hit the release toggle", "You land with that container still strapped to your leg you will break your ankles", "What are you going to do in the middle of Mozambique with broken ankles?", "Come on, come on, and get it right; it's your life you're playing with".

Day in and day out it continued: there was no time to relax or admire the scenery. By nightfall, we were so tired that we ate, went to bed and slept like the dead. We had sore muscles where we did not know we had muscles. Many of us were suffering from bad rope burns on our hands and legs, inflicted by the rope obstacles designed to emulate, as closely as possible, actual exits and landings from an aircraft.

After four days of back-breaking, morale-destroying training, we were ready for our first jump. Forgotten were the rope burns and aching muscles as morale shot through the roof. This was what we had come here to do: jump out of an aircraft.

Early the next morning we climbed onto the trucks and headed for a nearby deserted World War II airfield. The trip only lasted twenty minutes and was a subdued affair. The laughing, joking and bragging of the party the previous night was now replaced by headaches, sore eyes, upset stomachs, shaking hands and sweaty bodies. The moment of truth had arrived – talk is cheap: money buys the whisky.

Standing in a straight line with the parachutes at our feet in the hot sun, we tried to take in what the instructors were saying; maybe the other students were making sense of what was being said but my hangover was banging around my head making me unable to listen. I was using all my powers of concentration to stop myself from passing out. It was hot and there was no breeze, the heat of the sun bouncing straight off the tar of the runway back into my face. The glare was not good for my bleary, red eyes and even less so for my pounding head. My sweat-soaked shirt clung to my body. It was touch and go. Looking around, I noticed the odd instructor checking me out, shaking his head and smiling.

A lifetime later, at least that is what it seemed, we were seated in the aircraft, parachutes on our backs and waiting for take-off. I looked about to see how everyone else was taking the thought of jumping out an aircraft at three thousand feet. The black members looked solemn and resigned; I am sure they were thinking that all white men were crazy. The whites on the other hand were trying to put on a brave front, with plenty of smiles and thumbs-ups, none of which could hide the worry in their eyes.

The engines shuddered into life. The body of the aircraft shook violently as the pilot opened the throttle. Slowly the plane moved forward. By this stage, the rear of the aircraft stank of sweat, fear and farts; it was enough to bring tears to your eyes. A bit of fresh air would have been a godsend.

Before I could completely immerse myself in the world of the hangover that is full of self-pity, pain, remorse and excuses, I was standing up trying to keep my balance in the bouncing aircraft and at the same time checking that the person in front of me had put his parachute on correctly.

The adrenalin was pumping, the hangover was gone and I was three thousand feet above the ground, drifting gently earthward. The silence was almost mystical and the view was unbelievably beautiful. As I drifted down, I began to experiment with my parachute. In the Rhodesian army we were still using old World War II parachutes, over which you had little or no control: you landed where you landed and that was that. The parachute I was using was more modern and you could basically pick your landing spot and steer towards it, landing where you wanted to land, depending on your skill. It was impossible to register all the feelings that flashed through my brain – freedom, happiness, peace – and I could now understand why man had always wanted to fly.

The canopy of my parachute was hooked on the branches of a large tree and I was hanging about two metres above the ground. I had been so busy trying out the parachute's steering, admiring the view and generally behaving like a kid with a new toy that I had failed to keep an eye on the ground. I was lucky that the canopy had hooked up in the branches and had prevented me from hitting the ground, as I am sure I would have injured myself.

✂

Screaming, shouting, hitting, kicking, I was back in Rhodesia doing the parachute-conversion course at New Sarum. The difference between the South African course and this conversion course was like night and day. I had thoroughly enjoyed my course in South Africa. The instructors were highly skilled and their relaxed teaching methods made learning easy. The same could not be said of the Rhodesian instructors. Talking was not allowed: you had to shout out your instructions and whether the students understood or not was beside the point.

After being asked endless times, "What did they teach in South Africa?", we were deemed fully converted into the screaming, shouting, hitting, kicking Rhodesian system. Jumping from four hundred feet, with rifle, webbing and a twenty-kilogram container strapped to your leg, using the old Rhodesian army parachutes, was a completely different kettle of fish when compared to jumping from three thousand feet wearing only shorts and a T-shirt with a far more modern parachute.

From four hundred feet the parachute had no sooner developed than you were on the ground: you did not land, you arrived! If you did not release your container and pull your rifle into a horizontal position you could end up with a broken leg, a bent rifle barrel or both. I do not think there was another army in the world at that time where parachutists were dropped from four hundred feet. It was extremely dangerous as the slightest mishap could result in death.

God, the ground was close, too close as far as I was concerned. We were standing in the door of the DC-3 Dakota as it skimmed over the trees heading for the drop zone. The trees seemed close enough to touch. I was petrified, my body stiff as a steel bar, my legs leaden. As the lights changed from "Red light on" to "Green light – go", my training took over and like a robot I shuffled to the door. As I exited the aircraft, I was already trying to release the container attached to my webbing by a short piece of rope. The last thing I needed was a broken leg – a bent barrel I could live with but not a broken leg. Everything we had been taught went out the window. Looking up to check if your parachute had developed and to take note of the whereabouts of the other paratroops was a huge no-no. In the time it took to complete those two simple tasks you would have already hit the ground, with devastating results. There was no time for anything other than to release your container, pull up your rifle barrel, get your legs together and prepare for impact. I landed hard, very hard. I was winded by the impact but at least I had managed to release my container and pull up my rifle barrel. Staggering to my feet, I gave myself a quick once-over. I seemed to be in one piece and had no broken bones or bent barrel.

"What are you standing there for? Roll up your 'chute, get your gear together and get to the trucks. Why are you walking? Run! Run! You're not in South Africa now: the holiday's over!" The good old Rhodesian screaming-shouting-hitting-kicking system was back in full force.

In time to come several parachutists were to die due to pilot error. While deploying a stick of Rhodesian African Rifles paratroops into a contact in the Mtoko area, the Dakota pilot failed to notice how steeply the ground along his drop run was rising. The last members of the stick had no chance: their parachutes had no time to develop, at 150 to 180 feet they were too low and they died.

15

Mujiba: Operation Thrasher, 1977

I had deployed into the emerald-rich area of eastern Rhodesia. I was experiencing great difficulty. None of the pseudo terrorist groups under my command was being accepted by the local population as genuine terrorists. Our dress was correct, our weapons were standard AK-47s and our cover story was acceptable. Our problem was the *mujibas*. *Mujibas* were the youth of an area, who acted as intelligence officers for the real terrorists, supplying them with all the latest information on security force movement in the area. This was standard practice in all Tribal Trust Lands, the native reserves. However, in this particular area, the *mujibas* were king. Without their say so, the locals would not accept you.

The reason for our visit was to locate and eliminate the resident terrorist groups. Without the support of the locals, we would fail. One of the groups under my control was led by Corporal Thomas, a man who liked to use his own initiative. He was a tall, well-built individual with a weakness for *dagga* and women and a love for all things modern, especially his Afro hairstyle. A great operator who seldom failed, he decided that he had had enough of being made a fool of by the *mujibas* and was going to take matters into his own hands.

First, he accused the *mujibas* and local terrorist groups of being Rhodesian government agents. He then called a meeting of all the *mujibas* and local headmen in the area, threatening to shoot any who did not attend. The stars of the show were to be the *mujibas*. The roles of judge, jury and executioner were, of course, to be played by Corporal Thomas. The meeting was to take place at a camp established by Corporal Thomas and his group, situated on the banks of a small stream comprising several fairly deep pools that were to play a major part in the upcoming meeting.

By mid-morning, the headmen and *mujibas* had gathered at Thomas's camp. Thomas kicked off the meeting by giving his audience a long and detailed account of his career as a freedom fighter, outlining all the battles he had fought and areas where he had operated. He name-dropped well-known terrorist leaders and training camps in Mozambique, left, right and centre. The *mujiba* rank and file appeared impressed. Their leader, a short, well-built teenager, however, remained convinced that Thomas and his group were not the real deal. The more Thomas talked the more the *mujiba* leader questioned him. Thomas started losing his cool and accused the *mujiba* leader of being a police informer, pointing out that the only reason he kept asking questions was so he could pass information to his police handlers. Even the headmen appeared impressed with this gem of logic.

Finally, sick and tired of being continually questioned by the *mujiba*, Thomas decided to adopt the roles of judge, jury and executioner. According to Thomas, the punishment for being a sell-out was death, not by the run-of-the-mill 'beaten, stoned or hacked to pieces' death, but by drowning.

Ordering the other *mujibas* to tie their leader's hands behind his back, Thomas dragged the screaming, disbelieving *mujiba* leader to a pool at the nearby stream. Lying him on his stomach, he then forced his head under the water until the *mujiba* stopped struggling. He was dead.

This story was told to me by a member of Thomas's group. When I questioned him about it he told me his version of the events. He claimed that he and the *mujiba* had gone across to the pool so they could talk without being overheard by the people at the meeting when, unfortunately, the *mujiba* tripped over a log, struck his head on a rock and fell into the water. By the time he, Thomas, had dragged him out of the water, it was too late – the *mujiba* was dead.

Thomas said that whoever told me the other version of events was lying. He swore that he had had nothing to do with the *mujiba*'s death, that it was an accident. He related his version without batting an eye, even managing to look somewhat upset.

The fact is, it was a matter of survival and Thomas did what he had to do to survive. In the dark, misty world of pseudo operations, there is no black or white, no right or wrong. The end justifies the means. Survival is paramount. To understand how things worked, you had to have been there, felt the fear, the mental strain and the uncertainty of surviving on your wits alone, asking yourself the questions, "Did I say the right thing? Did they believe me? Will I get ambushed?" The pressure was massive, there was never time to relax and continual vigilance was the price of survival.

16

Pseudo op: Chiredzi, late 1977

I woke up cringing in the corner of the little rock overhang that I had been calling home for the past four or five weeks. I was filthy. I had not bathed, cleaned my teeth or brushed my hair since I had been here. I was operating alone: my normal companion, Peter, a tame terrorist, was sick.

To compensate for the missing Peter, I had booby-trapped the area around the overhang with white phosphorus and high-explosive hand grenades, which was fine as long as you remembered where you had set them. Picking the routes I thought most likely to be used by anyone trying to attack me, I had used brown tape to strap the grenades to trees and string as a tripwires. It was simple but effective.

The pressure was unrelenting, day and night, no chance to relax, not even for a moment. The burning questions were always at the back of my mind: had I been seen, was I going to be attacked or, worse still, captured?

My camp was on the only piece of high ground for miles around. It stuck out like a pimple on a baby's arse. The only vegetation in my chosen campsite was on top of the hill, where a fairly thick clump of trees provided shade and several large rocks gave cover from view and protection from small-arms fire were I attacked. The hillside was devoid of any trees or grass, the former having long been used for firewood, the latter eaten by the thousands of goats. As far as the eye could see were ploughed fields. The only trees to be seen were concentrated around the few water sources in the area that was turning into a desert due to overgrazing and poor farming practices.

What had woken me, I do not know. I had been lying down, trying to sleep. It was an uncomfortable, hot summer's night. The ever-present mosquitoes were giving me hell, not to mention the thousands of minute ticks crawling all over my body. No larger than a pinhead, they clung by the thousand to the long grass on top of the hill, waiting for any unsuspecting passerby to give them a lift to areas inhabited by livestock or humans, where they could obtain the blood they needed to survive. I spent many hours each day removing as many as I could, making sure, where possible, to remove the entire tick, head included. Failure to do so could result in tick-bite fever.

I had scratched large amounts of skin off my arms and legs which were now going septic and I needed to wash the affected areas in clean water and apply antiseptic cream. I had neither clean water nor antiseptic cream, so the best I could do was piss on the affected areas and hope for the best. The fact that I smelled to high heaven and was covered in several layers of black camouflage cream, in turn covered in many layers of dust, sweat and piss, did not seem to bother the mosquitoes – or the ticks – in the slightest.

Crouched under the overhang, sweating and slightly delirious, AK-47 firmly clutched, I tried to figure out what had woken me.

This had so far been a very difficult bush trip. The principal terrorist in the area was a guy by the name of Donkey. How he got the name I do not know but, one thing for sure, stupid he was not. He was clever, light on his feet and ran his area with an iron fist. His party trick was attacking police stations, as well as laying mines in the roads. Who detonated the landmines did not seem to bother him in any way, be they civilian or military personnel. Our job was to try and kill or capture him. This was easier said than done. We had tried all the normal approaches, including writing letters, to which Donkey had not replied. We had taken the odd *mujiba* to one side and had had some up-close and personal chats, all to no avail. The entire local population lived in fear of the man.

That he was in the area there was no doubt. The attacks on the police stations and the mining of the roads confirmed his presence. After much thought, we decided that if we could not beat him, we would join him, as it were. If he could attack police stations so could we. If he could lay landmines so could we. The information we were getting from the few locals who were talking to us, was that Donkey was telling anyone who would listen that we were sell-outs and working for the government.

The only way we could get to Donkey was through the locals, and the only way we could get the locals on our side was to start a misinformation campaign of our own. Pseudo attacks were carried out against the local police station by groups under my command. Each attack was verified by several *mujibas* who came along as witnesses. The attacks were harmless: no effort was made to hit the police station and all the rounds, including 60mm mortar and RPG-7s, were fired well off to the side. What the *mujibas* thought about the marksmanship of the pseudo groups I do not know, but I am sure they were impressed by the noise and the fireworks display as the sky was lit up by red and green tracer, accompanied by huge orange flashes as the mortar bombs and RPG-7 rockets exploded.

After each such attack, a large meeting was held where Donkey was accused of being the sell-out. Our one problem to overcome was the fact that we did not lay landmines and could not get permission to lay any, even fake ones. To overcome this, at each meeting it was explained to the locals that we, the real comrades, would not mine the roads and kill the very people who were supporting us, unlike Donkey who was doing this and proving to anyone with eyes and ears that he, Donkey, was the sell-out, killing innocent people on behalf of the Smith regime that he was working for.

Slowly but surely the tide began to turn against Donkey. The information we began receiving was more accurate and more current than anything we had received in the past. I knew we would pin him down in the next couple of days. Donkey was not your normal terrorist commander. Unlike most terrorists commanders who kept their groups together come hell or high water and only splitting up when attacked, Donkey did the opposite: he spread his group around, two in this village, two in the next, their weapons hidden in the thatched roofs of the huts they were staying in. They became part of the village and extremely difficult to locate.

The only time the entire group got together was to hold a meeting with the locals or to carry out an operation, be it killing a headman, laying landmines or attacking police stations. Due to the way Donkey operated, the chances of getting his entire group in one place at the same time were not good.

Still crouched under the overhang, trying to figure out what had woken me, I realized that I was in a bit of trouble myself: I had not eaten for several days, the last meal being a small piece of rotten chicken, the last bit of a whole chicken supplied to me by one of my pseudo groups. Commonly known as bubble gum among the local terrorists because of its rubbery flesh, it was nothing more than a parboiled chicken.

I was weak and becoming delirious, having difficulty in moving and keeping my balance. Trying to think logically was not easy. I could not concentrate for long. The septic sores on my arms legs had got worse, not out of hand, just worse. My clothing was rotting, as was the skin on my feet. On the odd occasion that it had rained, I had stood in the open and tried to use the rain water to clean the sores on my arms and legs, as well as wash away the rotting skin on my feet. It had helped a bit. It was the wet–dry combination, combined with sweat and urine that was causing my clothes to rot.

Due to the nature of Selous Scouts work, I had tried to keep myself looking like a terrorist at all times. My life, plus the safety of the pseudo groups, could depend upon how well I did this. The weapons, the clothing and the webbing were not a problem: my white skin was, so a long-sleeved shirt and long trousers covered my arms and legs; a face could be blackened up completely or disguised by the use of a combination of a balaclava and black camouflage cream. So here I was, in the middle of a hot African summer, dressed in long trousers, long-sleeved shirt, balaclava and gloves on my hands, wondering why I felt light-headed and weak, never mind the septic sores and rotting feet. During the day, I gave my feet as much fresh air as I could. At night, the shoes were back on. I could not take a chance that if something went wrong and I had to move quickly, having to start by putting on my shoes could cost me my life.

The last time I had had direct communications with my HQ was about four days ago when I had asked for a resupply of food and water. I was told there was no helicopter available due to other commitments. This was not the first time this had happened and I was not too worried. In the past, I had used one of my pseudo groups to supply me with food and water. The food normally tasted terrible and smelled worse and the water was drinkable, but only just.

This time it was different. None of my pseudo groups was near my position; they were spread far and wide as the frozen area where we were operating was huge. The last group in my vicinity had dropped off the parboiled chicken I had been living off for the past week. Luckily for me, I had discovered a small spring, or seep, for want of a better word, that briefly broke surface before disappearing back underground again. It provided me with a cup or two of drinkable water a day. Not a lot but enough. I was static so I did not need much. The only walking I did was from the overhang where I slept to the seep and back again, a distance of ten to twelve metres, no more. Apart from answering the odd call of nature that had become few and far between due to the lack of food, the water run was the only exercise I got.

I relaxed. I had not seen or heard anything suspicious. Concentrating hard, trying not to let my mind wander, I went through the events of the day, hoping this would provide some clue as to what had woken me and made me think I was under attack.

The day had started the same as the previous thirty or so had. As soon as it got light enough, I went to collect what little water there was in the hole I had dug in the seep. Only this time, it was different. I had noticed some movement in the thick grass that surrounded the seep. On closer inspection, I discovered a frog, a fairly large green one. The first thought that went through my mind was food. I had never eaten a frog before, let alone cooked one but I was willing to try. With a shaking hand, I grabbed the frog and threw it against a rock, killing it. Now I had the problem of how to cook it: boil or roast?

But somehow I bypassed a decision on the frog and had ended up pissing in a cup, using the piss to try and clean the sores on my legs and arms, and pouring what was left on my feet.

I had set several snares near the seep, hoping to catch a pheasant or two. In the thirty-odd days that I had been camped on the hill, I had neither seen nor heard any form of wildlife, be it birds or animals, so I don't really know why I bothered. Hobbling from one snare to the next on my rotting feet, I made a bad mistake. Instead of following the normal route which kept me well clear of the booby-traps I had set, I decided to take a short-cut. I was tired, hungry and slightly delirious – plus stupid.

I heard the pop as the striker lever struck the .22 cap that in turn ignited the fuse in the grenade. I had three to five seconds. I froze. My brain struggled to make sense of what my ears had heard. Instinct took over. I hit the ground. In that split-second it took to take cover, I knew I had walked into one of my own booby-traps. Now the big question was: what type of grenade had I walked into – high explosive or white phosphorus? I hoped with all my heart and soul it was white phosphorus then at least I was in with a chance. Or so I thought.

I had strapped the high-explosive grenades onto the trees at about waist height for maximum effect. If I was lying next to, or within, twenty metres of one of these I had no chance. The fact that I had used plenty of tape to secure the grenade to the tree would in no way affect the direction or the strength of the blast. I was a dead man. The white phosphorus grenades, on the other hand, I had strapped close to the bottom of the trees, also using plenty of tape. It was the large amount of tape and the relatively small explosive charge in the white phosphorus that, combined, I figured, would give me my best chance of surviving.

I heard a low, muffled pop, followed by a whooshing sound. I had heard that sound many times before, the sound of a white phosphorus grenade detonating. The sound had come from my rear. Jerking my head round, I saw what I was hoping to see. The excessive amount of tape I had used to attach the grenade to the tree was doing exactly what I was hoping: the explosive charge inside the grenade was not strong enough to tear it free from the tree. So, still tied to the tree, most of the white phosphorous was exiting the grenade casing from the top and bottom. I was in with a chance.

I was up and running before I knew it. Rotten feet? What rotten feet? Delirious? Not me! Weak from lack of food? What was I thinking, I was as strong as an ox! A couple of scratches were not going to slow me down. AK-47 in hand, I literally flew across the ground, the adrenalin gushing into my blood at a gallon a second.

"Stupid. Stupid," I told myself.

I was lying behind some rocks, about twenty-odd metres from the still-smoking grenade. My chest was heaving as I tried to get oxygen into my burning lungs. My head was pounding from the sudden exertion, my hands gripping the AK-47 shaking. I could not believe I could have been so stupid as to walk into one of my own booby-traps. It was not as if I had just set them; they had been there for weeks.

Five minutes later I was still lying behind the rocks, trying to decide what to do. One thing was for sure, if the locals had not known I was on top of the hill they sure as hell knew now. I was so pissed off at myself. I was having difficulty in thinking. One stupid move and I had not only put my life in danger but also those of the pseudo groups under my command. My anger began to subside and my breathing returned, my headache departed and everything went back to normal; even the mopane flies returned.

God, I smelled terrible. The odour of my unwashed body, coupled with the rotting black camouflage cream and piss I had been using to clean my sores was overpowering. I had gone for long periods of time before without washing and was to do so again, but never was I to smell as bad as I did now.

Lying in the hot sun, sweat dripping off me, trying my best to ignore the smell of my body, I realized I had to stay where I was, regardless of whether I had been seen or not. I was still safer up here on top of the hill than trying to hide down in the ploughed fields below. I needed to have communications at all times with my pseudo groups and the only way I could do this was to operate from the highest piece of ground I could find, which was where I was sitting right now. Moving was not an option.

Returning to the overhang, I removed my binoculars from their case and positioned myself on the highest spot on the hill and studied the scene below. Nothing unusual was going on, everyone seemingly going about their business as normal. No one was staring or pointing up at the hill. Maybe no one had noticed the smoke on the top of the hill? Highly unlikely but you never know. I was pretty sure that nobody had heard the muffled explosion of the grenade.

The nearest villages were situated at least a kilometre away from the base of the hill. But it was the smoke that worried me.

I spent the next couple of hours studying the area intently, looking for any sign that would indicate I had been compromised. The light was starting to fade, it was getting dark and still everything appeared normal. The smoke would have been visible from many kilometres away and all I could hope for was that the thick clump of trees under which the white phosphorus had detonated had dispersed the smoke and it had gone unnoticed.

Hobbling back to the overhang, I realized I was feeling much better. I still stank to high heaven, compliments of the *Eau de Piss* perfume I was wearing. My clothes were still rotten, as were my feet, the septic sores on my legs and arms were still there but the fever that had been my main cause of concern seemed to be easing. The hunger pangs did not worry me too much. I had been without food for longer periods than this and had continued to operate without any problems.

The green frog was still in the back of my mind. I had looked at it several times but I just could not bring myself to attempt to eat it. I was obviously not *that* hungry. Sticking to my original decision to stay where I was, I got myself ready for the long night ahead. To say I was nervous would be an understatement. Shit scared would be more apt. The darker it got the wilder my imagination became. Lying on top of my sleeping bag, trying to beat off the never-ending attacks launched by the mosquitoes and to refrain from scratching the sores on my arms and legs, my imagination ran wild. Every sound was transformed to sound either like people talking, footsteps or the sound of an AK-47 being cocked. Eventually, after several hours of tossing and turning and continually getting up to check all the sounds that my imagination had converted into imminent signs of attack, I dozed off.

Three bright flashes pierced my eyelids, followed by three loud cracking thuds as the 60mm mortar shells exploded around my position. Now I knew why I was crouched in the corner of the overhang: I was being attacked. It had taken all of two to three minutes to figure out what had woken me and it seemed a lifetime.

As the time passed and nothing further happened, I started to wonder if I had imagined the flashes and the three subsequent explosions, but the smell of cordite hanging in the still air of a hot summer's night put my doubts to rest. I had handled mortars most of my army career and knew the smell given off by an exploded mortar bomb as well as I knew the smell of meat being cooked on an open fire. And to confirm my conclusion, dogs suddenly started barking in one of the villages situated near the base of the hill. It was about one o'clock in the morning. All the locals were sleeping: the only people who could be walking around at this time of the night were terrorists, most certainly my attackers.

As the barking receded, I began to relax. My attackers were leaving; they had just wanted to show me that they knew I was up there, firing off the mortar bombs on the off-chance of hitting me.

Time dragged. The mosquitoes were having a field day (or night). I was just too tired to try and brush them away. As the adrenalin wore off, a deep sense of peace and contentment descended on me. For the first time in four days I was without a fever. The piss I had been using on the sores seemed to be working. Even my feet were improving. As I sat there idly feeling around my ankles for any of the tiny little ticks that swarmed all over the hill, I tried to figure out what had caused the fever I had been suffering from. Then, out of the blue, it hit me: I had just survived a quick four-day bout of tick-bite fever. I had spoken to other operators who had worked the area before and they had warned me that due to the vast amount of ticks in the area, I was likely to suffer a bout of tick-bite fever, just as they had. They had described the symptoms in detail. It all tied up. Things could only get better from now on.

It was becoming hard to stay awake. As the barking of the dogs moved ever farther away from my position, I became ever-more confident that I was not going to be attacked again. To try and stay awake I wedged myself between two rocks so that every time I dozed off my head would hit the rocks and wake me up. It was crude and painful, but effective.

After what seemed a lifetime, the sky gradually began to lighten. I had spent hours wedged between the rocks. I was stiff and sore and my head was throbbing from the many contacts it had had with the rocks. I was also extremely thirsty. It had been a hot, moonless night and I had sweated non-stop. How the smell of decay emitted by my body and clothing had not caused me to pass out, I will never know.

I would have loved to have visited the seep during the night, but after my nearly fatal short-cut experience, I had decided to wait for first light. As I made my way towards the spring on my healing feet, I felt a pang of hunger. The frog I had killed the previous day sprang to mind, still lying on the rocks where I had left it. After drinking most of the water that had collected overnight, I had a close look at the dead frog. It had swollen up and looked like a green tennis ball. The skin was starting to split and out of the slits oozed a vile yellow liquid. I was hungry but I was not sure if I was hungry enough to eat it. Deciding to give it a try, I took the small pocketknife I was carrying and holding the frog by one leg against the rock, plunged the small sharp blade into its swollen belly. Foul-smelling air accompanied by an equally foul-smelling yellow liquid exited the hole in the stomach and ended up all over the front of my rotting foul-smelling shirt. Dropping the frog, I stumbled backward, trying to get away from the smell. I started retching. I couldn't stop myself the smell was so vile. I had never smelled anything like it before. I had dug up dead bodies in the past and eaten rotten baboon that was more maggots than meat and smelled like a burst sewer, but they paled in comparison to the rotten frog. This won hands down.

Tears running down my face, bent over in pain caused by the retching, I drew long deep breaths into my lungs. Retching on an empty stomach is extremely painful. It felt as if somebody had grabbed hold of my gut and was busy tying knots in it. Bent over as I was, with my face almost buried in my shirt that was covered in the yellow liquid from the frog, I was not getting anywhere fast. Using a nearby tree as support, I managed to get myself into an upright position and get the retching under control. There was no way on God's green earth that I was going to eat that frog. I would rather die first.

Making my way back to the overhang, keeping well clear of the booby-traps, I sat down and, trying to ignore my newly acquired aroma and the maddening mopane flies, attempted to come up with a plan. My radio communications with HQ were not good. I had not heard from them for several days, which was strange, to say the least. The standing order in the unit was that if you had not heard from a call sign in twenty-four hours then you find out what the problem was. Twenty-four hours was long past. The only HQ contact I had was with the air force, via a relay station, which was better than nothing.

My train of thought was broken by the radio coming to life. As I picked up the handset, I prayed to the gods – all of them – that it was one of my pseudo groups and that they had located Donkey. I got what I had wished for. It had taken me, and my call sign, well in excess of thirty days to pin down Donkey. We had handled the heat, the hunger, the thirst, the ticks and everything else that had been thrown at us, and now we were about to receive the fruits of our labour.

In the ensuing contact, two terrorists were killed and one captured. I had no idea if Donkey was among the dead or captured, neither did I care. However,

I was to learn later that the mining of the roads stopped and the attacks on police stations petered out.

Later that same day I got my entire call sign uplifted by helicopter and dropped at the fort in Chiredzi. I could not help but notice that the pilot and tech of the helicopter were both wearing surgical masks. As I got in, the pilot looked at me, rolled his eyes skyward and shook his head. Not that I blamed him as I did indeed smell like the dead.

On arrival at the fort, I was greeted by the sole occupant: the caretaker. There was no signaller, no security branch and no fort commander. No wonder I had been unable to establish communications. Thank God for the relay station and the air force. As to what happened to the staff at the fort, that's another story.

17

Chiredzi, Operation Repulse, 1978

I was operating in a Tribal Trust Land in the Chiredzi area, a terrorist stronghold. Every member of the local community was a staunch ZANLA supporter; the youngsters would patrol the roads, check the high ground and report any signs of security force activity to the resident terrorist groups that had been operating in the area for some time, and that knew each other. To make matters worse, the area was not generally used for transit by other groups, which meant that it would make our pseudo operations more problematic.

After two weeks of operating without success, the three pseudo groups I had operating in the area were slowly starving to death. Every village they approached refused to help them, saying they were not real comrades. No support from the locals meant no food to eat and no blankets at night to keep warm. Things were not going well. I needed to meet and speak with the three groups. Looking at the map, I selected an isolated hill feature a good distance from where we were operating but still within my frozen area. I passed the grid reference to the three group commanders and told them I would meet them there in two days. I intended to move there that night.

It took Peter, the tame terrorist, and I, most of the night to get there. By seven the following evening, the three groups had arrived, tired and hungry. After speaking to the group commanders, I knew we were wasting our time. We were not compromised as such but because the resident groups did not know us, they would not meet with us and had warned the locals against feeding us. I got on the radio and explained the situation to my controller, requesting a helicopter uplift the next morning.

"Not possible," I was told, "the helicopters are busy tomorrow morning."

It would have to be the following day. That meant another night on the hill. The biggest problem I was facing was the fact that no one had any food.

I called the group commanders together and explained the situation. I asked them how far it was to the nearest village.

"Not far," they said.

An African person's idea of not far and a European person's idea of not far are like chalk and cheese, so I asked how long it would take me to walk there.

"No more than an hour," they said.

"Okay," I said, addressing Thomas, one of the group commanders, "go to the village and get a goat, some chickens, anything." I did not mind what it was as long as it would feed us for the next two days. As he left smiling broadly, I added, "Thomas, I do not want Special Branch asking me about a local being killed in an area where I was operating at the time of his death."

Thomas assured me there was no need to worry: they would not harm anyone. Thomas had a weakness for *dagga* that had made him do some amazingly stupid things in the past and, as you may have read earlier, was known for taking the initiative. I just hoped he had run out of his supply of *dagga*, otherwise anything was possible.

An hour and a half later, I heard a peculiar noise. It sounded like a bull or an ox being driven up the hill towards our position. It could not be Thomas returning so soon. I estimated it would take him an hour to the village, half an hour to find some chickens or goats and an hour back, making the return trip approximately two and a half hours. Only an hour and a half had passed, so it could not be Thomas. I went across to where the other group commanders were sitting and asked them what they thought was happening.

"It's Thomas returning with an ox," they replied.

"An ox?" I queried. "What are we going to do with an ox? I told Thomas to find some chickens or goats, not an ox."

They just smiled, "You know Thomas: anything is possible," urging me not to worry as there were nearly thirty of us and we would manage to eat a whole ox without a problem.

Sure enough, ten minutes later, Thomas and his group appeared pulling an ox behind them. The ox was not as big as I'd thought but it still took four men hanging on to the rawhide thong around its neck for all they were worth to control it. Shaking my head, I looked at Thomas and asked where were the chickens and/or goats that he was supposed to have returned with. Grinning from ear to ear, he explained that at the foot of the hill he and his group had come across this ox roaming around all by itself; there was no herdsman in sight and seeing that it already had a rope around its neck, he decided that it would far easier to bring the ox to the top of hill than going from village to village trying to steal chickens and goats. He paused, looked at me and then informed me that the chances of stealing chickens and goats without having to kill a local were not good, and seeing as I had told him that killing a local was not on the agenda, he figured he had done the right thing by taking the ox. As an afterthought, he added that some of the guys did not eat goat as it was their clan totem. There was nothing to say: what Thomas said made sense.

The next problem was how to kill the ox. I was carrying a silenced AK-47, which was fine for dealing with people up to a range of maybe ten metres but for any greater distance you were pushing your luck. In order to silence the weapon without using a silencer, grains of gunpowder were removed from the cartridge cases of standard AK-47 rounds to help reduce the noise. This subsonic ammunition was standard issue for silenced AK-47s. Whether this could kill an ox was another story but there was only one way to find out. Four shots later, at point-blank range, the ox finally gave up the ghost.

The feast began. Each group had its own task. Whether it was cutting up the meat, collecting firewood, keeping the fire going or cooking, everyone went about his task with a smile on his face. It was already eleven o'clock at night and the fire had yet to be started. The plan was to cook and eat as much of the meat as possible that night. The remainder was to be partly cooked or smoked the next day and taken with us that evening when we moved to a new position to await uplift by helicopter the following morning. Eventually, sometime after midnight, the fire got going and the cooking and eating began. I was a bit worried about the fire but looking at the time I knew it would be light in four to five hours, plus we were quite far from the nearest village. It was unlikely anybody would be awake at that time of the morning.

Making sure there were sentries posted, I went across to the fire to see how things were going. The ox was only half-skinned and the gut had only been partly removed. Everyone helped themselves to whatever piece of meat they fancied, cut it off, threw it in the fire and ate it when they thought it was cooked. Most of the meat I saw eaten seemed raw, with blood still oozing. Any stranger coming across the gathering would have been convinced he had stumbled on to a large group of terrorists having a party. There were AK-47s and RPG-7s, leaning up against trees, their owners crouching next to them eating half-raw meat, blood running from their mouths and dripping off their chins into the fire, the heat from the fire making their black skins shine, the flickering light turning their features monster-like, only made worse by the Afro-styled hair which constantly changed colour in the firelight. A white Rhodesian's nightmare!

A drying–smoking rack of sorts had been constructed using wooden poles and large rocks, on which a large amount of meat was smoking, cooking or burning, I was not sure which. The smell of the roasting meat and burning blood was overwhelming and could surely have been smelt miles away. Looking again at the amount of the ox still left, I could see it was going to take most of the next day to smoke or cook. Doing a final check on the sentries and confirming with Thomas that smoking the meat was going to continue through the remaining hours of darkness, I went and tried to get a bit of sleep.

A couple of hours later I was awake, drinking a cup of tea and watching the sun rise. I just hoped the owner of the ox did not come looking for his missing animal. The rest of the meat was either smoked or eaten by midday. Luckily, the owner of the ox did not appear. The smell and the tracks would have told him what had happened to his ox. By the time we left the hill that night, the smell of rotting guts and ox hide was bad, not helped by the summer heat. When we got picked up by the helicopters the next morning the smoked meat was almost completely finished. Thirty men had eaten an entire ox in a day and a night – amazing.

18

Tete Province, Mozambique, 1978

East of Mukumbura, the small border town situated on the north-eastern border of Rhodesia and Mozambique, was a large Frelimo army base. The commander of the Ruya camp was an ardent ZANLA supporter. Nothing was too much trouble: he would feed them, care for the sick, use the vehicles at his disposal to move them to and from the border, provide guards for their camps – a real fan!

It was time he was taught a lesson.

The border was demarcated by two fences running parallel to each other, about two metres apart, the gap between the two fences full of anti-personnel mines.[1] It was evening. We were sitting on the Rhodesian side of the fence, opposite a breach in the minefield made by our engineers. And as usual, due to the long trousers, long-sleeved shirts, jackets, balaclavas and a thick layer of vile camouflage cream, we whites were sweating buckets. Our group consisted of black and white Selous Scouts. We carried the same weapons and webbing and wore the same clothes and shoes as the terrorists; in the moonlight there was no telling us apart. Most of us had terrorist packs on our backs containing TMH46 anti-tank mines and CE4 plastic explosive. Terrorist packs were like canvas bags onto which two straps were attached, no padding or support of any kind. They were not made to carry weight, especially not landmines. After an hour or two, your arms and hands would go numb and your back would be bent forward from trying to take the weight off your shoulders. You looked like the Hunchback of Nôtre Dame as you walked in, trying to give your shoulders a break and at the same time not fall flat on your face.

Around 19h00, under the light of a full moon, we crossed the cleared section of the minefield into Mozambique. Getting through the two-metre-wide breach was a slow, nerve-wracking, time-consuming exercise. With thumbs-ups, false smiles of confidence and back-slapping, the men in front of me crossed one at a time, each man desperately trying to place his feet into the tracks of the man preceding him.

---

1   Instituted by the Rhodesians and known as the *Cordon Sanitaire*

Sitting there in the moonlight, sweat pissing down my face, waiting for my turn, I could not but help remember that, six weeks earlier in the same area, a Selous Scout had lost a foot in the very same minefield. By the time my turn came, I was a bunch of nerves, my whole body as stiff as a board, my leg muscles felt as if they had cramp, heavy and painful, to say nothing of the pounding headache and burning eyes now full of liquefied black camouflage cream. Getting the nod, I lurched unsteadily to my feet. Pausing for a second or two, I stamped my feet, trying to get some feeling into them. They felt like two lumps of dead meat. Slapping a devil-may-care grin on my face, pushing all my fears, which were many, to one side, I headed for the crossing point.

My face was buried in the ground, fixed there by the weight of the landmines in the pack I was carrying. I had to breathe but my neck muscles were not strong enough to lift the twenty-odd kilograms the landmines weighed. I had tripped over the bottom strand of wire of the fence marking the minefield. I was on my knees, bum in the air, arms outstretched, face buried between them like I was praying. My heart was pounding, the adrenalin was flowing and I was starting to panic. I tried desperately to supply my burning lungs with the oxygen they required by breathing through my mouth but all I got were mouthfuls of sand. I needed to breathe but at the same time I did not want to lose an arm or leg. Talk about a rock and a hard place! Suddenly, the weight was gone and I was breathing.

"For fuck's sake, Andy, keep it down. You're making enough noise to wake the dead."

Three hours later and six kilometres into Mozambique, the adrenalin had worn off, and with it the sense of well-being. My shoulders were one mass of pain. My arms and hands were numb: the straps on the pack had cut off blood flow. Another couple of hours of this and I would be on my last legs.

My whole world now revolved around my aching shoulders and numbed arms and hands. Even though the going was slow as we tried to steer clear of the paths and game trails, some of which were thought to have been mined by Frelimo, I was dropping behind.

To keep up, I 'switched off'. Head down, doubled over at the waist, glazed eyes staring unblinkingly at the ground, I stumbled along. I had become an unfeeling, unseeing, unhearing blob of flesh.

We were moving along the edge of an old road that was not really more than a game trail, in single file, a metre or two apart. The area was thickly wooded and, even though it was full moon, it was still pretty dark beneath the trees. Walking at the back of the patrol, I was about to stop for one of my numerous ten-second breaks when out of the corner of my eye I noticed movement on the other side of the road. I straightened up. Forgotten were the aches and pains of the previous four hours: this was survival time. I watched the area where I had seen the movement, weapon at the ready. My body was as taut as a steel spring, my hands throbbed in pain. I was gripping my AK-47 like a vice, the cold, rancid sweat of fear running down my back. The seconds ticked by. Nothing. Shaking my head, I checked again: still nothing. I began to wonder if the combination of shadows caused by the moonlight filtering through the trees, the slight breeze and my imagination, had me seeing things.

Glancing in the direction of the patrol disappearing down the side of the track, I knew I could not stay where I was much longer. Having one last look and seeing nothing, I continued on my way. My breathing was fast and shallow, legs weak and rubbery, body ice-cold. Someone was walking next to me. I did not know what to do other than continue walking. My brain was struggling to move from the 'this is it; we are dead' mode to the 'we can handle this' mode. Turning my head slowly, I glanced at my new travelling companion. Carrying his weapon over his shoulder, he appeared completely relaxed. Maybe too relaxed! I wondered if he was not a sentry posted by Frelimo to keep an eye on the roads. Seeing us coming from the direction of Rhodesia, he had perhaps assumed we were a group of returning ZANLA terrorists and had decided to join us for a chat. I hoped not. He looked like one of us, was dressed like one of us but his appearance out of nowhere made me very nervous. While my brain, using the few facts available, fought to make sense of what was happening, my new friend indicated with the use of his hands that he wanted a cigarette.

Shaking my head and shrugging my shoulders to indicate I had none, I glanced down the track to see how far I was behind the rest of the patrol. When I looked back he was gone! I stopped dead in my tracks. My blood went cold, my hair stood on end. I frantically looked around, eyes searching the shadows, ears straining for the slightest sound: nothing. Had the combination of fear, exhaustion and pain caused me to hallucinate?

A long, pain-filled hour later, we arrived at the road we intended mining. We split up into two groups, put out sentries and started digging holes. I was a bundle of nerves; I had the jitters and could not concentrate. My eyes continually scanned the surrounding bush, trying to penetrate the moonlight shadows in the trees. What I was looking for I did not know, but try as I might I could not stop myself. Every shadow took on a human form; like a cowboy of old who saw an Indian behind every bush, I was seeing a terrorist.

A lifetime later, we were finished.

Into each hole that we dug, we placed two landmines plus a couple of kilograms of plastic explosive. We did the same in each water-filled pothole we found. Once we had covered over the holes, we used a piece of old car tyre to run over the top to make everything look as normal as possible.

We crossed back into Rhodesia at first light.

In the days that followed, the Frelimo commander, his second-in-command and several Frelimo soldiers were to die in landmine explosions.

19

Pseudo op: Fort Victoria, 1978

It was dark, very dark, clouds hung thick and heavy overhead blocking out the moon. The wind tore through the trees and up the dry riverbeds, whipping up the desiccated soil and creating a mini-dust storm. Multiple lightning strikes pierced the darkness and thunder rumbled in the distance.

It was October. The heat was unbearable. The long-awaited rains were about to arrive. Crouched over in a small, dry riverbed, tired and dirty, covered in ticks and shielding my face from the stinging, wind-driven sand, I was puking my heart out.

Food and water had been in short supply of late. I had been living off what the terrorists called bubble gum. To create bubble gum you have to take a chicken and gut it, then remove the feathers and throw it in a pot of boiling water for no more than ten minutes. Then remove it, let it cool down and you have bubble gum. And, like bubble gum, it was rubbery and tasteless. My particular piece of bubble gum had been supplied to me by one of the pseudo terrorist groups under my command four days ago. Old and long past its sell-by date, it was rotten. Having nothing else, I continued to eat it.

As I was continually on the move at night in order to try and keep up with my pseudo groups, and hiding from the locals by day, I had little time to devote to finding food. Several hours earlier, while on my way to fill up with water from the local supply point, I had come across several large *majotas*. Similar in size to a watermelon, but not as sweet, they were a godsend. I was hungry and thirsty.

Throwing caution to the wind, and relying on the ever-worsening weather to keep all the locals indoors, I had sat down next to the *majotas* and started eating. I ate as if there was no tomorrow. Even as I ate, I knew I was overdoing it and I would probably end up being sick. Pushing the thought to the back of my mind, I had continued to gorge myself, alternating between a piece of rotten bubble gum and a mouthful of *majota*. Now crouched in the riverbed puking my heart out, I was paying the price for my stupidity.

Pulling down my balaclava to protect my face from the stinging onslaught launched by the huge, wind-driven raindrops, I left the puke-strewn riverbed.

Using the almost continual lightning flashes to help see where I was going, I began climbing what appeared to be a small ridge. It was a beautiful morning. The air was crystal clear and everything looked and smelled clean. The sky was a deep purple with splashes of pink and orange. Nothing moved and silence reigned supreme.

Wedged between the rocks where I had spent the night, cold, wet and miserable, with a bongo-drum headache, damp cigarette in hand, I watched the sun rise. The night had been long and hard. The rain and wind had turned the ridge into a slippery, knee-breaking, ankle-twisting, branch-flying nightmare. Using the lightning to assist me to see where I was going was fine in the open countryside. However, once I reached the maze of huge boulders, thick undergrowth and trees that formed the side of the ridge, the lightning became more of a hindrance. Reflecting off the shiny wet rocks, glistening leaves and soaking tree trunks straight into my eyes, it had blinded and disoriented me. After walking into several large rocks and even larger trees, I had decided to call it a night. Still weak from my *majota*–rotten bubble-gum orgy and the ensuing puking, I figured enough was enough.

It was mid-morning by the time I reached the top of the ridge. Battered and bruised, bleeding from what seemed like hundreds of cuts and grazes, my AK-47 covered in mud, I needed a place to hole up for the day and do a few running repairs. My trousers were badly torn, exposing my white legs and the rain had removed most, if not all, of my black camouflage. Even from a distance I would not pass as a terrorist.

I could smell what seemed like raw sewage mixed with rotten eggs, thick, heavy and overpowering. Standing at the edge of a small clearing and trying not to retch, I tried to locate the source of the smell. As my eyes took in the details of the clearing, alarm bells started to ring. There was a single path in to and out of the clearing that had small bare patches of ground every couple of metres around it, which appeared to be sleeping places. I was tired, wet and hungry, my body battered and bruised, my brain a blob of unthinking grey matter, so it took a few seconds to register.

Into my semi-frozen, fear-riddled brain, the thought stuttered: a terrorist base camp! I froze, the cold, rancid sweat of fear running down my back, my pounding heart blocking out all other sounds, my eyes darting left and right looking for an escape route like a cornered animal. Seconds passed and nothing happened. No bullets flew over my head, no mortar bombs exploded around me. I began to relax. My once-stiff, taut, sweat-covered body started to shake as the adrenalin rush disappeared. Sitting down before I fell down, with my back against a tree, the smell forgotten, I dug in my pocket for a cigarette.

"God, my man, you're so lucky," I thought, as I tried to light a soggy cigarette with an equally soggy match held in a violently shaking hand. Ten or so soggy cigarettes later, trousers repaired, dirty balaclava pulled over my nose and mouth in a futile attempt to block out the smell, 'black is beautiful' plastered all over any exposed skin, AK-47 in one hand, long stick in the other, I poked around a small grave-like mound.

Once I had finished smoking myself hoarse and the shock of stumbling into a deserted terrorist camp had worn off, I had decided to have a look around to see if there were any terrorist tracks and try and locate the source of the smell before moving on. With my stick in hand, I began moving the wet soil on top of the mound. The smell was horrendous: the more soil I moved the worse the smell became. Memories of unearthing the two pilots in Mozambique came flashing back. Into my head popped the memory of the wet ground, the smell, the strange silence, the feeling of being watched; all familiar and all frightening.

The face had been eaten away, the eye sockets were one mass of white, heaving, twisting maggots. Why I was digging up a dead body I had not a clue. I could not stop. I would dig a bit but my head was never still, eyes darting from one clump of rocks and trees to the next in a constant search for danger. Every couple of minutes I would stop, light up a cigarette, huff and puff, smoke half, kill it and start digging again.

It was October – 'suicide month' in Africa – and the heat was awesome. And here I was in the midday sun, wearing long trousers, shirt and long-sleeved jacket, balaclava, covered from head to toe in black camouflage cream, sweat dripping off me, with flies crawling up my nose, digging up a dead body.

If Corporal Thomas had not called me on the radio reporting that he had located the group we were looking for, I probably would have stayed there until I had dug up the entire corpse. Who it was and how he or she had died, I had no idea. Terrorists had their own disciplinary code and any infringements were harshly dealt with. Maybe the body was that of a discontented terrorist who had decided that the life of a terrorist was not his idea of fun and had dared to say so.

"One day, Corporal Thomas," I muttered to myself, looking through the binoculars and shaking my head, "one day you and your love of *dagga* will lead to you having your arse shot off."

Across a narrow valley, about five hundred metres from where I was sitting, was Corporal Thomas perched in the top of the largest tree in the area, radio on his back, AK-47 in one hand, red flag in the other, awaiting the arrival of the Fire Force.

The terrorist group we had been searching for was led by one Comrade Che, who had introduced a reign of terror into the area. Nothing and no one was safe. Headmen and their families were brutally assaulted. Cutting off lips and bayoneting innocent civilians – men women and children – was the order of the day. Police stations were attacked, army vehicles ambushed and what appeared to be the group's favourite pastime: attacking buses and killing the passengers. It was so bad that the Selous Scouts had taken a bus and converted it so that the sides could be dropped. A bit of armour plate was added here and there and various types of machine guns were installed. It was then loaded up with a bunch of Selous Scouts dressed as locals and driven up and down the local roads. It was a futile exercise, as other buses were attacked but the one carrying the Scouts was left strictly alone. Having no choice, we reverted to plan B, passing ourselves off as terrorists and relying on information from the locals to try and pinpoint the group's location for the Fire Force to deal with.

Two frustrating weeks later we were no closer to locating Che and his group than when we had started. Then luck played a hand. The small, rocky, thickly wooded hills were silhouetted against a sky of red and orange, the silence broken only by the screech of a rooster and the footsteps of Corporal Thomas and his group of pseudo terrorists as they searched for a place to base up for the coming day. After a long night of speeches and the singing of *chimurenga*[1] songs, they were tired and hungry. Heading for a nearby thickly wooded ravine, they had no sooner settled in when they noticed a group of real terrorists approaching. It could only be Che and his group. Chance had delivered him into Corporal Thomas's hands – and Corporal Thomas was determined to take full advantage of his windfall. Sitting on top of the small hill where they had moved to avoid being seen by Che and his group, Corporal Thomas realized he could not see what was happening in the ravine. Leaving his group on the hill, he had gone down to try and find a position from which he could see the terrorist camp and at the same time guide in the Fire Force. Finding no place suitable on the ground, he had climbed a tree. The precariously balanced, wildly waving figure on top of the tree belied the voice guiding in the Fire Force. In a calm, measured voice Corporal Thomas talked the Fire Force over the target and twenty minutes later a reign of terror had mercifully ended.

---

1   War of liberation (Shona)

20

My last operation in the Selous Scouts: Chiredzi, 1980

O ne handshake, one thank you for all you've done, and it was all over. We had lost: all the effort, all the sacrifice had been in vain. We had lost. Shoulders hunched, head drooping, empty inside, standing on a muddy dirt road in the middle of nowhere and rotting clothes falling off my body, I tried to make sense of what had just happened.

The British and Commonwealth advisers had arrived and were busy establishing safe camps, collection points, disarmament centres, call them what you will. These camps were for what were previously known as terrorists – who had suddenly become liberation fighters – to gather in safety and hand over their weapons in preparation for the upcoming election. Confusion was the order of the day. What was going on? Was the war over? Were the elections going to decide the fate of the country? These and many other questions flashed through my mind as I sat under the overhang, cold, wet, miserable and stinking to high heaven.

The new tactic being employed by the terrorists was simple: put a political commissar in each village to make sure the locals voted for whom they were told to vote for. My mission and that of my troop was equally simple: capture as many of these planted political commissars as possible and hand them over to Special Branch. Why? I had long stopped asking.

It had been raining non-stop for the last couple of days. It was wet, cold and miserable. Unable to make a fire or erect a shelter because of nearby villages, I had tried unsuccessfully to keep dry by cutting a hole in my groundsheet and using it as a poncho. Crouched in the small overhang on the side of a hill that had been my home for the last four weeks, I watched the rain come down. My clothes were damp, as were my blanket, webbing and pack. Everything smelled like rotting meat. I no longer wore my wet shoes. The soil on the side of the hill had turned into a morass of slippery, sliding mud. I found it safer to walk around barefoot and only put on my shoes when I had to. As always, the only thing clean and dry was my AK-47.

With my nerves stretched to breaking point, balaclava pulled down over my nose and mouth, AK 47 in my hand, kneeling in the slushy, thick, red mud, trying to use the thatched roof of the mud hut to keep the rain off, I observed Sergeant Elton. His shoulders slumped, his feet dragging as he approached a group of blanket-wrapped locals standing around a smouldering, smoking fire. The strain and uncertainty were beginning to take their toll. I had grown tired of sitting on my behind trying to keep dry under the overhang and had decided to join Sergeant Elton for the night.

The whole operation had a feeling of desperation to it, a 'half a loaf is better than none', 'we have to do something', 'anything is better than doing nothing' scenario. The icing on the cake was that there was no Fire Force. Staring through the rain at the flickering fires from the distant villages, I pulled my blanket closer around my wet shoulders, put my head on my knees and tried to get some sleep. Not wanting to think about the uncertain present and equally uncertain future, I fell into a troubled sleep.

Ten metres in front of me, barely visible through the pouring rain and smoke, I watched Sergeant Elton talking to the locals around the fire. I could not help but wonder what thoughts were going through his mind and that of his group. That they were many and varied and very similar to my own I did not doubt. The big difference was that I was white. I could always move to South Africa and try to start again. They were black, their families were here and this was their land. They had no choice: they had to stay. I could not in my wildest dreams imagine the South African government welcoming a flood of black Rhodesians.

Here we were, sitting on a major route to an assembly area: there were terrorists to the left of us, terrorists to the right of us; what the hell, the truth be known, there were terrorists all over the place – we were falling over them. Instead of calling in the Fire Force, we were walking around in the mud and rain trying to remove the political commissars as fast as the passing terrorists dropped them off. To this day I have not figured out why.

Through the darkness and pouring rain came a scraping sound. I froze, my muscles tensed, I started to sweat. I was as nervous as a cat on a hot tin roof; there was literally a terrorist behind every bush. Peering through the gloom, ignoring my pounding head and the rain-diluted black camouflage cream running into my burning eyes, I stared in the direction whence the sound had come. Nothing. Silence. Apart from the sound of the rain hitting the grass roofs of the mud huts and the murmur of voices from the group gathered around the fire, there was only silence.

Before I could stop myself, I was lying belly down in the thick mud: the door of the hut three metres to my right was being forced open. Rolling around like a beached whale, with a bulky twenty-five kilogram pack on my back, I tried desperately to get into a position facing the door. I was too slow. I was not going to make it. The pack sitting high on my shoulders was forcing my head down, making it impossible for me to see the doorway. Panicking, I tried to sit up and face the potential danger. As I sat there, flat on my bum in the pouring rain, firmly anchored in the thick mud by the weight of the pack, staring at the slowly opening door and the emerging AK-47 barrel that was close enough to touch, I knew I was in big-time shit. In my effort to face the door, I had lost my weapon. This was as close as I had ever been to an armed terrorist, bar once, and all the memories came flooding back.

Tearing my eyes away from the doorway, I frantically tried to locate my weapon. It was dark, the rain was coming down in buckets and I was panicking. Sobbing in frustration, now on my hands and knees, the pack resting on the back of my head restricting my head movement, scurrying to my left then to my right like a headless chicken, I tried to find it. "Jesus wept, get a grip of yourself!" screamed my brain. "If you're going to be shot at least try to be shot standing up." A strange feeling of calm descended upon me, with an acceptance of what was to be. Closing my eyes and taking a deep breath, I struggled to my feet. I turned to face the doorway and opened my eyes. A fleeting shadow obscured my vision. An AK-47 was thrust into my muddy hand. The doorway was empty: its occupant was being hustled away by my saviour towards Sergeant Elton and the group of locals standing around the smoking fire.

I could not stop shaking, my teeth were chattering, my body felt numb as did my brain, my legs were heavy and unresponsive. I was not sure if I had tick-bite fever or my body was reacting to the narrow escape I had just had.

Several hours later, in almost complete darkness, buffeted by a gusting wind and crouching under a small bush in the pouring rain near a muddy, flooded dirt road awaiting the arrival of a vehicle to uplift our latest captured political commissar, I wondered how many more operations I would last before I got shot.

I need not have worried.

Here I was less than eighteen hours later, after handing over our last capture, standing on the same water-logged road in the middle of nowhere trying to figure out what happened. It took time. But in the end, my brain accepted the inevitable. We had lost. With the feelings of pain and anger also came one of overwhelming relief and guilt – relief from the stress, pressure and the morale-breaking uncertainty of a war effort that seemed to have stalled. The guilt because you had survived where others had died, and deep inside you were glad it was finished.

Part III
South Africa:
Homeland Security, 1982–88

21

Port St Johns, Transkei, 1982

We were lost – stuck on a mud bank in the middle of the Umzimvubu River.

Pete Mac and I had entered a night fishing competition that was taking place at Port St Johns. We had arrived at the launch site earlier on in the evening with our canoe, fishing rods, bait, one bottle of Old Brown sherry to keep us warm, and a dozen Black Label beers, the kind with the screw-off cap, a torch and two paddles. We joined the rest of the teams at the braai – the barbecue – where we ate too much, drank too much, talked too much and should have gone home.

Needless to say, we did not. After we were called many times to "get the show on road", the teams finally got down to fishing. By this time it was dark. Pete and I were the only team using a canoe: all the other teams had motorboats. Maybe they knew something we didn't – for example, after drinking too much you need to pee and trying to pee when half drunk in a canoe is not easy, as we soon found out. On launching our canoe, we decided to paddle upstream towards the main bridge. The tide was still coming in so it should not have been a problem. We kept an eye open for the other teams' boats as we made our way upstream. It started off fine but once out of sight of the lights from the supermarket, we realized how dark it really was.

The river flows through a gorge; we could not see any landmarks which we were hoping we could use to tell us where we were. After paddling for half an hour or so, we figured we were where we wanted to be, dropped anchor and began fishing. By now the Old Brown sherry and Black Label beer were starting to have their effect. The simple task of putting a mud prawn on a hook became mission impossible. To try and have a pee was dangerous: drunk people swim like a rock – straight to the bottom, with no hope of coming up again. The choice of using the canoe for the competition, especially a night competition, was a bad one. It was cramped and difficult to move in without capsizing and being drunk did not help. As time went on and we had still caught no fish, I could not help noticing how quiet it was. Earlier on we could hear talking and laughter, but now – nothing. I knew something was wrong but my alcohol-soaked brain was working at a snail's pace. As I got to my knees in an attempt to pee, it dawned on me that the canoe was no longer trying to flip over every time we moved. I put my hand over the side and it sank into thick mud. After quite a search, I managed to find the torch and switched it on. Lo and behold, we were firmly stuck on a mud bank.

The tide had long since gone out and the nearest open water was about five metres away. Getting out and pushing the canoe was out of the question as there was no way of knowing how thick the mud was. Our only choice was to pull up the anchor and, using the paddles, try to manoeuvre the canoe off the mud bank. It took twenty minutes of huffing, puffing and swearing to reach open water. In the distance we could hear the waves breaking on the beach, so we pointed the canoe in the direction of the breakers and started paddling. We were pathetic; we couldn't get it together, first going left then veering right and turning a two-kilometre trip into four.

By now the booze had worn off and we were cold and hungry – with terrible hangovers on top of it. It was the worst fishing trip I had been on. The fishing trip to end all fishing trips and to top it all off we caught nothing.

22

The Lesotho Liberation Army: Qacha's Nek, 1983–4

I had been in the Transkei some four years, living a life of luxury and ease when the subject of training the Lesotho Liberation Army came up. Alarm bells should have started ringing immediately. We were here to train the Transkeian army, not liberation armies. We had just spent the last fifteen years fighting against liberation armies or, as we called them, terrorists.

The powers that be were looking for somebody to assist Major Bob MacKenzie, Vietnam veteran and former Rhodesian SAS, in the training and deployment of liberation fighters-cum-terrorists to destabilize the unfriendly Lesotho government on behalf of the South Africans. Volunteers were few and far between. Most of the advisers were married with families and had no intention of leaving their homes and families to train a bunch of terrorists. Not if they could help it. That left me: I was the only single adviser around apart from Major Bob.

The area chosen to conduct the training was the Drakensberg Mountains on the border between the Transkei and Lesotho. Warm and pleasant during summer, it was freezing cold in winter.

A couple of days later Major Bob and I were bouncing along pothole-infested farm roads, along the base of the Drakensberg range, viewing abandoned farmhouses. We were looking for premises that were isolated enough to give us a bit of privacy and at the same time provide accommodation and protection from the harsh winter, both for us and the trainees.

Several back-breaking, bum-numbing, bouncing hours later, we came across a farm that met the requirements we had set. It had not one but two large houses, one road in and out and no other farms nearby; the layout of the property was ideal. The area was beautiful, with high mountains, deep blue skies, crystal-clear streams full of trout and air so clean and crisp you could taste it.

Both houses were very old, built in the early 1900s out of local wood and rock. They were a cross between a house and fort. In those days, the natives still got restless. Then, as now, cattle theft was a major problem. The rooms were large with wooden floors and high ceilings, and the kitchen had a large wood-burning stove. Electricity was available, however running water was not. Both dwellings originally had earthen canals running from nearby streams to supply them with water. These were now blocked by fallen trees and, in some cases, washed away by rain. The houses were separated by a fairly large stream, a small concrete bridge and a distance of about five hundred metres. The house we chose to live in was situated at the bottom of a small hill and directly opposite across a small, steep-sided valley was the second house that, with all its outbuildings, would be ideal for housing the trainees.

In an effort to pre-empt any stories and rumours, we introduced ourselves to all the farmers in the immediate area. Our cover story was that we were advisers to the Transkeian army and had been tasked with setting up a training camp in the area to teach mountain warfare. On the face of it, everybody seemed to accept the story; what they thought was another matter. The pot was somewhat sweetened when we informed them that we would be buying all our fresh meat and vegetables directly from them. Plus, we would assist in any way possible to help stamp out the cattle rustling that was rife in the area.

Two weeks later, shirts off, sweating like pigs in the hot sun, Major Bob and I were trying to clean out the canal supplying water to our new home in the mountains. Talk about an exercise in futility! As fast as we fixed it up, it collapsed. After four days of back-breaking work, we finally got water into the holding tank – and there it stayed. The pipes leading in to and out of the house were so rusted up that there was no way on God's green earth that water was going to travel along them. Running water was out, buckets were in. On our next trip to Matatiele, the closest town, we picked up four large buckets.

We did several long walks around the area looking for any human signs but the whole place seemed to be deserted. There were no footprints or vehicle tracks on any of the mostly overgrown farm roads and paths.

In the evenings I would do a bit of trout fishing or sit on the veranda, have a couple of beers and marvel at the beauty of the place. The silence, the mountains, the huge trees, the crystal-clear streams and air clean enough to bottle and sell. After having spent the last fifteen years in the hot, mostly arid Rhodesian countryside fighting a losing battle, this was indeed heaven on earth.

But soon, even this isolated piece of heaven would have its silence shattered by men practising war. And with men would come all the ingredients required to pollute the streams and turn the countryside into a garbage pit.

Two days before the arrival of the trainees, we returned to Umtata, the capital of the Transkei, for a final briefing. Unfortunately, I was not invited to attend so I have no idea what was discussed. Talk about being kept in the dark and fed on shit. I was to conduct the training but was not privy to why we – the former Selous Scouts – had changed sides and were now training liberation armies, our old enemy whom we had called terrorists! The only reason that made any sense was money.

Two days later we were travelling in front of a convoy of trucks loaded with everything from beds to TMH46 anti-tank mines supplied and paid for by the South African government via their security services. The weather was overcast and raining and the roads were narrow and slippery – a recipe for disaster.

Things started off badly. Just outside Kokstad, the lead vehicle, while trying to negotiate a sharp corner, slid off the road and rolled two or three hundred metres down a steep embankment and came to rest in a stream. How the driver survived, Lord alone knows. Unfortunately, this vehicle was carrying the arms and ammunition. All you could see scattered all the way down to where the vehicle lay on it its side were AK-47s, mortar barrels, landmines, RPG-7s and boxes of ammunition.

It could not have happened in a worse place or at a worse time. It was not long before cars stopped and the locals started to gather to see what was happening. Then, to make matters worse, the police from Kokstad arrived. An AK-47 to a South African policeman was like a red rag to a bull. All common sense, logic and reason disappeared to be replaced by "HANDS UP, HANDS UP", backed up by a tightly gripped pistol, wide eyes and quivering mouth. Luckily for us, the accident took place just inside the Transkei. Unluckily for us, we still had to travel through South Africa to get to our base where we were to train the Lesotho Liberation Army.

Four cold, sweaty, wet, mud-covered, hill-climbing hours later, we finally finished recovering all the weapons and ammunitions and were on our way once more. Major Bob, in the meantime, had gone into Kokstad and had spoken to the South African police and security police. After a couple of phone calls, all the problems were sorted out and we were given the all-clear.

The first part of the journey along tarred roads went fine and we had a good chance of reaching our destination before it got dark. The last forty kilometres from Matatiele to our base were a nightmare, putting to bed any hope of arriving while it was still light. The farm roads were too narrow, the trucks too big, the potholes to deep. After three hours of gear-changing, wheel-spinning, pothole-dodging misery, we finally arrived at our base in the foothills of the Drakensberg Mountains. It was dark, cold and still raining.

It was now early morning and the rain had gone. The silence was awesome, the mountains magnificent, their peaks painted red and yellow by the rising sun. We were already sweating from moving all the ammunition and weapons that we had offloaded from the trucks the previous night into the farmhouse that was to be our HQ.

Two days later, in unmarked trucks, the forty trainees arrived. One look at the hard-faced, dead-eyed white drivers and I knew whom we were working for. It could only be the South African government security services. Which of the many branches, God knows.

I hoped Reid-Daly knew what he was doing. This was not Rhodesia, this was South Africa. He might have been a 'heavy' in Rhodesia but here in South Africa he was nothing, just somebody to be used and, when no longer required, tossed on the pile of the other used and abused people. I had known Reid-Daly a long time. He had been my training officer; he had, in fact, failed me on my first recruit course. Apparently I was lazy and had a bad attitude. He was my commanding officer in both the Rhodesian Light Infantry and Selous Scouts. Did we like each other? No, we tolerated each other. We respected each other but at the same time I was always a bit wary. The Selous Scouts, as in most units, had, for want of a better word, a clique, led and presided over by Reid-Daly. If you were in the clique – fine; if not, you had to mind your Ps and Qs. Having said that, I must also say Reid-Daly was a good leader who had, on many occasions, put his cock on the block in support of the men under his command. As time passed, I was to realize that the Reid-Daly of Rhodesia died in Rhodesia. The Transkei Reid-Daly was a different kettle of fish. The only thing that was the same was the clique. Now it was all about the money. If it meant abusing the trust and loyalty of the people working under him, so be it. If it meant training terrorists-cum-liberation armies instead of fighting against them, so be it. If it meant trying to overthrow governments and people were to die in these attempts, so be it. It was all about the money. Most people will disagree with what I have written and insist that Reid-Daily was a great leader and soldier, and it is all a case of sour grapes.

That evening, as Major Bob and I sat outside on the steps discussing what we were going to do the next morning, I could not concentrate. Glancing across the valley at the other farmhouse, I could see two large fires burning, each surrounded a group of trainees. I wondered what motivated them to risk their lives. What promises had they been given by their political leaders? I had spoken to many captured terrorists during the Rhodesian bush war and I always asked them same question: "Why did you join?" The answers ranged from "They promised to train me as a pilot/doctor/lawyer" to "I was forced to join or they would kill my family". Nobody ever said, "I joined to fight for the freedom of the oppressed masses."

Unbidden, the thought entered my mind: "And *you*, what are you doing? Why are you doing what you're doing? What is it with the holier-than-thou attitude?" Not wanting to go down that road, I pushed the feeling of uncertainty and guilt to one side, hoping it would go away. Needless to say, it did not. Even today, thirty years later, I still ask myself the same question – and still refuse to answer.

I was sweating like a pig, my breathing sounded like a steam engine with a hole in the boiler, as I desperately tried to supply oxygen to my burning lungs. It was early morning and I was struggling to keep up with the Lesotho Liberation Army trainees. What should have been a nice, slow, early morning road run had turned into a road race for the trainees and a survival mission for me. Barely an hour later and we were back at the river where we had started. Ordering everybody to have a swim, I collapsed in a heap. I had thought I was fairly fit but compared to these guys I was like an old man on crutches. Nevertheless, we started each day with a road run and a swim. Apart from the fitness aspect, it also gave me a chance to get to know who was who in the zoo and keep an eye out for potential leaders.

Day five and the silence of the valley was shattered by the sound of gunfire, the sound echoing again and again in the foothills of the mountains surrounding our base. Major Bob and I were testing our newly constructed rifle range. We had spent the previous four days converting an old overgrown maize field into a shooting range. With the help of a bulldozer it would have taken a couple of hours. With picks, shovels, pangas (machetes), gallons of sweat and a pint or two of blood, it had taken us four days of toil, literally from dawn to dusk. The construction of the range had given me a further opportunity to get to know the men I was to train. I was pleasantly surprised to learn that they could all speak English, which would make instruction so much easier.

So after four days of hard work, the training began. We issued no notebooks: everything would have to be learned by repetition. There were no motivational speeches: politics were best left to the politicians. We were there to train and to train only. I am pretty sure among the forty trainees there were at least two or more political commissars.

The training on the weapons' side was to cover the AK-47, 60mm mortar, 40mm grenade launcher and, most terrorists' favourite weapon, the TMH46 anti-tank mine. If the need arose they would also learn the RPG-7 rocket launcher. On the tactics side we were going to concentrate on ambushing, the laying of landmines and, most importantly, lots and lots of live fire and movement. And in between we would also teach a bit of first aid, demolitions and the dos and don'ts of a pseudo operator.

The next five weeks consisted of hard training. Learning how to strip and assemble the AK-47 and doing it again and again until they could do it blindfolded. The same went for the 60mm mortar, 40mm grenade launcher and the arming and laying of the TMH46 anti-tank mine.

Then we concentrated on the bread and butter of tactics: fire and movement. The first couple of times we did it without live ammunition and I ran them up and down the range until they were exhausted. I then issued them with live ammunition and we did it again and again. After many hours of training and countless thousands of rounds, things started coming together. No one flinched any more as rounds went over their heads. Firing into the ground directly to their front ceased and they showed no hesitation in running forward when commanded to do so.

As one week blurred into the next, there was no let-up. Ambushes, night shoots and laying anti-tank mines took up many hours on most nights. By day the road runs, carrying all their personal kit plus landmines and mortar bombs, as well as the never-ending range work, including fire and movement, made sure that everybody, including the instructors, were on their last legs come evening.

The closer it got to deployment time the more worried I became. When the trainees first arrived, I had issued them with blankets, mattresses, pots, pans and toiletries, but no clothing of any sort. They had arrived wearing denim jeans, shirts, running shoes and the odd jacket, all well past their sell-by date. Now, after five weeks of intense training, their clothing was hanging in tatters from their bodies and their running shoes were held together by plastic packets and wire.

Major Bob had requested warm clothing on several occasions but his pleas had fallen on deaf ears. The fat, shiny, black politicians arrived and departed amidst much clapping and cheering but still no warm clothing. The dead-eyed people, the ones who would not piss on you if you were on fire, came and went, saying little. The winter had arrived, it was bitterly cold and there was still no sign of clothing, never mind warm clothing.

During training, four group leaders were chosen by Major Bob and me. Each group was to consist of ten men, including the leader. Not too big, not too small – big enough to conduct an attack and small enough to hide. In terms of weapons, all group members would have an AK-47. In addition, each group would also carry a 60mm mortar and a 40mm grenade launcher. The carriers were nominated by the group commanders and the extra ammunition was shared out among the group.

By the time the training of the Lesotho Liberation Army was completed, winter had arrived. It was extremely cold. The river froze over as did the canal supplying water to the house. The ice was so thick we had to blow a hole in the river using plastic explosive to get drinking water.

Against this backdrop of frozen rivers, snow-capped mountains and howling winds, it was decided by the powers that be, who were sitting in their warm houses wearing the latest and warmest in winter clothing, that the first mission to be carried out by the Lesotho Liberation Army was to lay landmines on the roads leading to Lesotho security force bases in the Qacha's Nek area. The fact that the men who were to carry out the task had no warm clothing or shoes was beside the point. As I sat there listening to Major Bob's briefing on the upcoming mission, I could not help but think about the last time I had laid landmines. With all my experiences of the dos and don'ts of laying landmines fresh in my mind, I gave the group tasked with the mine-laying one last briefing, hoping they would learn something from the re-telling of my experiences.

By mid-morning, the sun had not shown its face, visibility was down to ten metres, the wind was screeching through the trees, the snow falling thick and fast and temperatures were below freezing. Into this world of cold, stepped Tokyo and his group of Lesotho Liberation Army fighters. They were dressed in thin, worn-out shirts and trousers, old running shoes held together by wire and bits of plastic, packs on their backs, weighed down with landmines and little else. This was a recipe for disaster if ever I saw one. No jackets, gloves, balaclavas and, most importantly, no socks or boots.

Looking at them as they sat drinking hot coffee, AK-47s lying on tops of packs in the room where I had just given my final briefing, I could not help but shake my head in admiration. There was no way in hell that I would go out dressed as they were into the snow, wind and sub-zero temperatures. Remembering that I had extra blankets in my storeroom, I offered them to the patrol. An hour or so later, the patrol, looking like they had just returned from an extremely tough operation instead of beginning one, stepped out into the raging storm. The extra blankets I had given them were turned into ponchos by some; others had cut the blankets into strips and had bound their feet, trying to keep the cold at bay. Looking like survivors of Napoleon's retreat from Moscow, they disappeared into the storm. Their mission was simple: lay the landmines on the roads leading to Lesotho security force bases, be they police or army. Outside, the snowstorm continued. One minute it sounded like a demented animal as the wind howled and screeched its way down the valley, threatening to destroy the house and everything in it, the next it was soft, clean, white and gentle, like a beautiful woman, as it slowly transformed the dark, bleak countryside into a white, breath-taking paradise.

Unused to this type of weather – I was more into the heat of the Zambezi Valley – I spent all my time huddled round the old wood stove, listening to the civilian radio. We had no direct communications with Tokyo and his group. We relied on the local radio stations to try and find out what was happening, when it was happening and where it was happening. This was sad but that was the way it was. If things went wrong for Tokyo and his group, they were on their own. Their existence would be denied by all and sundry, including the South African government, and condemned by the rest of the world.

The storm had died down but it was still incredibly cold, the ground covered in snow and the rivers still frozen. Major Bob and I had spent the last three days in the kitchen listening to our civilian radio that we had tuned in to Radio Lesotho but we had heard nothing concerning landmines or terrorist activity.

After spending three days and nights huddled around the old wood stove, the only source of heat in the house, we were beginning to smell. A combination of wood smoke, sweat, unwashed bodies and the smell of old cooking oil had turned us into a bad advert for fish and chips: like old fish and chips reheated in dirty oil, we smelled like a cross between a mountain man and a public toilet – rancid, sweaty and overpowering.

To get our minds off Tokyo and his group, we decided to go for a swim; besides, we needed drinking water. Arming ourselves with a kilogram of plastic explosive, carrying two plastic buckets for water and our washing gear, we headed down to the frozen river. Our plan was simple: blow a hole in the ice, have a swim, fill the two buckets with water and return to the farmhouse – or 'the fridge' as we now called it.

Twenty minutes later, we reached the river, a mere two hundred metres from the farmhouse. It had been a long, painful walk, the ground covered in a thick layer of snow, beautiful to look at but concealing numerous obstacles. Dressed only in shorts, T-shirt and shoes without socks, we arrived at the river's edge, bleeding and missing large patches of skin, courtesy of the snow-covered rocks, holes and broken branches. Blue and shaking from the cold, we finally managed to detonate the explosive and blow a hole through the ice. By this stage, I was so cold I could not stop shaking and my interest in having a swim and cleaning myself up had waned to zero. Barely a minute later, I was standing on the snow-covered bank, gulping in great gulps of fresh air. My naked body was blue with cold from my swim as I tried to soap down my body. The soap was like a block of ice; it would not lather and kept slipping out of my numbed hands. In desperation, I used my shampoo but to no avail – it was just too cold and nothing would lather. Throwing caution to the wind, I once again plunged into the icy water.

Later, with my head sunk into my shoulders and my shaking hands holding a cup of hot coffee, I felt exhausted; my teeth would not stop chattering. All I wanted to do was sleep. I was back in the kitchen, sitting as close as I dared to the wood stove, attempting to listen to the civilian radio and get warm at the same time. The warmer I got, the sleepier I got. I was already half asleep when my still-thawing brain partially registered what my ears were hearing – something about landmines and terrorists. Shaking my head, I tried to concentrate on what was being said. The words sounded distorted, like they were travelling down a tunnel bouncing from one side to the next. By the time I was fully awake and realized it was the Radio Lesotho news, it was too late.

Drinking a coffee a minute and burning my lips in the process, when the next news bulletin came on an hour later, I was ready. I had not been imagining things. Several landmines had been detonated in the Qacha's Nek area on the border between the Transkei and Lesotho. The Lesotho government claimed that only innocent civilians had been killed and injured and that the act was carried out by terrorists. It sounded so familiar, I did not know whether to laugh or cry. The big difference this time was that I was training the terrorists, not fighting them. How times had changed. How easily labels had changed: freedom fighter or terrorist – it all depended on what side you were on and how much money you were being paid.

The radio report confirmed that Tokyo and his patrol had survived the deadly weather and had succeeded in their mission. Early the next morning I was standing outside on the veranda. I needed a bit of fresh air after too much coffee, stale air and a sleepless night that had left me feeling nauseous and light-headed. It was bitterly cold outside and we had not seen the sun for days; the icy wind had returned and with it the rain. The wind and rain now exposed the once snow-covered rocks, dead trees and grass. The once-beautiful white countryside now looked grey and ugly and was somehow menacing like a great beast waiting to pounce. The heavy, brooding silence was broken by the wind as it whistled and moaned its way up the valley. I had had enough fresh air and, with the cold wind cutting through my clothing as if I was wearing nothing and slowly turning me into a block of ice, it was time to go back inside.

Having one last look around, I saw what appeared to be an animal of sorts, on all fours, crossing an open patch of snow a hundred metres away. I was about to turn when what I thought was an animal stood upright. Shaking my head, I looked away for a couple of seconds hoping I was not seeing things. Looking back, I could see seven or eight of what could only be humans, crossing the same patch of snow. Crossing tends to insinuate that they were walking. Walking they were not: falling, staggering and crawling would be a more accurate description. This could only be Tokyo and his group returning from Qacha's Nek.

Frozen, I stared in disbelief and horror at the approaching patrol. Like a bunch of drunks, they staggered forward, tripping and falling, getting to their feet, staggering forward again and again tripping and falling. Even the use of their AK-47s as walking sticks was not helping. Nobody seemed to be able to stay on their feet for more than a pace or two without falling. Cold forgotten, I ran to the approaching patrol.

Looking into Tokyo's eyes as I half carried, half dragged him to the house, I could see he did not recognize me. This was not Tokyo the human being, this was Tokyo the animal, fighting for survival. His hair and eyebrows were covered in snow, his mouth wide open as he struggled to get air to his lungs, his eyes large and unseeing and his skin a chalky grey and splitting across the cheekbones. Another hour and I figured he would be dead.

The kitchen was as warm as it was ever going to get. I had taken the top off the old wood stove and built a fire in the oven to try and warm up the huge kitchen. Looking more dead than alive, shaking uncontrollably, sitting around the stove, backs against the wall, legs stretched out in front of them, were the nine members of Tokyo's patrol. Most of them were wearing only trousers, no shoes, no jackets or shirts, their torsos grey from the cold and covered in cuts and scratches. I wondered what had happened to their shirts and jackets. One look at their feet and I had my answer: they were massive, at least the size of rugby balls, the skin bluish grey in colour with deep splits caused by the swelling. Many had toenails missing and deep cuts on the soles of their feet. There was no blood, yet no one showed any signs of pain. The strips cut from the extra blankets that they had wrapped around their feet were long gone, replaced by their shirts and jackets, not that they seemed to have helped.

I had heard of frostbite but never in my wildest dreams did I think I would have to treat anyone for it. I had done a medic's course in the Rhodesian army where we had dealt with gunshot wounds and bleeding but frostbite was not even mentioned. Keeping the fire alive and dishing out hot, sweet tea to anybody who would drink it, I waited for the doctor to arrive.

With the weather going from bad to worse and no warm clothing forthcoming, we stopped any retraining. The last thing we needed was a repeat of the frostbite saga. Luckily for us, all nine patients fully recovered and in a short time were ready to go back on operations. The sun seldom made an appearance. It was extremely cold, the rivers were iced up, it rained or snowed continuously and the wind never seemed to stop blowing. The nights were the worst – cold and never-ending. I passed the dark, cold hours sitting in a chair with my blankets wrapped around me, drinking coffee and keeping the fire going. On the odd occasion that the moon did break through the clouds, I spent hours staring through the window, transfixed by the strange beauty its yellow light produced. The trees with their broken branches, and the rocks all took on strange animal-like shapes. The old, creaking house, the snow eddies produced by the moaning wind, the sea of snow, eerie, silent, menacing and medieval, all an ideal setting for a horror movie.

※

One cold, wet, miserable day led to the next. Most of our retraining was now done indoors. On the odd occasion when the weather cleared up we did plenty of live firing. There appeared to be no limit to the amount of ammunition available. Whatever we requested, we got. It was always delivered by the same light aircraft to a dirt airstrip just outside Kokstad. This same aircraft would later be used for the distribution of propaganda pamphlets over the Ciskei.

I wish I could say the same about the money to buy food and warm clothing. We found it difficult to keep everybody fed and warm. After buying much-needed shoes for the trainees, we were flat broke. In desperation, we had started to buy meat on the hoof – it was much cheaper. The Lesotho Liberation Army members were now using their blankets as both ponchos to keep warm during the day and to sleep with at night.

Needless to say, the smell of sweat, unwashed bodies, wood smoke and cordite, mixed with blood and cow dung from slaughtering animals, made the blankets smell anything but pleasant. In our hour of need we received no visits from the smiling, fat, black politicians or the dead-eyed people, both probably deciding that discretion was the better part of valour.

I had never been so cold for so long in my life. Days dragged into weeks, weeks into months. The wind never stopped blowing and if it was not raining it was snowing. My whole life revolved around the wood stove in the kitchen. When I was not conducting training I was sitting by the stove. I slept next the stove, I ate next to the stove and I smelled like the stove. As far as I knew, I probably looked like the stove. I had heard of cabin fever and wondered if I was not suffering from it. I had not changed my clothes in weeks; neither had I bathed, cleaned my teeth or brushed my hair. My mouth tasted like the bottom of a birdcage and I stank like a putrid piece of meat, confirmed by the strange looks I was getting from Major Bob.

Gradually the weather began to warm up. The wind died down and the sun started making regular appearances. The snow melted as did the ice on the rivers. As the weather improved, so did my morale and with my morale, my personal hygiene. I started to pull myself towards myself and felt a lot better for it.

After one final week on intensive retraining, we were ready for operations again. The days were warm, the countryside green; throw in the crisp, clean air, the sparkling, clear rivers overflowing with trout, the majestic mountains and you had a piece of paradise that people would pay a fortune to visit. Into this little piece of heaven on earth came the politicians. Now that the roads were dry they came in their numbers with their big cars, big bellies, big smiles, big stories and even bigger promises.

While awaiting instructions on future operations, I passed the time trout fishing and training Peter to be a sniper. Why the Lesotho Liberation Army needed a sniper was beyond me. However, orders were orders. The only weapon we had that came anywhere near a sniper's rifle was an old .303 rifle dating back to the Second World War, fitted with an equally old telescopic sight. Peter had volunteered. He was in fact the only volunteer. None of the other Lesotho Liberation Army members had showed any interest, especially after they learned that snipers invariably operated alone. Peter was in his early twenties, tall and slim with long, neatly braided hair. He was a smooth talker and an even smoother dresser – a bit of a ladies' man, a trait that would cost him dearly. Even though his clothes were torn and the worse for wear from the training, they were clean. His shirt was neatly tucked into his trousers and the shoes we had bought him were clean and shiny. He was also a quick learner and it was not long before he was hitting targets from four hundred metres.

The days were getting longer and warmer. My trout fishing skills were improving by the day, as was Peter's shooting. Man, talk about a life of luxury and ease: this was what it was all about. All that was missing was a bit of wine women and song!

⚓

I was brought back to reality by Major Bob calling my name and asking if everything was okay. It was summer in the Drakensberg Mountains: lovely and hot during the day, refreshingly cool in the evenings. The scenery was picture-postcard perfect, the blue-green mountains rising to an ice-blue sky with air so clean you could see forever, crystal-clear streams and singing birds, truly magnificent and in complete contrast to the cold, bleak, grey, dangerous winter.

I spent the next couple of days, while awaiting the return of George from his mine-laying operation and John from his deep-penetration reconnaissance mission, doing a lot of trout fishing and a bit of sniper retraining with Peter.

Peter the sniper was becoming aggrieved by the fact that he had not been used as yet. The big problem was how to use him. Guerrilla warfare is all about movement, hit and run, no front line. The only way that I could see him being used as a sniper was to position him close to a border crossing, such as Qacha's Nek, and let him attempt to take out the Lesotho troops patrolling the border or those manning the actual border post itself. However, even a simple plan like that presented problems. Where should he position himself: in Lesotho or the Transkei? Should he have a spotter for protection and to help locate targets? He was only armed with a bolt-action .303 rifle, no match for a modern assault rifle. If he was seen while operating in Lesotho itself and chased by Lesotho security forces, could he run back into the Transkei for safety? The list was endless.

I sat Peter down and did my best to explain all the problems involved in deploying him. He listened to and agreed with everything I said. Thinking that was that, I got up and walked away. I was wrong! Early the next morning he was back with what he considered a better plan. Having no choice, I sat down and listened. The more I listened the more alarmed I became. Peter's plan was to operate in and around the area where he was born that, according to him, was well wooded and would provide good cover for a sniper. Talk about shitting on your own doorstep. Every question I threw at him, he came back with an answer. Yes, he knew everyone in the area and they were all anti-government. They would help him if he needed it. He would travel only at night and if anybody asked him about the rifle, he would tell them he stole it from a farmer in South Africa. And so it went on – for every question I asked, he had an answer.

Realizing he was going to return to his village regardless of what Major Bob or I said, I decided to help rather than hinder. Once again, I went through the weaknesses of his plan. It was like talking to the trees: he would not listen. As I sat there looking at him, I went cold, the hair on the back of my neck stood up: I was looking at a dead man walking. In my mind's eye I could see it all, his arrival at his village, weapon in hand, the fireside bragging, the beer, the girlfriend, the clumsy, failed assassination attempts, the trust he had for his fellow villagers, all contributing to his death. He was indeed a dead man walking.

Four days later, John returned from Lesotho having completed his information-gathering patrol, complete with three beautiful head of cattle direct from the Lesotho Royal Herd. It was early in the morning. I was down at the river trying to catch a trout or two for breakfast. The air was crisp, the water clear and the sun was just starting to make its presence felt when the silence was broken by somebody calling my name. Turning to the direction of the voice, I saw a short, thin man with a crazy hairstyle, waving his hands above his head. There was only one person with a hairstyle like that and it could only be John. He seemed extremely excited, literally jumping up and down, pointing at the hill where their camp was situated. I froze. My heart was pounding. "No," I thought, "it could not be. Surely the Lesotho army had not followed John into the Transkei." God – and the day had started off so well.

Dropping the fishing rod, I grabbed my AK-47 and started running to John. My mind was churning: what the hell was I going to do? Run, fight, cry or laugh? This was one scenario I had not envisaged. I crossed the river in one leap, barefoot. I hardly felt the sharp stones and broken branches cutting my feet. Adrenalin pumping, I covered the hundred metres to John in a matter of seconds. Stumbling, sliding, chest heaving, I came to a halt in front of him. His yellow Bushman-like features were split into a huge smile. My instant reaction was anger. "Jesus," I thought, "what's the matter with the man, why is he standing here shouting and waving his hands as if something is wrong? Damned arsehole!"

The next second I was laughing and hugging him, partly from relief and partly because it was good to see him again. Still laughing, with tears running down my cheeks, I held him at arm's length and asked what the problem was.

"No problem," he replied, he had something he wanted to show me. Hobbling along next to him on my battered, bruised, bleeding and gently throbbing feet, we made our way up the old farm road, heading up the hill to where they were based.

Many thoughts crossed my mind as I tried to figure out what it was that John wanted to show me. Maybe a prisoner captured from the Lesotho security forces. God, I hoped not, I had enough problems as it was. Or perhaps, my personal favourite, possibly a bag of diamonds he had taken from one of the many diamond mines in Lesotho. The heavy wooden door to the large dilapidated old barn was difficult to move. With both John and I pushing, it reluctantly squeaked and moaned its way open. It took a couple of seconds for my eyes to adjust to the light. There, standing in the middle of the barn, surrounded by the rest of John's group, were three big, fat head of cattle! This was indeed an answer to a prayer. The remains of the ox we had slaughtered several days ago were already looking a bit thin on the ground. Thirty to forty men eat a lot of meat. Once the initial burst of euphoria had worn off, I began wondering where John had managed to get the three head of cattle. I hoped he had not stolen them from the local farmers.

I am no cattle rancher but looking at the three head of cattle now being driven out of the barn into the sunlight by members of John's group, I could see the quality. Turning to John, I asked him where he had got the cattle from.

Looking at my dubious face, he burst out laughing. "Free cattle," he laughed, "free – compliments of the Royal Cattle Herds of Lesotho."

I wanted to pry further but was afraid of the answers I might get, so I decided to let sleeping dogs lie. All I knew was that we had meat for months to come, kindly donated free of charge by our enemy, the Lesotho government. But in the back of my mind lurked the feeling that this was not the last I was to hear of this.

Very early the next morning, while it was still dark, I was sitting on the veranda relaxing and enjoying a cup of coffee, my fishing rod lying on the ground next to me. The sky was slowly changing colour, the black giving way to a gorgeous array of pale yellows, fiery reds and subtle pinks; in the distance I could hear the sound of running water and the lonely call of a pheasant, the only sounds in an otherwise silent world. The beauty was such that it brought a lump to my throat and an understanding as to why some peoples worship the sun.

It had been a long and sleepless night. I was on my third or fourth cup of coffee and had smoked numerous cigarettes when the cause of my sleepless night came walking down the road. I had decided to have one more go at trying to convince 'Dead Man Walking', Peter the sniper, to abandon his plan of returning to his village in Lesotho and using it as a base for his sniper activities. One look at the determined walk and defiant face and I knew I had a hard job ahead of me. Watching him walk away an hour later with a pack on his back containing his ammunition and the old .303 rifle wrapped up in a blanket over his shoulder, I knew with utter certainty I would never see him again.

In the following weeks, the groups returning from Lesotho began bringing back strange stories of a man being stoned to death after trying to kill a policeman. The area and the time where the incident was supposed to have taken place all pointed to Peter the sniper. To put the stories to bed, it was decided to send a patrol, led by Henry, to the area to try and find out if, in fact, Peter was the person concerned. Wearing glasses, highly intelligent and nobody's fool, Henry was ideally suited for a task requiring a bit of brains, as in this case where it would be necessary to sort out the truth from the fiction. Seven days later, Henry returned from Peter's village and filed his report that went roughly as follows.

On his arrival at his village, Peter threw everything I had tried to teach him out the window. Wine, women and song were the order of the day. Much time was spent around the fire at night bragging of, among other things, his intention to kill members of the Lesotho armed forces. The old .303 rifle was shown around to all and sundry and was on permanent display. Somewhere along the line, amid all the drinking, bragging and womanizing, his alcohol-soaked brain must have decided that the time for action had arrived. His target was a policeman living in a nearby village, the time late afternoon. The condition of the would-be assassin: drunk as a lord.

After firing several shots to no effect, Peter had decided to call it a day, return to his village and revert to his life as a high-flying socialite. Later on in the evening, still sitting around the fire bragging, a group of men arrived. They came from the village where his intended victim lived. Twenty minutes later Peter was dead, stoned to death, deserted by the very people he thought would protect him. What thoughts went through his mind as the stones thudded into his body, nobody knows, but maybe, just maybe, he would have remembered how many times I had told him not to trust anyone and that wine, women and song had been the death of many a man.

Since John had returned from Lesotho with the three head of cattle, there was no shortage of meat and the camp was a happy place. We trained in the morning and played football in the afternoons. A period of peace and quiet descended on the base.

George was expected back any day, his progress from Sani Pass towards Qacha's Nek marked by reports of landmine explosions and threats of hell and damnation from the Lesotho government. Things were looking good.

Our short period of peace and quiet came to an abrupt end. The heavens opened and down came the politicians, from both South Africa and the Transkei, closely followed by the heavies from the Transkeian army and the South African security police, all jumping up and down, all frothing at the mouth. Our little training camp was as busy as a shopping centre on Christmas Eve.

"YOU HAVE CAUSED AN INTERNATIONAL INCIDENT!" they all shouted.

I was confused. What did they think sending an armed group or two of so-called freedom fighters into an innocent neighbour's territory was? Offering a helping hand maybe? Of course it was an international incident: what was the matter with them. But it appeared I was missing the point.

The armed groups, the landmines, the destroyed trucks, the dead people, were not the problem. We could carry on killing people, blowing up trucks, planting landmines for as long as we wanted. But under no circumstances were we to take cattle from the Royal Herds of Lesotho! To steal cattle from the good old locals was fine, but the Royal Herds – definitely not! I sat there and stared at them in disbelief; I could not believe my ears: here were my bosses condoning all the acts of terror carried out by the various groups against a by-and-large innocent civilian population, but throwing their toys out of the cot over a few head of cattle! God help them, I thought. The hypocrites had more blood on their hands than I ever would.

After the delegation had left in their big, shiny cars, acting as if they had just averted the Third World War, I spoke to Major Bob to find out the finer details of what had happened. According to what he had been told, John's group had killed the herder looking after the cattle which, according to Major Bob, did not seem to bother anybody too much: it was all about the cattle and the fact that they had been tracked to the South African border. It is important to mention that Lesotho did not recognize the Transkei as an independent country, so, as far as they were concerned, the transgression was committed by South Africa. Hence, an official complaint was presented to the South African embassy in Lesotho, causing the floodgates to open.

Once again I was confused. I don't know; maybe I was just stupid or maybe I was not seeing the bigger picture. Landmines were exploding, people were dying and there were no complaints, so why all the drama about a couple of cows? If you can track three head of cattle you sure as hell can track a group of ten men.

Later that evening, I took a walk to the camp on the hill where the members of the Lesotho Liberation Army were based and spoke to John about the incident.

It was early morning, dark, the clouds low and heavy, the wind was blowing and in the distance were rumblings of thunder and the occasional flash of lightning: rain was on its way. John and his group had made their way back to the Transkei through an upcoming storm. Hampered by the wind and lack of light, the going was slow. On one of their many breaks the sound of bells could be heard. In Africa the sound of bells is associated with livestock, be it sheep, cattle or goats. On investigation, the source of the bells was found to be a large herd of cattle. Not any old herd but one belonging to the royal family of Lesotho. Remembering the problems we were having back at the base in the Transkei trying to get enough meat to feed everybody, John decided a couple of head from the Royal Herd would be a great help. What should have been a simple job of separating two or three head of cattle from the main herd and driving them off, however, had become a mission. The rain had arrived and with it the thunder and lightning, the cattle were nervous and refused to be separated from each other.

Soaking wet, slipping, sliding, tripping and falling in the mud and over the rocks, struggling to make themselves heard above the thunder and pouring rain, a miserable half an hour later, they had finally managed to get three head separated from the herd. As they were preparing to drive the three beasts off, four men appeared out of the rain, one appearing to be armed but, as John explained, it was difficult to see. The men, who claimed to be herders looking after the cattle, were wrapped up in blankets for protection against the elements. Each carried a walking stick, or knobkerrie, and the wood, being old and worn, took on a shine of its own. When wet it could easily be mistaken for a rifle barrel. According to John, while he was busy trying to explain to the herdsmen who he was and what he was doing, he mentioned the Lesotho Liberation Army. One of the herdsmen, on hearing the name, shouted something and lunged at him with what John thought was a rifle, so he shot him. The remaining so-called herdsmen disappeared as quickly as they had appeared. Simple. End of story. I asked him if he did not think to check and see if what he thought was a weapon was indeed a weapon.

"No," he replied, adding that there had been no time to waste. The weather was bad and his priority was to get his group plus the three head of cattle across the border into the Transkei before it got light. Whether the herdsman was armed or not was not his problem; besides, he was dead. How he knew the man was dead or not without checking, I did not ask; some questions are better left unasked.

A couple of days later George returned with his group. At first I did not recognize them. They had left looking like escapees from a Russian gulag, wearing torn, worn-out shirts and trousers, no jackets and in desperation the odd guy had converted his blanket into a poncho by cutting a hole in the centre and slipping it over his head. The tattered clothing had been replaced, courtesy of the locals, with what appeared to be brand-new shirts, trousers and jackets. Whether the locals had done it of their own free will was another story.

The cattle-rustling incident seemed to have put the fear of God into the politicians, as all operations were put on hold. Major Bob had gone to Durban for a break. Three weeks had passed and we still had no word on our fate. I passed most of my time trout fishing. I had tried to keep the Lesotho Liberation Army members busy by doing a bit of retraining but nobody seemed interested, so I let it be.

Morale was low, the three weeks of inactivity and uncertainty was starting to take its toll. What had been a highly motivated, well-disciplined group of men was slowly turning into a disinterested mob. I knew the cause: there is nothing worse than being kept in the dark and fed on shit. Thank God for the three stolen head of cattle; at least there was enough food.

Lying in the cool waters of the mountain stream a month later, almost to the day after the cattle rustling, I watched Majors Bob's vehicle bouncing its way up the narrow track leading to the farmhouse. I hoped he was the bearer of good news. By the time I had got dressed and reached the farmhouse, Major Bob had already unloaded his vehicle and was waiting for me on the veranda. I took one look at his face and I knew everything was back to normal. The powers that be had decided to press forward with the venture, but we were to make sure no more embarrassing incidents, like the dead herder and missing cattle, took place. We were, according to the briefing received by Major Bob, to enter a new, more aggressive phase of the attempted overthrow of the Lesotho government. Included was the ambushing of Lesotho army and police patrols plus attacks on government buildings, with the ultimate aim of expanding our operations from the border area farther into the hinterland. This sounded great – but we had only four groups of ten men. To expand on any scale at all we would need more men, which meant more training. Maybe the powers that be were getting serious or maybe time was running out and they could see the writing on the wall and it was unpleasant reading. Whatever the reason, it seemed it was full steam ahead.

From information gleaned by the debriefing of the different groups that had operated in the Qacha's Nek area, we knew patrols were done on a daily basis along the border by the Lesotho security forces. Patrol strength was normally ten-plus men. Ambushing one of these patrols seemed a simple and reasonably safe way to commence the more aggressive phase that was deemed necessary.

Two groups were selected to carry out the ambush. One was led by Tokyo, now fully recovered from the frostbite and raring to go, and the other by John, the cattle thief. The two groups had just been briefed by Major Bob and were getting ready to move to the Lesotho border and the selected ambush site.

It was late afternoon and already it was getting cold. The sun was slowly disappearing, the valley was covered in shadow and the mountain peaks catching the last rays of the sun were bathed in a strange reddish glow. Standing there admiring the sunset, I glanced at the two groups preparing to move out. They were still wearing the same old, oft-repaired, torn and tattered clothing they had arrived in almost a year ago. With no jackets available for protection against the cold, they were all wearing their blankets that they had converted into ponchos. The only serviceable item of clothing they possessed was their shoes. I felt blinding anger, shame, pity and humiliation, most of it directed at the politicians but some of it at myself for being part of this farce, and some at the Lesotho Liberation Army members for accepting the way things were without complaint. With the new orders to attack and expand had come no new warm clothing or shoes. Shaking my head, I turned and walked away before I said something I would regret.

As our base was not too far from Qacha's Nek, situated at the base of the Drakensberg in a narrow valley, we should be able to hear the firing taking place in the mountains above us. It was nearly ten o'clock in the morning. I had been awake since six, had drunk countless cups of coffee and was on my second packet of cigarettes. I was beginning to wonder if something had gone wrong and the ambush had been called off.

Suddenly I heard one solid wall of sound echoing and re-echoing as it faded into the distance. This had been created by twenty AK-47s firing on automatic. It rolled across the peaks and down the mountainsides. The ambush had been sprung. Hopefully none of the groups had suffered casualties and, all things being equal, would be back in camp by the evening. Twenty minutes later, fishing rod in hand, I was making my way down to the river to try my luck when I heard what sounded like a burst of automatic fire. Stopping, I turned and faced the area where I knew Qacha's Nek was. Sure enough, in the distance, I could hear the sound of rifle fire, punctuated by the sharp crack of an exploding 60mm mortar bomb and every now and again the duller thud of the 40mm grenade launcher.

The fighting continued off and on well into the afternoon. This was no ambush; it sounded like a mini-war. I was to learn later that most of the farmers in the area, on hearing the continual firing coming from the border post at Qacha's Nek, had jumped in their vehicles and had driven up to the border to see what was going on. Some of the more curious had climbed the surrounding hills to get a better view. It was like Christmas, the most exciting thing that had happened in the place since Lord knows when.

The icy-cold waters of the river kick-started my brain and got the blood flowing. It had been a long night that I had spent around the wood stove in the kitchen, drinking sweet, black coffee, smoking myself to death and worrying. Sunrise had found me on the veranda trying my best not to puke. Too much coffee and nicotine, combined with the heat from the stove, had made me feel nauseous, my eyes felt like piss holes in the snow, my head throbbed and my breath tasted bad enough to peel the paint off a car. Standing in the sun towelling myself off, I wondered what the day was going to bring.

The sun was big and hot, the fire was big and hot, the two sheep cooking on the big and hot fire were big and hot and everything not big was definitely hot. It was midday and we were having a barbeque, commonly known in this part of the world as a braai. I had no sooner finished dressing when I was surrounded by twenty smiling, happy faces. John and Tokyo had returned. Light headed with relief, I grinned back. Looking around, I could not help but notice the odd man carrying two weapons. Immediately, all my thoughts on death, capture, live interviews on Lesotho TV, parading though the capital, Maseru, came flooding back. Forcing my way through the throng, I made my way across to John.

Two hours later, I had blood from the 'burnt on the outside, alive and well on the inside' sheep running down my chin and onto my shirt. I was relaxed, happy and even a bit proud. John and Tokyo had done well; the extra weapons had come from dead members of the Lesotho government security forces.

The next morning, at the debriefing of the two group commanders, several captured weapons, including AK-47s and pistols, were handed over to Major Bob. Among the captured weapons, I noticed a Galil, the Israeli version of the AK-47. I claimed this weapon for myself. This was the same weapon I was to bury at King William's Town golf course many months later after a failed attack on the palace of the president of Ciskei, Lennox Sebe. Sitting on the floor, stinking to high heaven of wood smoke and sweat, listening to the two group commanders explaining what happened at the ambushing of the Lesotho border patrol, a picture formed in my mind. It was as if I was there looking down on them, watching as the drama unfolded.

It was early morning, cold and misty in the mountains. The two groups led by John and Tokyo – twenty men in total and armed with AK-47s, carrying two 60mm mortars with ten bombs for each plus two 40mm grenade launchers with twenty rounds per launcher – had split into three smaller groups, consisting of a killer group and two stop groups. The split was done quickly and quietly. It had been practised many times back at base: every man knew in which group he belonged and what his job was. The killer group, whose job it was to spring the ambush and kill as many of the enemy as possible, consisted of twelve guys, all of them good shots. The two stop groups consisted of four men per group. Their tasks were twofold: firstly, to kill any enemy running away from the killing ground and, secondly, to act as an early-warning post for the killer group. In the case of the Lesotho Liberation Army, not having radios for communications, the role of listening post was extremely important. It meant that both stop groups had to have visual contact with the killer group to warn them of any approach by the enemy and civilians who might have to be taken into custody, so as not to compromise the ambush.

At first light the commanders of the two stop groups and killer group went on a quick reconnaissance to select their positions, bearing in mind the early-warning problem of no radios. Once the positions were chosen, the groups moved in and waited.

The Lesotho army border patrol was heard long before it was seen, walking along with weapons over their shoulders, calling to one another, laughing and joking with not a care in the world. After the international incident involving the death of the cattle herder and the theft of the three cattle, all operations by the Lesotho Liberation Army had been put on hold while a decision was made whether to continue or cease operations. So it had been very quiet of late: no landmines going off, no stories of strange armed groups in the area; everything seemed back to normal. The noise made by the approaching patrol gave the ambush party plenty of time to get themselves ready and any noise they might have made was covered by the approaching enemy.

Suddenly they appeared, as if out of nowhere, weaving their way around the many large rocks that made a zigzag path just before it reached the flat, open, marshy ground of the vlei. Dressed in a mixture of military uniform and civilian clothes, carrying mainly AK-47s, they continued along the path that would lead them into the killing ground. There was no scouting party up front to clear the ground ahead, no flanks out, nothing but a happy group of guys about to have one of the worst days of their lives.

The distance between the killer group and the path was no more than ten metres. Into this death trap walked the Lesotho army border patrol, still chatting and joking. The noise was deafening. The enemy was too close to miss and surprise was complete. Most of the enemy in the killing ground were either killed or wounded. Once the shooting had stopped and the dust settled, the search party went forward to check the dead and wounded, as well as weapons. There appeared to be nine bodies lying in the killing ground, some dead, some wounded. The dead were not a problem, the wounded were. The sun was starting to warm up and the smell of blood, combined with the stench of the liquids leaking out of the dead and wounded who had been shot in the stomach, was enough to make you puke your guts out. The stress was starting to show. Once the weapons had been collected and the bodies searched, there was the matter of what to do with the wounded as no orders had been issued regarding captures. It was a subject nobody wanted to broach. John and Tokyo had a problem on their hands: what to do with the two prisoners, both wounded in the legs and bleeding. They were unable to walk any great distance. To leave them alive after having seen most of the ambush group and being able to identify them in the future was not a wise thing to do. It not only put the individuals' lives at risk but also their families.

They had no radio contact with the base in order to seek advice. Half an hour or more had passed since the shooting had stopped, but they had still not come up with a plan of what to do with the prisoners. The decision was taken out of their hands as they came under fire from a large group of Lesotho soldiers. Luckily for John and Tokyo, they had already called in the two stop groups and all twenty of them were under cover, lying in extended line and able to return fire. Using the 60mm hand-held mortar and the 40mm grenade launcher, they forced the Lesotho army patrol to break formation and take cover. The liberation fighters then tried to break contact, with one group giving covering fire as the other withdrew, and vice versa. The commanders faced two major problems, i.e. ammunition and time. Ammunition because they were not carrying any extra: they each carried five thirty-round magazines for their AK-47s that was plenty for an ambush, but now that they were involved in a full fight with the Lesotho army they would have to ration their ammunition carefully and use the two 60mm mortars and 40mm grenade launchers to keep the enemy at bay, and use their AK-47s only when they had to. Time was probably the bigger problem of the two: there was no way they could cross back into the Transkei, or even South Africa, in broad daylight and still in contact with the Lesotho army, the consequences of which were unimaginable. So they had only one course of action and that was to break contact completely with the Lesotho army before attempting to cross back into either safe haven.

The Lesotho army had no intention of letting the killers of their comrades escape that easily, yet at the same time they did not press too hard, fearing they might end up in the same condition as their friends – dead. The firing continued throughout the day with the time between the outbursts of firing getting longer and longer, the last being late in the afternoon. Contact was finally broken and the Lesotho Liberation Army managed to cross back to the safety of the Transkei.

23

The Lesotho Liberation Army: Sani Pass, 1984

With spinning wheels, straining engine, grating gears and clouds of black, evil-smelling diesel smoke, we inched our way up the Sani Pass. The dirt road was cut into the side of a mountain and, like most mountain roads, it had huge drops, numerous potholes and large rocks scattered all over the place, as well as deep gullies caused by erosion. Feet firmly placed on the dashboard of the old Transkeian army truck, one eye on the driver, the other on the huge drop just below my door, I was relaxed and feeling positive. Things had gone a lot better than I had expected. In an hour we would have completed our mission and be on our way back to our base in the Drakensberg Mountains.

My sense of well-being and confidence did not, however, extend to the driver of the truck: Chris Robbins was a founder member of the Selous Scouts and as cool as they come but even he was muttering and swearing under his breath, his shirt soaking wet from sweat as he struggled to keep the truck on the road while at the same time trying to avoid the rocks and potholes. It had been a long trip: we had spent the last four hours travelling through South Africa with a truck load of Lesotho Liberation Army members, all black, all dressed in civilian clothes and all armed to the teeth. I shudder to think what would have happened if we had got caught in a roadblock manned by a nervous group of South African policemen.

George, the commander of the group travelling in the back of the truck, was a short, aggressive man and took no shit from any one. His mission was twofold: one, to hold meetings with the local population and gauge the strength of the support for the movement in the area, and, secondly, to lay landmines on the roads used by the Lesotho security forces.

As we neared the top of the pass, we found what we were looking for: a place where the road was wide enough to turn the truck around and the bush thick enough to conceal George and his group after they had disembarked from the truck. I watched as an official-looking green *bakkie*, a pick-up truck, approached from the top of the pass. My heart dropped, my world in tatters, my confidence shattered, my feeling of well-being a mere memory. I had to fight back the tears of frustration, anger and, I must admit, of self-pity. "Why now?" I thought to myself. An hour earlier or later would not have mattered but no, the arsehole driving the bakkie had to choose this moment to come driving down the fucking road. My frustration and self-pity were quickly replaced by anger.

Pulling the truck over to one side so as to make room for the two vehicles to pass, Chris stopped. We both watched with bated breath as the green bakkie drew level. The driver was white, young and dressed in some sort of uniform.

"Please do not stop, my friend; whatever you do, please do not stop," I muttered.

We were high up and the air was cool but we were both sweating. Chris was gripping the steering wheel so tight his knuckles were white.

The bakkie slowed to a crawl and for a minute I thought it was going to stop, but the driver just wanted a good look at us. Our long hair and beards, scruffy civilian clothing and the old smoke-belching Transkeian army truck would not have inspired much confidence in him. One look at his face and I could see he was confused: what was a Transkeian army truck driven by two hobos doing heading up the pass for the Lesotho border? I knew he would be back real soon to find out what was going on.

As soon as he was out of sight, I jumped out the cab and opened the tailboard. Within seconds the truck was empty as George and his group were swallowed up by the thick bush. We were trying to reverse the truck and turn it around when the bakkie reappeared. Stopping about ten metres from the truck in the middle of the road and effectively blocking our escape, the driver got out. He was younger than I had thought, tall and slightly built, but there was nothing slightly built about the 9mm pistol he held in his hand. He looked unsure of himself, the tell-tale shaking of his hand clutching his weapon giving away his nervousness. I could see the sweat running down the side of his face. We were scared but so was he. We were used to weapons and the stress and uncertainty that accompanied them: he was not. That made him dangerous and totally unpredictable. He needed to be handled with extreme caution.

With a stiff-legged gait, eyes the size of dinner plates, mouth quivering, stumbling over the loose stones on the road, he approached. One look at the wild eyes and we knew we were in big trouble. Any sudden movement on our part would result in one, if not both of us, being killed. Neither Chris nor I spoke Afrikaans. I can only assume that the driver of bakkie was demanding to know who we were and what we were doing. Not being able to speak the language did not help our cause. The tension was such that you could cut it with a knife. We had to do something before the shooting started.

The only option available was to try and talk our way out of the mess we found ourselves in. We tried the 'we are lost' story, talking slowly, while at the same moving forward, hoping to get close enough to overpower him. As we moved forward, however, he moved backward, keeping the distance between us constant. Young and nervous he might be but stupid he was not. God, I thought to myself, would this not be poetic justice: shot dead by some unknown amateur on a lonely road trying to protect the type of person I had spent the last ten years in Rhodesia fighting against.

I could see he was not buying our story but he was starting to relax. His quivering mouth now had a self-satisfied smirk plastered all over it as if to say, "Who do you think you're talking to? If you think I believe any of the rubbish you're telling me, forget it." I don't know who he thought we were but the smirk on his face seemed to indicate that he thought he had captured two notorious criminals and that fame and fortune were just around the corner.

The cell was small, dirty and smelled of sweat and urine, the only furniture being a bench on which Chris and I were now seated. The past hour had been nerve-wracking as we fought to buy time for George and his group.

Finally, growing tired of listening to our bullshit, the owner of the green bakkie had ordered Chris to reverse the truck and get it pointed up the road towards the Sani Pass border post, with his weapon trained on me the whole time. After much wheel-spinning, gear-changing, stalling and revving, amidst large clouds of vile, black diesel smoke, Chris finally got the truck turned around. Chris was an old hand: he knew just as well as I did that George needed time.

On his next visit to the cell, I gave the owner of the green bakkie who had turned out to be the border post commander, a telephone number to call. Three hours was more than enough time for George. A couple of minutes later, he was back, all smiles as he unlocked the cell and asked us to follow him. After a short walk, we ended up in his house where he apologized, explaining that he was only doing his job and that if he had been informed of what was going on, this would never have happened. After a cup of coffee and much shaking of hands and back-slapping, we departed the best of friends, promising that if we were ever in the area again and needed help we would come straight to him.

As we made our way down Sani Pass the sun seemed brighter, the air clearer, the view more heart-stopping than usual, the road smoother and even the old truck seemed to have shed a couple of years and was going like a dream. Man, that had been close.

Several days had passed since the near-disaster of the Sani Pass deployment. Back at our base in the Drakensberg, I was listening to Radio Lesotho trying to find out how George and his group were doing. For the first couple of days I had heard nothing and was beginning to wonder if George had made it. Now, three days later, the Radio Lesotho presenter announced that several landmines had been detonated in the Sani Pass area, followed by the announcement that only civilians had been killed and injured and that the terrorists would be hunted down.

George was alive and kicking.

Flushed with success, we decided to send in another group, only this time deeper into Lesotho, purely on an information-gathering operation. The man chosen to conduct this mission was John. John was in his early thirties, short and wiry and somewhat older than his comrades. He was softly spoken with a light-yellow skin and the features of a Bushman. Calm and patient, he was a good leader, ideally suited for the deep-penetration reconnaissance coming up.

But all was not well in our little piece of paradise. The dead-eyed people came and went, as did the fat and shiny people, and still we struggled to keep everybody fed. Money always seemed to be in short supply. Little did I realize at the time but this continual shortage of food would later lead to an international incident.

After much bargaining with a local farmer, Major Bob managed to get a live ox delivered to the farm gate. An hour later it was lying on the ground dead, shot through the head. After building a huge fire, the butchering began in earnest. The knife wielders, specially chosen by their Lesotho Liberation Army comrades, were experts. In no time at all they had skinned the dead ox and removed the stomach. It was a hot afternoon and already the stench of the congealing blood and the contents of the stomach were attracting flies. They arrived in their thousands. Fearless, they covered the carcass in a heaving mass of tiny, black bodies. Sparing no one, they attacked butchers and spectators alike, driven into a feeding frenzy by the smell of blood and offal.

Unfazed by the flies, amid much banter, the butchering continued. Onto the fire went the heart, liver and kidneys. Ten seconds later, still raw, they were removed from the fire and thrown onto the blood-covered hide of the ox.

The cutting-up of the morsels had no sooner finished than the flies descended. What had been, though somewhat raw and covered in congealed blood, tasty morsels were now transformed into a moving, breathing mass of flies.

I watched fascinated as, undeterred, the onlookers devoured the pieces of par-cooked heart, liver and kidneys. A holiday atmosphere prevailed. Laughter and the smell of meat cooking on the fire filled the air. This was the happiest I had ever seen the group. For once there was enough food to feed everybody. At least John and his group, who were leaving later that evening for Lesotho, would have full stomachs.

Turning around, I made my way back to the house Major Bob and I were sharing. Sitting on the veranda, I thought back to the last time I had seen AK-47-wielding black men cooking an ox over a fire.

24

Last throw of the Lesotho dice: Zastron, 1985

I t was a dark, hot summer evening in the small farming town of Zastron in the south-eastern Orange Free State. I was sitting in a covered bakkie about two hundred metres from the police station in a dimly lit side street. I was, to put it mildly, shit scared. It was not a wise thing in apartheid South Africa to lurk around police stations, especially at night. After the success of the ambush at Qacha's Nek, it was decided to open a new area of operations around Zastron. The fact that our base was hundreds of kilometres away from our new operational area was neither here nor there.

I heard rifle shots. "God, not again," I thought.

It was a lovely warm summer morning, with a slight breeze and not a cloud in the sky. We were driving around in the farmlands along the border between South Africa and Lesotho. We were lost. I was standing in the back of Major Bob's bakkie to see if I could see anything that would help us pinpoint our position. My eyes felt as if they were going to burst and my head was light and empty as if it was floating free, unattached to my body. My movements were clumsy and uncoordinated. Like they were going out of fashion, I had been popping the 'stay awake' tablets that had been given to us by the dead-eyed people.

Gripping the canopy bars as tightly as I could to counter the floating, I looked around. As far as the eye could see in all directions was maize, not a tree, not a house, just a sea of green, white-topped maize. Faintly in the distance I could hear more gunshots. God, what a disaster: I knew what those gunshots meant. We had left our base camp in the Drakensberg the previous evening. Morale was high and things had been going well. Using the back roads, we had headed for Zastron. Six or seven hours later, in the early hours of the morning, our trucks were running out of fuel. We were now in South Africa, driving around with three truckloads of black people dressed in civilian clothing and armed with AK-47s. Talk about living on the wild side. No wonder I was popping the tablets with gay abandon.

The small town we pulled into was in darkness, the only garage was closed and the only building that showed any sign of life was the police station. An hour later, trucks refuelled, we were back on the road. What Major Bob had said to the station commander, I do not know but within minutes, the garage owner appeared, opened up and refuelled the vehicles himself. Who paid? Lord knows. It was now a race against time.

Everything from here on became a bit blurred as the tablets, fatigue, tension and pressure started to take effect. The police roadblocks, the escorts, the daylight deployment, the local farmers taking pot shots at the deploying groups of Lesotho Liberation Army fighters, all merged into one blurred, mind-boggling disaster as the wheels fell off.

I stared in dismay and fear as the elephants and rhinos crossed the road in front of our truck. Shaking my head, I looked away. This was the Transkei: there were no elephants or rhinos around here; you'd be lucky to find any wild animals at all! I was sitting in the passenger seat of the old Transkeian army truck and we were on our way back to our base in the Drakensberg. My body was shaking and covered in a cold sweat, my eyes large and unblinking, my ears filled with a high-pitched buzz, my brain slow and clumsy as it tried to make sense of what my eyes were seeing. Trying not to think, I closed my eyes firmly and tried to relax.

"Hallucinating. You're hallucinating," announced my brain. The 'stay awake' tablets, the lack of sleep and food and the disaster that was the deployment of the Lesotho Liberation Army had all contributed to my present condition. Thus began and ended the longest journey of my life. I was staring through the windscreen of an old truck looking at animals that were not there.

Four days later, I was back to try and pick up the pieces. One of the groups we had deployed had got lost and had given themselves up to the Zastron police. It was for this reason that I was lurking in a dimly lit street near the police station. At exactly 20h00, I entered the police station as I had been instructed. It was dark and murky inside and the bulbs hanging from the ceiling were doing little to illuminate the place. I had no doubt that I was being watched. Nor did I have any doubt that while looking at me, they were laughing and shaking their heads. Then again, after our disastrous deployment of the Lesotho Liberation Army a couple of days prior, who could blame them?

Standing in the centre of the charge office, more embarrassed than anything else, I let my eyes adjust to the light. It was an old, oblong-shaped room, clean and well maintained. Black with age and shiny from use, along the one side ran an old wooden counter, on the middle of which was a large bunch of keys – for the cells, no doubt. Staring at the bunch of keys, I moved forward cautiously. The feeling of being watched was starting to play on my mind, my body had tensed up and I had broken out into a sweat.

"God," I thought to myself, "get a grip of yourself, there are people watching, you are supposed to be a hairy-arsed Selous Scout, fearless, and here you are tiptoeing around the place looking like you're going to burst into tears any second!"

Grasping the keys, I headed for what could only be the door leading to the cells. It was green in colour and made of steel with numerous locks of various types and sizes all over it. The smell stopped me in my tracks. It had taken me a couple of minutes to unlock all the locks and open the door. As I stood in the passageway to the cells, I was having difficulty in breathing. The smell of urine, faeces, unwashed bodies and sour sweat was enough to make even the strongest stomach complain.

The first two cells were empty. In the third, looking somewhat dejected, were, for want of a better word, the prisoners of war.

The walk from the police station to the bakkie had a strange, pre-ordained feel to it. It was only 20h30, in the evening, the police station was situated in the middle of the town, yet there were no cars driving around or people, either black or white, on the streets. Be that as it may, ten minutes later, the cell keys left where I had found them, we were loaded up and ready to say goodbye to Zastron.

Two weeks later I was back running selection courses in Port St Johns. The trucks arrived at our training base. The members of the Lesotho Liberation Army got on and departed to places unknown. No thank you, no goodbye, no nothing.

25

The Ciskei Liberation Army: Transkei, 1986

The plan was to replace the present Transkei government of Lennox Sebe and his corrupt ministers with Charles Sebe and his equally corrupt cronies. I hoped with every sinew in my body that this plan would work out better than the Lesotho Liberation Army saga. Where the money was coming from, and the real reason for attempting to replace one government with another, was beyond me. Even if the new government was to be friendly to the South African white minority government, it was, after all, only a small homeland government, unrecognized and with no power on the international stage. Clutching at straws, this was the last throw of the dice by the South African government. Who knew what was happening in the dark corridors of power in Pretoria. I could imagine the poorly lit rooms, the hunched bodies, the brooding eyes, the gesturing hands and the guttural voices, all trying to delay the inevitable – all refusing to read the writing on the wall.

Major Curtis was to do all of the undercover work. The meetings with the head of the Ciskei intelligence, around which the whole plan revolved, and all related subjects, were all his responsibility. I would go along when required, mainly as his bodyguard. My primary task would be training the Ciskei Liberation Army. The more I heard of the plan the less positive I became. There were just too many people in the know. My fears would be confirmed later when, among the many VIPs who visited the Ciskei Liberation Army fighters during their short training phase was none other than the author Peter Stiff. So much for security! Even at this early stage, I knew in the back of my mind that the whole thing was doomed to failure. As hard as I tried, I could not get rid of the feeling that too many people were in the know.

The training was to include the AK-47, landmines and explosives, including booby-traps, and, most important, how to conduct pseudo operations – something the Selous Scouts had been masters of during the Rhodesian bush war. I was to have nothing to do with the political side of the operation: this was to be handled by the visiting politicians, all fat and dressed in shiny suits with shiny shoes and even shinier smiles. Talk about great white sharks: I was seeing the human version.

The world of the so-called freedom fighter is dark and dangerous, with little or no glory, no colourful uniforms, no bright, shiny marching bands, no adoring public – just the constant fear of betrayal, hunger and a less-than-dignified death.

The training was to take place at the Special Forces training ground in Port St Johns. The camp was situated on top of a mountain surrounded by thick, natural bush and pine forests. It was extremely isolated, with only one road in and one road out, with no possibility of any prying eyes or flapping ears. The camp consisted of a small wooden office, wooden dining room/kitchen and a couple of toilets. A Rhodesian-type boiler supplied hot water to the showers. The trainees were to live under canvas. In the case of the Ciskei Liberation Army, the need for secrecy was paramount and as such they would have to do their own cooking, laundry, etc. No cooks or bottle-washers were allowed.

Finally the big day arrived and I waited with bated breath to see what it was going to bring. I had spent the previous two days getting the camp in order. All my questions regarding the number of persons to be trained and length of time I had to train them had fallen on deaf ears, so I did what soldiers had been doing since the beginning of time: I hurried up and waited! I was standing in front of the small wooden office that was to serve as my HQ. It was early morning, the mist still clung to the branches of the taller trees and the sun was struggling to burn its way through the low clouds, the air was fresh and clean, the silence soft and beautiful, I was young and strong: it was good to be alive. In the distance I could hear the sea smashing against the cliffs many miles away in the continual battle between the land and the sea. Relaxed and at peace with the world, I waited for my charges to arrive. I could make out the sound of a straining truck motor, sometimes loud, sometimes soft, as it made its way up the twisting, potholed, narrow track that served as the road to the training camp.

Forty minutes later, an old, green, battle-scared Transkeian army truck came to a shuddering halt in front of the office. Looking at all the steam pouring out from the engine, I was surprised it had managed to navigate the track leading up to the camp. Walking across, I greeted the driver, a corporal. About forty years old, he had a happy, round face, slightly bloodshot eyes and a mouth filled with badly stained teeth from smoking too many cigarettes or *dagga* or both. Not even bothering to switch off the engine, he screamed at the top of his voice for everybody to get off. Grinning down at me, he explained that if he switched off, he would never get it started again. Grinning back in understanding, I made my way to the back of the truck.

Huddled together amidst the thick, black diesel fumes belching from the exhaust, stood the future liberators of the Ciskei – all ten of them. I had expected at least twenty. Dressed in the latest brand-name shoes and clothing, complete with fancy, wheeled suitcases, this was the most unlikely group of liberation fighters I had ever seen. I do not know what they had been told by their recruiters, but it appeared that somewhere along the line the wires got crossed. These guys were dressed as if they were coming to Port St Johns for a seaside holiday: training as liberation fighters seemed to be the last thing on their minds.

I introduced myself to each individual, shaking each proffered limp hand, as is the tradition of Africa. I was looking for the ingredients most needed for any liberation movement to succeed: Passion and Belief. Moving slowly from one individual to the next, I tried to make eye contact to get an indication of what was going on in their minds. Their eyes kept sliding away, their laughter shrill and nervous, their hands soft and unused to hard labour. This was the complete opposite of what I had seen in the faces of the Lesotho Liberation Army recruits: one look in the face of any one of them and you could see the fire, the passion and the will to succeed and continue, no matter what the odds. Commitment was not my problem – that was something the politicians had to sort out – I just had to train them. At the same time, a bit of commitment on their part would not be a bad thing and would definitely make my job a whole lot easier.

The next morning, dressed in green overalls and wearing black army boots, smelling heavily of wood smoke, with eyes red from lack of sleep, the future liberators of the Ciskei gathered outside my wooden office to begin their training. Gone were the Nike and Adidas shoes and shirts, and with them went what little confidence the wearers had had. The wide grins on the happy faces were now replaced by sullen uncertainty. And this was day one!

"This lot will soon learn that the life of a liberator is not all beer and skittles," I mused.

First on the agenda was the assault course. I had built it myself with the help of several other instructors. It was a bitch! Starting in a river, it ran up a small ravine shielded by huge trees from the direct rays of the sun. The ground was always wet and muddy, making keeping your balance difficult, if not impossible. Using all the experience we had gathered over the years, we made sure that everything was bigger and better. The rope bridges were longer and higher off the ground than any I had seen, the barbed wire was tighter and strung closer to the ground than before, the ditches were wider and deeper, the walls were higher with less grip: we had made everything as challenging as we could. To top everything off, because the course had been built in a ravine, little or no breeze ever reached it, so it was like operating in a steam bath. If you were fit, strong and determined, it would take at least forty to forty-five minutes to complete, after which you would need an hour to recover.

Leaving the camp at a slow trot, we headed down the track to the assault course. After the first three or four hundred metres, we were spread out over a distance of two hundred metres. Looking behind me, I could see some members were walking. Others were attempting to run but were moving no faster than the ones who were walking. I could see I was in for a hard time trying to get this lot sorted out. This was day one and already signs of discontent were showing. How would they react after four days with no food and plenty of physical exercise, lots of shouting and very little sleep? The only food they would be getting for the next four days would be what they could catch in the surrounding bush. I intended to keep them fully occupied during daylight hours, leaving them only an hour or two in the evening to look for food. And seeing the size of the fire that they had built the night before and how close they had huddled around it, I could not see any of them venturing into the big, dark forest to forage.

Arriving in ones and twos, some staring at me defiantly, others looking everywhere and anywhere except at me, eventually all ten recruits joined me at the start of the assault course. Showing no displeasure or anger – I was not going to let this lot make me lose my temper – I took them around the assault course, explaining the purpose of each obstacle and how to cross it. By the time I had reached the end of the course, all the laughing and talking that had greeted each obstacle as I had introduced it had ceased, replaced by sombre silence and nervous grins.

Pathetic was the only word I could think of as I watched my charges attempt the assault course for the first time. I did not scream or shout, I just stood there and watched. A less enthusiastic group of people I had never seen: everything was treated as a joke; it was becoming a circus, a stage show. On arriving at each new obstacle, the group would hold a meeting to see who should attempt to cross it. The selected recruit would then make several half-hearted attempts, cheered on by the remainder of the group, and he would invariably end up lying in the mud feigning a serious injury. And so it carried on, obstacle after obstacle. On reaching the end, they stood in a tight group, the laughing had died down and the party was over. They all stared at me as I walked up to join them. I had not said a single word during the entire one-hour circus act. They had expected me to scream and shout or at least threaten them. I did neither and could see they were confused and did not know what to expect. The ball was in my court and I had just the guy to hit it back to them.

Telling them I would meet them back at camp, I turned and walked off. I had taken no more than three paces before they started arguing among themselves. They had not got the reaction from me that they were hoping for. Maybe they did not know what to do next but I sure as hell did.

An hour later, I called a meeting in the dining hall. With me was Corporal Jonas. As I had come to expect, after dealing with this rabble for only a few hours, doing everything at their own pace – slow, very slow – I had briefed Corporal Jonas on what had happened down at the assault course and what I was trying to achieve. Twenty minutes later we had come up with a plan. As we stood waiting at the entrance to the dining hall, the first of the recruits, Richard, the ringmaster, sauntered up, trying to put a swagger in his walk and a look of disinterest on his face, continually glancing at the rest of the recruits to make sure they were watching. He looked ridiculous: his overalls were too short for his lanky frame and the legs ended halfway between his knees and the top of his boots, his thin legs making his boots appear way too big for him. The closer he got, the more he looked at the other recruits who were now no longer smiling and waving but watching intently to see what would happen next. As he drew level with Corporal Jonas and me, he nervously flashed us a dazzling smile. He was still smiling when he hit the ground. Corporal Jonas was a dedicated karate man, big, fit and strong and he took no shit from anyone, especially not from fools like Richard. Bending down over the stunned recruit, he whispered a few words in his ear. What was said I do not know, but the result was unreal. Staggering to his feet, the smile gone, his face almost grey in colour, he unsteadily made his way back to his now-silent comrades.

Two hours later they were still running. The earlier clouds had long since been burned away by the sun and the heat was now intense. Corporal Jonas had put two piles of stones on the track that ran through the training camp. About three hundred metres apart, he had had them running up and down between the two piles for the last two hours, shouting continually, "I MUST

SHOW RESPECT."

As the third hour ended, there was no more shouting, the running had deteriorated to a drunken stagger and the overalls were soaking wet from sweat. Hands and knees were bleeding from the frequent falls, but there was no let-up. Corporal Jonas had, by this stage, joined the recruits on the track, picking up the ones who fell, forcing them to continue, swearing, shouting, kicking and hitting, giving them no rest. As the saying goes, 'No one is crueller to a black person than another black person'.

Getting bored watching the recruits staggering and falling all over the place, Corporal Jonas called a halt to proceedings. Leaving them to recover as best they could, he walked across to me. Squatting down with a broad grin on his face, he suggested a quick trip over the assault course would be a nice way to end the day. The thought was appealing but looking at the exhausted, bleeding clowns and their equally destroyed ringmaster, Richard, I realized it was too dangerous. If somebody got killed while attempting the assault course, I would be in big trouble, especially if they found out about the 'run till you drop exercise' preceding the attempt. Coming to a compromise, I agreed to let Jonas run them down to the assault course where he could talk up a storm and scare the living daylights out of them, but keep them off the obstacles. He was not too happy with the idea but agreed.

Barely a minute later, the 'nearly dead' recruits were attempting to leapfrog each other on their way down to the assault course. Progress was slow, bloody and painful as recruit after recruit, unable to bear the weight of the recruit trying to leapfrog him, collapsed in a heap. Not easily discouraged, Corporal Jonas changed plan and the last I saw of my charges they were piggybacking each other in their run to the assault course.

Returning just before dark, goaded by the tireless Corporal Jonas, the future liberators of the Ciskei were a sorry sight to behold. Gone was the arrogance. With heads hung low and feet dragging, some wearing boots and some not, overalls soaking wet and covered in red mud, it was a pitiful sight to behold .Corporal Jonas brought them to a stop in front of me. I could not help but feel sorry for them. Even from where I was standing I could see large blisters and areas of no skin on the feet of the recruits who had removed their boots, and all had large, swollen welts on parts of their bodies not covered by the overalls. The welts looked very familiar. I joined Corporal Jonas and asked him what had caused the large welts.

"Stinging nettles," he replied with a wide grin on his face and went on to explain that, since the recruits were so exhausted and they could hardly stand, he had decided to teach them to leopard-crawl. Using the ground on either side of the assault course as his training area, he had got all the recruits to lie flat on their stomachs and using their arms and legs to propel themselves, he had made them move through the undergrowth that was alive with stinging nettles and all sorts of biting, stinging insects. Hence all the swollen body parts.

"God," I thought, "some of them looked like they've done ten rounds with Mike Tyson." I also knew from experience that it was not as bad as it looked and by the next morning, most of the swelling would have disappeared.

Pushing all thoughts of pity to one side, I walked up and down in front of the demoralized group, stopping in front of each individual and asking how they felt and if they had any complaints. The answer was always the same: "I am fine, no complaints … sir." Obviously they had received a bit of coaching from Corporal Jonas. I was not complaining: it was a start and Rome had not been built in a day.

Dismissing them, I told them to report to the dining room in one hour. As they hobbled away to their sleeping area, heads hanging, no joking or laughing, I couldn't help but smile. How things had changed; for the worst as far as they were concerned, the party was over. An hour later, with Corporal Jonas by my side, I addressed my charges. Some had showered and changed into their brand-name clothing, looking clean and alive, contrasting drastically with the remainder of their comrades who were still wearing their dirty, sweat-soaked, muddy overalls, looking more dead than alive. The losers.

In great detail I explained what I expected from them and that I expected it all the time, not just sometimes. In the heavy silence that followed I added that if there was anyone who had a problem with what I said and wanted to leave, now was the time to say so.

Leaving them to digest this, I went outside to think about my next problem – food. To feed them or not to feed them, that was the burning question. I was not running a Selous Scouts' selection, but at the same time I also needed to be sure the people I was going to train believed in what they were doing, and if they had to suffer a bit of hardship along the way, that they were quite prepared to do so.

The day before, I had been given a dead porcupine by one of the white instructors who had accidentally ridden over it on his way home. I had taken it and hung it up in a large tree near the training camp. It was not ready yet: it still needed three or four days to become the maggot-infested rotten piece of meat I was wanting.

In the end I came to a compromise. This was the recruits' second day of training. I had not given them anything to eat and they had not asked. Whether they had brought food with them or not, I did not know and was not going to ask. A search was out of the question as I needed their trust and co-operation. I was not going to achieve this by searching their belongings, which would probably prove them to be liars. I was sure if I asked them if they had brought food with them, they would say no – I would have done the same.

Returning to my office, I got together two pots, five tins of bully beef, one kilogram of rice, the same amount of sugar, a couple of loaves of bread, coffee and tea. Bundling it all together, I returned to the dining hall. While I had been deciding what to do, Corporal Jonas had stayed behind in the dining room and had continued to address the recruits. As I walked in, the two pots in my hands, they all stood up. I now knew what the talking had been about. I told them all to sit down and then I took a long careful look at each individual face. I was not interested in the cuts, the bruises, the blisters: I needed to know what was going on inside their heads. In a couple of days these self-same recruits would be carrying AK-47s, complete with live ammunition. I needed to know I could trust them. I did not need to be shot in the back by a half-trained freedom fighter. After a minute or two of soul-searching and a quick consultation with Corporal Jonas, I was happy. Breaking the awkward silence that had developed, I asked if anyone had changed their mind about the training and wanted to leave. "No," was the answer, they all wanted to continue. A job was a job. There were worse things than training terrorists, I thought to myself.

It was a beautiful night, warm and clammy. In the distance I could hear the sea pounding against the rocks. The slight breeze that was blowing did little to cool me down and failed to blow away the mosquitoes attacking me. Standing outside my office having a cigarette, I could see the recruits sitting around the huge fire they had built. There was plenty of talking and gesturing, even the odd laugh. It was amazing what a bit of food could do. I was tempted to go across and join them but I knew it was too early for that: we did not know each other well enough yet to feel comfortable in each other's company. Killing my cigarette, I went back inside the office. It had been a long day and I needed to get a bit of sleep. Corporal Jonas had returned to Special Forces HQ. He had done a very good job in getting the message across to the recruits concerning who was who in the zoo.

I got up early the next morning feeling like death warmed up. It had been a long night, as between the mosquitoes, the heat and the hard wooden floor of the office I had not got much sleep. A cold shower and a couple of cups of sweet, hot coffee would sort me out. Wearing only a pair of shorts, I grabbed my towel, soap, toothbrush and toothpaste and headed for the showers. Passing the recruits' sleeping area, I saw they were all still asleep around the now-dead fire. Some were still dressed in their mud-caked overalls, others in their designer clothes. Yesterday had been a hard day for them. I was feeling bad but nothing compared to what they were going to feel like when they woke up. Their muscles would be stiff and sore, the swelling from the stinging nettles would have disappeared but not the raw patches of skin caused by the scratching and, to top it all off, they would have huge blisters inflicted by the heavy, new, morale-destroying army boots.

The cold water from the shower started to get my blood moving and I began feeling human again. After cleaning my teeth, I actually felt alive. Once I had got the sleep out of my eyes, I felt ready to face the world. Towelling down, I returned to my office/bedroom and put on a pair of clean camouflage shorts, a T-shirt and a pair of soft running shoes. I was ready for the day's training.

By the time I had changed, all the recruits had assembled in the dining hall. Before I could start the day's training, I had to do a check of the injuries they had sustained the day before, courtesy of Corporal Jonas. Calling them out of the dark, thatched-roofed dining hall, I lined them up on the track running past my office. It was eight o'clock in the morning. The sun was up and already I could feel it was going to be another hot, clammy day. As I moved closer to the line of uneasy recruits, the first thing that hit me was the smell. The combination of sweat on unwashed bodies, damp, smoke-inundated clothing and some serious athlete's foot problems, produced a smell capable of stopping a charging bull elephant in his tracks. There was no breeze, so the smell hung in the air like an invisible barrier.

Going slowly from one recruit to the next, looking each one in the eyes, I asked how they felt and if they had any injuries to report, all the while trying not to retch. My eyes were watering, I could live with that, but I knew if I started puking I would not stop till there was nothing left in my stomach. Everybody claimed to be fine, apart from a couple of blisters. There are blisters and there are blisters but these were massive, the smallest being the size of a 5-rand coin. They needed to be treated but first and foremost was a shower.

After what seemed an awfully long time, I finally came to the end of the line. Stepping back a couple of paces, trying in vain to escape the smell, I told the recruits that, since yesterday had been so difficult, I was giving them a break until after lunch, during which time they were to shower, wash their overalls and generally relax, adding that if their overalls were still wet after lunch, they could wear what they wanted as we would be doing weapon training.

Four hours later I met a happier, cleaner, smiling group of recruits. Some were dressed in damp overalls, others in a mixture of denims and T-shirts. No one, I noticed, was wearing their army boots. Armed with my medic pack, I went from one to the next, cleaning and dressing their blisters as best I could, after which I got 'Richard the troublemaker' to help me to carry the ten AK-47s and twenty empty magazines for the upcoming training.

Using old blankets as a groundsheet, I laid out the ten AK-47s, each with two empty magazines, positioning a recruit behind each one. I did not bother with the characteristics of the weapon or any other such useless information. My job was to teach the recruits how to use them safely and efficiently and that is what I intended to do.

Hour after hour I continued: Load, Ready, Aim, Fire, Make Safe, Unload.

As always, safety came first. Once everybody had the safety procedures firmly implanted in their brains, I would move on. Until then, Load, Ready, Aim, Fire, Make Safe, Unload would continue. By late afternoon, I was hoarse. I had almost lost my temper on numerous occasions but at last I could see signs that what I was trying to teach was beginning to sink in.

Early the next morning, we were at it again. Load, Ready, Aim, Fire, Make Safe, Unload. By lunchtime, I was happy that the basic safety procedures were understood and could be enacted by all of the recruits.

The next step was stripping and assembling. As with everything in the army it too has a set sequence. As the AK-47 is a simple-to-operate weapon, it was a lot easier to teach the stripping and assembling than the safety procedures. An hour before dismissal time, I had started to combine the stripping and assembling with safety procedures. Things were moving along nicely and the fact that all the recruits spoke English was a great help.

As always, I was worried about time. I still did not know how much time I had to train these people. I had put the physical fitness on the backburner, not that I had much choice: some of the recruits were still suffering from their encounter with Corporal Jonas, so I had to concentrate on the need-to-know stuff.

The next day, after lunch, I decided to take a chance and do a bit of live firing with the recruits. We had spent the morning practising aiming, holding and the different firing positions. I had touched on the possible stoppages one might experience but being simple and extremely robust, stoppages on the AK-47 were few and far between, the main one being an empty magazine. Taking one recruit at a time, I issued ten rounds of live ammunition that the recruit would then load into the magazine. Using a blanket to mark the firing point, I began the sequence that, if everything went according to plan, would result in the recruit firing his first live round.

Nerves on edge, I started with 'Lying position, down'. This is normally shouted by the instructor at the top of his voice, which is fine if you have twenty well-trained men on the firing point. I had only one scared, undertrained individual, with shaking hands, big white eyes, a sweaty brow and a very nervous, fleeting smile. Talking softly, smiling often and correcting gently, I got all ten recruits to fire their ten live rounds without mishap.

Feeling good, I decided to give the recruits the rotten porcupine for dinner. Taking Richard with me, I headed off where I had hung the squashed animal. I had not checked on it for a couple of days and was not even sure it was still there. My doubts soon disappeared. Still a hundred metres away, I got my first whiff: it was still there, of that there was no doubt. Arriving at the tree, I noticed a large, brown, wet patch directly under the hanging porcupine. On closer inspection, it turned out to be body fluids and maggots dripping and falling from the rancid meat. I was amazed at how quickly the meat had rotted. Two days ago it had appeared fine – a slight aroma, sure, but that was all; now it was completely rotten. Untying the rope, I gently lowered the carcass to the ground. The slightest jerk or sudden stop would cause thousands of maggots, and also several quills, to rain down. It was so rotten I was afraid it would fall to pieces. Most of the stomach had disappeared, eaten by the maggots. The leg around which the rope was tied was attached to the body by a bit of skin. A day longer in the humid heat and the whole porcupine would have turned into a mass of putrid, dripping jelly.

I did not know how hungry the recruits were. As far as I knew, today was only their second day without food. Now was a good time to find out if the fact that the meat was rotten and they were not so hungry would influence their decision to eat it or not. I gingerly lowered the meat to the ground, ending up in a maggot-covered, brown patch directly beneath where it had been hanging. I stared at it in fascination, lying there in its own thick, brown juice, covered by maggots. Would I eat it? I would not!

Soon the whole porcupine was one mass of flies fighting each other tooth and nail to get at the rotting flesh. The smell was unbelievable: how such a small piece of meat could create such a stench was beyond me; it was like a heavy weight on my shoulders making breathing difficult. It was like being in a jail cell without walls with nothing preventing me from moving except the stench.

Gesturing to the carcass, I said to Richard, "Dinner," watching carefully for any reaction as I said it.

He just gave me a happy smile as he gathered up the meat and put it in the pot I had told him to bring along.

I headed back to camp. Once I had got out the clearing with its invisible steel bars, away from the stench, the flies and rotting flesh, all of which reminded me of a less-than-pleasant experience I'd had in the past when I had had to dig up two dead pilots, I began to feel better.

It was a lovely, quiet, warm evening with not a cloud in the sky, only a slight breeze that carried the sound and smell of the sea with it. I was sitting outside my office and had had my usual bully beef and bread sandwich for dinner. I was smoking a cigarette, fighting the mosquitoes and watching the recruits cook the rotten porcupine.

When I had offered the rotten meat to Richard I was surprised that he had accepted it. He and the group did not appear to be the type that would eat rotten, maggot-infested meat. They were now out to prove me wrong. From where I was sitting, about twenty metres from the fire, I had a good view of what was going on. They had two pots of water on the fire. While they were waiting for the water to boil, they were taking pieces of the rotten meat and hitting them against the logs burning on the fire, trying to get rid of the maggots. The quills were not a problem: the meat was so putrid they were easily pulled out. The smell appeared to have no effect and a holiday atmosphere seemed to prevail. There was plenty of talking and laughing as they mimicked each other's mistakes made during the earlier live-firing exercise. Five minutes later, the water in the two pots was boiling. The laughing and joking stopped as it was time for the serious business of cooking the porcupine. The rotten meat was thrown into the first pot of boiling water for about three minutes, just long enough to kill the remaining maggots which, once dead, floated to the top. The meat was then removed and thrown into the second pot of boiling water to continue cooking and the water in the first pot was thrown away.

Barely ten minutes later and it was all over. There was no sign of the porcupine, apart from the odd quill and bone lying in the ashes of the fire. A contented silence fell over the group. Some were already asleep while others talked softly, picking their teeth with quills.

The training now settled down into a routine. Every morning would start off with live firing with the AK-47. I knew from experience that it is not easy to teach African troops to shoot straight. By straight, I mean being able to aim at a target and hit it, not point the barrel in the general area, put the selector on automatic, pull the trigger and hope to hit something. Day after day we practised, getting in as much shooting as possible.

African troops have two major problems when it comes to handling weapons. The first is that they tend to close their eyes and push the rifle in front of them when pulling the trigger, as if throwing a spear. The other is that in a firefight they tend to believe the side making the most noise is winning, so they love firing on automatic. The only way I knew to overcome these problems was practice and more practice. Load, Ready, Lying Position Down, Aim, Fire, Unload, On Your Feet – and so it continued day in, day out, week in, week out, until they did it right.

I had to be sure everybody knew how to handle their weapons efficiently and safely before I moved on to the next phase of the training, which was fire and movement with live ammunition. Fire and movement is a method used by small groups of soldiers to move forward and at the same time provide each other with covering fire.

On the last day of the third week of training, I decided to introduce the recruits to this sometimes frightening method of advance. After an hour of explaining the ins and outs and the dos and don'ts on a blackboard, I reckoned the time was right to do the real thing. Thirty minutes later, I was struggling to control my temper, the pounding of my heart blocked out all other sounds, I was shaking from anger and fear and my eyes felt as if they were going to pop out of my head. My breathing was shallow and rapid, as if I was about to have a stroke, and even my legs felt like they were going to collapse under me. Walking slowly away, I went and sat down on an old tree stump. I needed to cool down because I knew if I started to say something I would lose my temper and end up hitting someone, the last thing I wanted to do. Everything had started well, a bit slow in the beginning maybe but that was because I had broken everything down into stages, as I did not want any accidents. Safety was my paramount concern. I had no intention of having to explain to my superiors how I had managed to get a recruit killed on training or, worse still, to the wife or mother of that recruit.

On arrival at the large clearing in the thick bush that I was using as a firing range, I got the recruits into one straight line facing the targets that I had put in place. They looked a real sorry bunch, wearing torn, dirty overalls, unpolished, worse-for-wear, clumsy army boots and all carried cuts and bruises courtesy of the assault course. I once again went over all the safety precautions and slowly introduced them to the dangerous art of fire and movement. I broke the movement down into a step-by-step sequence, shouting out at the top of my voice what each individual should do in each different step. After about thirty minutes of shouting, my throat was raw, so I stopped calling out instructions, believing everybody by that stage should know what to do and when to do it. I was wrong.

Walking behind the line of recruits as they dashed forward in short spurts, one half moving forward, the other half giving covering fire, I failed to notice that one recruit had experienced a stoppage with his AK-47. Once the firing stopped and all movement ceased, I ordered, "On your feet, up!" As they got to their feet, a burst of automatic fire shattered the silence, the bullets sending up little spurts of sand as they passed within centimetres of the heads of two recruits lying to the left of the firer. Recovering from the shock, I stepped forward and grabbed the AK-47 from the offender's hand, made it safe and threw it on the ground in disgust. I then turned to the recruit to vent my anger and frustration on him. One look at his grey face, bulging eyes, quivering mouth and shaking body and I knew that nothing I said would make him feel any worse than he already did.

My anger forgotten, I walked across to the stunned recruits. Nobody looked at me: they were looking at the sky, the trees, the ground – anywhere – but not at me. Stopping in front of the now weapon-less recruit, I asked him what had happened. He explained that he had suffered a stoppage and had been unable to fix it which was why he had not fired off any rounds. When I had shouted "On your feet, up!" somehow in his efforts to get to his feet the weapon had cleared itself and he had unfortunately kept his finger on the trigger; hence the burst of automatic fire. I did not bother asking any questions: I was just happy that nobody had been killed so I let it go. I really enjoyed my bully beef and rice that night. It had been a close shave but I had made it through the day.

During training the recruits were visited on many occasions by what I can only describe as VIPs. Some I knew were from the South African security police, given away by their white skin, the way they dressed, their arrogant faces and dead eyes, thin unsmiling lips and guttural English that said it all. I had met the same type before when training the Lesotho Liberation Army. On the other end of the scale you had the politicians: big and fat, wearing shiny black shoes, shiny black suits, shiny black skin and flashing shiny white smiles. Once again, I had met the same type when training the Lesotho Liberation Army. In between the two types was author Peter Stiff.

The politicians were the easiest to figure: power and money is what they wanted and they were prepared to go to any lengths to achieve their goals. They would lie, cheat and sacrifice innocent lives on the altar of ambition – it was all part of the game.

The pan-faced South African security police were something else again. Why the continual visits? I do not know and can only guess. Perhaps to check their money was being spent on what it was supposed to be spent on? Or to assess the standard of training? To hold secret meetings with the opposition members of the Ciskei government away from glare of the media? The list of reasons was endless. I would have given an arm and a leg to sit in on one of the meetings between Ron Reid-Daly and his new bosses. What was discussed? How much money changed hands? What was the ultimate aim of the exercise? To what lengths were they prepared to go?

One thing I do know for sure is that we ex-Selous Scouts, led by our ex-leader, were being used by the South African security police to train terrorists to destabilize the whole region. The Transkei had been turned into a training camp for dissidents. I am not saying we were forced to do what we did but maybe we had trusted too long and too deeply and our trust was abused. It was no longer about us as a unit but rather one person and the money.

Peter Stiff, the joint author with Reid-Daly of the book *Top Secret War*, had, I assumed, been invited by Reid-Daly who had briefed him on what was happening, with the intention of writing a book in the future. As I have said before, there were just too many people in the know. Compromise and failure were guaranteed.

A couple of years later a tiff developed between Stiff and Reid-Daly. Stiff, in a book he had written, or was about to write, would claim that I had told him I had taught the Ciskei Liberation Army recruits how to booby-trap a car in thirty seconds and that I had escaped from King William's Town after the failed attack on the Ciskei presidential palace disguised as a black woman. Sad to say, it all ended up in a court case.

During the training I did not get into or discuss anything of a political nature with the recruits, and I did not let my personal feelings in any way influence the standard of training. I trained them as best I could in the time available.

By the end of the training, they were reasonable shots, had a fair knowledge of explosives and booby-traps, could plant a landmine as quickly and efficiently as most and had a good understanding of guerrilla tactics.

This was the first and last and group I trained. One minute they were there, the next they were gone. I was never to see any of them again. Several weeks later, I heard of protests taking place in the Ciskei against the government of Lennox Sebe, the president. These were brutally put down by the army, resulting in the deaths of civilians. Whether the protests were organized by the recruits I had trained, I do not know and did not care.

26

Preparation and double-cross: Ciskei, January–February 1987

Suddenly I sensed a change in tempo. Charles Sebe, the proposed new king of the Ciskei, arrived in Port St Johns, moving into the house between my house and the that of George Matanzima, the prime minister of the Transkei, to set up shop. A worse place could not be found if you tried: it was a bodyguard's nightmare. The house was right next to a main road, with easy access in and out for any potential attackers. Open high ground to the rear of the house provided the ideal position for any would-be sniper. And into this nightmare steps none other than yours truly, the night time bodyguard.

The powers that be had decided that since I was living next door to Charles Sebe, it made perfect sense that I should be the one to keep an eye on him. According to what I understood, I was not to concern myself too much about the daylight hours as he had his own bodyguards to protect him. The night was the problem when, according to what I was told, the bodyguard contingent went to sleep en masse, with the blessing of the man they were supposed to be guarding. My job, therefore, was to make sure nothing untoward happened to Charles Sebe while his bodyguards were sleeping.

I had received many ridiculous instructions since arriving in the Transkei and this definitely ranks in the top three. If anyone thought I was going to spend the night creeping around Charles Sebe's house armed with an old Second World War .38 revolver to ensure nothing happened to him, they were crazy. Nevertheless, I agreed to keep an eye on things and do what I could to ensure that no harm came to him.

I had also learned not to argue: it was a waste of time – some people do not like to hear the truth and ignorance is bliss. All I could do was point out how dangerous the situation was and how easy it would be for anyone determined enough to kill Charles Sebe and hope the powers that be would take notice of what I said. A week later the penny dropped and it was decided to move the future president of the Ciskei to a more secure location, namely Msikaba, an old deserted ex-South African naval base.

Situated on the Wild Coast of the Transkei on a windblown, treeless piece of ground jutting out into the sea, it was a lot safer than the house in Port St Johns. The nearest town was Lusikisiki that was situated about forty kilometres inland and known up and down the coast for its high-quality *dagga* and its abundance of *dagga* fields. The base itself consisted of several brick buildings and round mud huts, with only one road leading into the base and no locals for miles around. It was ideal. Several other advisers and I were sent in to upgrade the security. Combining trenches with claymore mines, hand grenades, flares and the odd booby-trap, we turned the area into a mini-fortress, ready for Charles Sebe to move in.

The operation now moved up a gear. On my return to Port St Johns, I was informed that I would have to make several trips to Umtata to assist in the propaganda war against Lennox Sebe. My task would be to throw out pamphlets at night from an aircraft as it flew over the Ciskei.

Two evenings later I was in the cargo section of a small aircraft sitting by the open door and hanging on for dear life. Behind me, also hanging on for dear life was Ron Reid-Daly. What he was doing in the aircraft I do not know, as there were plenty of other advisers who could have done what he was about to do. Maybe he was trying to keep the people in the know down to a minimum, but after the Peter Stiff visit I did not think so. Always lurking at the back of my mind was the money. How much were our new bosses paying Reid-Daly to organize the overthrow of Lennox Sebe? How much money had changed hands for the training of the Lesotho Liberation Army? And after that failure, had he been warned that the overthrow of Lennox Sebe was his last chance? Failure would see the money dry up and he would be left standing alone to face his accusers. So, this could be the last throw of the dice as far as he was concerned and he intended to make sure that the right numbers came up.

I was sweating. The door of the aircraft had been removed and a cool wind was blowing in my face and all over my body, but still I was sweating. It was the foul-smelling sweat of fear: I was scared to death. All we had to do was hit a large air pocket and I would be history. There were no safety lines to attach myself to and the only thing keeping me in the aircraft was my grip on the door frame.

The interior of the aircraft was dark, cold and cramped and had no lights anywhere. It was as if we were in the Second World War, flying over Nazi Germany on a highly dangerous mission. For God's sake, I thought, this is small defenceless Ciskei: they had never heard of anti-aircraft guns, let alone owned any. But a bit of light in the rear of the aircraft so we could see what was going on would have done no harm.

Clutching onto the door frame with one hand, I used my other to grab bundles of pamphlets from the boxes that Reid-Daly was pushing towards me. It was dangerous, tiring and never-ending. Hand in the box, grab a handful of pamphlets and throw them out the door. As fast as I finished one box, another took its place. My back was aching. I could not stand upright to relieve the pain as the aircraft was too small. Every time we hit an air pocket the aircraft would lurch all over the sky. I was petrified that I would slip, get caught in the slipstream and be ripped out the aircraft. As a result, I did not lean out far enough and a lot of the pamphlets blew straight back into the aircraft.

Two hours or later we were back on the ground. I was exhausted, my back was sore, my eyes felt and looked like piss holes in the snow and I had to walk around a bit to get the blood flowing into my cramped muscles. A couple of minutes later I was back in the aircraft trying to gather up all the pamphlets that had blown back inside. I also took this opportunity to study the aircraft more closely. The more I looked at it, the more it reminded me of the aircraft that Major Bob MacKenzie and I had met on the dirt airstrip outside Kokstad. Whenever we had required additional ammunition, mortar bombs or landmines, this was the aircraft that did the delivery, of that I am completely convinced.

I never read any of the pamphlets and have no clue what they contained.

As I stood there in the dark waiting for my lift back to Port St Johns, I thought about the night's activities, the lurching plane, the air pockets, the lack of lighting in the back of the plane, and it all reminded me of my parachute course.

※

During the same period of the pamphlet night drops, I was tasked with the job of checking out the roads in the area of the Ciskei presidential palace, together with my good friend and fellow ex-Selous Scout, Pete Mac. It was important to know which roads went where, their condition and their usability for the upcoming raid on the palace. The only time this could be done was at night. Our cover story, if we got caught, was that we were looking for the casino that was not too far away from the palace and that we had got lost. Thank God that story was never put to the test: it had more holes in it than a sieve.

Night work of this type is extremely nerve-wracking. There is no front line, there is no war and you do not know whether someone is an enemy or a friend. For several nights in a row we blundered up and down the roads, torches flashing, engine revving, pliers cutting, as we tried to sort out a safe route for the forthcoming attack. This might sound like an exaggeration of the reconnaissance that Pete Mac and I carried out on the roads but to my staring eyes and straining ears, everything was magnified many times over, the light seemed super-bright and the sound of the pliers and revving engine seemed super-loud. It is amazing how a bit of fear can sharpen the senses. The landscape where we were working was flat and open, crisscrossed by several small rivers and miles of old barbed-wire fences.

The lights of the vehicle we were using would have easily been seen from the wall surrounding the palace, not to mention the sound of the revving engine. Yet we were left strictly alone and no one approached us to find out what we were doing driving around at night in the area of the palace. At the time, I did not really think about it too much and put it down to luck, plus the fact that the soldiers guarding the palace were probably sleeping. Little did I know at the time but we were being set up.

Major Curtis's undercover work seemed to be going from strength to strength. I was to join him for his next meeting with the head of Ciskei intelligence. My role was to be observer/bodyguard. The meeting was to take place at the Hogsback Ridge Hotel cocktail bar. This was the make-or-break meeting. The Ciskei government by this stage must have been desperate and I am sure they knew about the propaganda leaflets and the training of the Ciskei Liberation Army. South Africa at this stage was full of informers – sell-outs – as we were to find out to our cost.

Add to this the fact that Charles Sebe was a now a welcome and fully supported guest of the Transkei government and you now have a Ciskei government willing to go to extreme lengths to get their hands on the person they consider to be the cause of all their problems: Charles Sebe.

In their hour of need, like a knight in shining armour, appears none other than Major Curtis, a highly recommended mercenary leader who, for the small price of one million rand in used, small-denomination notes, offers to deliver Charles Sebe into their hands, alive and well. These were desperate times for the Ciskei government: they had no choice and Major Curtis was the only light in a long, dark tunnel leading nowhere. They had to hire him. It was a brilliant piece of undercover work.

The meeting at Hogsback Ridge was the last in a series of meetings between Major Curtis and the head of the Ciskei intelligence who was representing the Ciskei government. At this meeting all the finer details of the handover of Charles Sebe were to be finalized. At half past ten in the morning, dressed in my Sunday best, I seated myself at the bar in the cocktail lounge. The meeting was to take place at eleven o'clock. I had never seen the interior of the lounge before and had decided to arrive a bit early so I could get the lie of the land, as it were. Ordering a beer, I took a slow look around. Everything appeared normal. One way in and out, with ladies' and gents' toilets, swing doors leading to the kitchen, large glass windows to let in the light, eight or so tables scattered about – nothing suspicious at all.

Standing up slowly, I walked to the gents' toilets. I was going because firstly, I wanted to check the toilets were safe and, secondly, I had been issued with the vintage .38 revolver without a holster and I had stuck the revolver into my belt beneath my shirt where it felt comfortable and I could get at it if needed. Everything was fine while I was standing but the moment I sat down, the barrel and front sight started digging into my crotch. It was painful to say the least. In the back of my mind lurked the question: what if the hammer got caught on my clothing and the weapon discharged and I did myself a serious injury? Hence the trip to the toilet.

An hour and three beers later I was really nervous. I was not worried about the meeting being late; after all, this was Africa where time meant nothing. I had forgotten what I was there for – I had drunk three beers which was three beers too many. As the bodyguard, I needed to have a clear mind and quick reactions; beer did not help with either. The minutes passed slowly. God, what a mess! I needed to go to the toilet but was worried that Major Curtis would appear and, not see me sitting at the bar, would think something was wrong and abort the meeting. To make matters worse, the .38 I was trying to hide in my pocket felt as if it was going to fall out, resulting in some strange looks from the black barman. I was now standing up, my eyes were watering and I was sweating like a stuffed pig. Unable to stand still, I was shifting my weight from one foot to the next. I had no choice – standing next to the urinal, all I could do was curse my own stupidity and hope I did not have to pay too high a price.

Barely ten minutes later, Major Curtis appeared, closely followed by the Ciskei intelligence chief. For a final meeting it was short and sweet, a handshake, a smile and the stage was set for the next phase of the attack on the Ciskei presidential palace: the kidnapping.

Meanwhile in Umtata, the capital of the Transkei, tension was mounting at army HQ. The HQ was staffed by three different factions: the advisers, the pro-African National Congress (ANC) and the pro-George Matanzima (the prime minister) supporters. Pro-ANC leaflets began appearing on advisers' and pro-George officers' desks. The writing was starting to appear on the wall. The tension mounted; the atmosphere was thick enough to cut with a knife. Throw in the fact that the Transkei and the Ciskei were both created by the South African government and that the inhabitants of each were the Xhosa people. With one brother in the Ciskei army and the other in the Transkei army, there were no secrets. It was against this background of mistrust and politics that an attempt to replace the Ciskei government was to be made. As the saying goes, fools rush in where angels fear to tread.

On my ride back to Port St Johns with Major Curtis, I could not but help but think of the last time I was involved in an attempted snatch. I hoped our attempt to capture the head of Ciskei intelligence would go a lot smoother.

'Kept in the dark and fed on shit', 'Hurry up and wait'. Both of these sayings continually popped up in my mind as I tried to relax. I had tried everything, from the wine, women and song bit, to a round of golf, but nothing seemed to work. I was tired and irritable and had big, black bags under my eyes. I had not had a good night's sleep in days; my mind gave me no rest as it continually put obstacles in the way of the success of the upcoming operation. Everything hinged on the capture of the Ciskei intelligence head going well, as he was the key to the whole operation. As a close friend of the president and a regular visitor to the palace, he was well known to the guards who should, in theory, open the gates without hesitation as soon as he approached. Once inside the palace, the actual capture of the president should not pose too many problems.

The Selous Scouts had used a very similar modus operandi in their very successful raid on Nyadzonya base in Mozambique during the Rhodesian bush war. The major difference between the two operations was time. In the war in Rhodesia we were dealing with an unsophisticated enemy. Having no radios or cell phones, it took weeks, sometimes months, for the news of the death or capture of an important person to filter through to the enemy HQ. However, in the Transkei and Ciskei this was not the case as both governments had access to the latest communications equipment available. The longer the head of the Ciskei intelligence stayed out of circulation, the less our chances would be of capturing Lennox Sebe, the president.

That the Ciskei government already knew of the plan to replace Lennox Sebe with Charles Sebe I did not doubt: the security surrounding the entire operation was very poor and any doubts they may have had would have been put to rest by the night pamphlet drops. The only thing they did not know was when and how. That they were prepared to go to extreme lengths to prevent this was evident in the hiring of Major Curtis to deliver Charles Sebe to them, dead or alive. And lurking in the background pulling the strings, as ever, was Big Daddy, the South African government: the Paymaster.

The more I thought about it, the more depressed I became. We were underestimating the Ciskei government. This was not a bunch of semi-educated blacks from a Tribal Trust Land in Rhodesia that we were dealing with: these guys were clever, streetwise and light on their feet – they had to be; they had not only managed to survive in an apartheid South Africa but had ended up running a country.

The more important ministers would, including the president, know about the hiring of Major Curtis. I think that a select few would know about the date, time and place of exchange. To think that they did not have a plan in case something went wrong is not thinking. The man we were dealing with was the head of their intelligence service; he may not have been a J. Edgar Hoover but to think he was stupid would be a great mistake as, above all else, he was a survivor and as such he would have taken all the necessary steps to ensure his survival.

We had arrived several hours earlier and as I stood on the high ground looking down on the exchange point, I had to admit Major Curtis had chosen well. He had selected the old low-level road bridge across the Kei River. This was the border between the Transkei and Ciskei. The river was about thirty metres wide at this point; the bridge was basically a concrete slab stretching from one side to the other, wide enough for one vehicle only. The ground on the Transkeian side was slightly higher and more broken, with clumps of rocks and trees that were ideal to hide in. The Ciskeian side, on the other hand, was flat and appeared to be used as a campsite or picnic ground. As far as the location was concerned, we had the advantage.

The exchange was to take place in the early hours of the next morning at 04h00. It was summer and it started getting light at around 04h30. By 05h00 a helicopter could fly. Time, time, everything revolved around time. If everything went according to plan, the head of the Ciskei intelligence would be winging his way to the new detention barracks in Port St Johns by 05h00.

By the time it got dark, we were all in position. Dressed in a mixture of civilian clothing and the odd bit of Rhodesian uniform that we still had, carrying AK-47s, we really looked the part. We were all nervous; nobody seemed able to sit still. We continually scanned the other side of the river using our night-vision binoculars and gun sights. Time after time we checked but the result was always the same: nothing.

Time passed slowly. Unable to smoke and too pumped up to sleep, I leaned up against a tree and tried to relax. All the doubts came flooding back. Surely our intended victim had put someone in place to observe the exchange. Someone he could trust to report back to the necessary people if the plan backfired. Yet try as we might, we could not see anything out of place. My brain, however, refused to give me any rest. I spent the next couple of hours trying to convince myself that everything was going to plan and there was no need to worry, but in the background my brain continued to shout, "Rubbish! You've been doing this sort of thing for years, you know, and it's just too easy. Something is wrong."

Before I could take this argument with myself any further, a set of headlights pierced the darkness on the Ciskeian side of the river. The wait was over. I watched the vehicle, its headlights lighting up the road as it slowly made its way towards the large trees near the bridge. Even with the assistance of the headlights, I could see nothing suspicious. Maybe I was overreacting, "Bullshit!" my brain retorted. "You know there's something wrong; maybe you can't put your finger on it, but something's wrong."

On reaching the trees, the vehicle stopped and the lights went off. Apart from the murmur of the water running over the rocks in the river below, a deadly hush shrouded the area; even the mosquitoes had fallen silent. Time and time again we checked the area where the vehicle had parked but everything seemed safe. The all-clear message was passed to Major Curtis. Headlights flashed and the final phase of the kidnapping began.

Nothing happened for the first couple of minutes and I began to think that maybe the Ciskei intelligence chief had got cold feet. Watching intently through the night binoculars, I saw the front door on the driver's side open. A man stepped out and I saw him take a good look around before proceeding to the boot of the car. Once again he stopped and had a good look around. He was unhappy about something. I am not sure what was bothering him but he spent the next minute or two walking back and forth from the boot to the open driver's door. The sky was starting to change colour, patches of pink, red and yellow appearing on the horizon. In twenty minutes it would be light and with the light would come a whole new set of problems.

The tension mounted and even though it was a cool, crisp morning, I was sweating. Would all the hard work we had put into the operation be for nothing?

"Come on, my man, come on, everything's alright, there's nothing to be afraid of, it's only your old friend Major Curtis waiting for you," I muttered under my breath.

As if hearing me, he stopped pacing, had one last look around, opened the boot of the car, took out what appeared to be a small suitcase and started to walk to purposefully towards the bridge. Showing no sign of nerves, head held high, suitcase clutched firmly in one hand, the intelligence boss of the Ciskei began his walk into history.

Whatever had been bothering him previously he seemed to have put aside. Maybe the thought of getting his hands on Charles Sebe and all the praise and money he would receive from his grateful president had dampened his natural instinct for survival. If he was in any way suspicious that he might be walking into a trap, he kept it well hidden. But then again, why should he worry: he was going to meet his trusted friend Major Curtis who was going to hand him Charles Sebe on a plate for a mere million rand – cheap at the price.

Looking down on him as he crossed the bridge, I could not help but feel a bit sorry for him: his whole world was about to come crashing down. Little did I know that within ten days the shoe would be on the other foot and it would be my world that would come crashing down.

When he arrived at Major Curtis's vehicle, the truth dawned on him. He had been set up. The feedback I got suggested that, on realizing he had been fooled, he put up little or no resistance as he was handcuffed and a hood put over his head.

Once again, it was all about time: the longer he stayed out of circulation, the less chance we had of success in our upcoming raid on the presidential palace. Within half an hour, bound and gagged, he was sitting in a helicopter on his way to the army detention barracks in Port St Johns, where he would be persuaded to turn on his government and friends.

It was now broad daylight. Pete Mac and I were half way across the bridge on our way to collect the Ciskei intelligence chief's car. To say I was nervous would be an understatement: shit scared would be more appropriate.

Everything so far had gone according to plan, smooth, without any hiccups, twists or turns. It had gone too smoothly as far as I was concerned. I still could not believe that our captive had not at least had an observer in position to check that everything went according to plan and whom he should inform if it did not. If he had, then the wheels had already fallen off.

Tense, crouched over, sweaty and unsure of what to expect, Pete Mac and I approached the car. Parked in the open under some large trees, it was in an ideal place to be observed – and ambushed – if so desired. Carefully we approached the car; crossing the bridge was bad enough – this was worse. At least if we were fired upon while on the bridge we had a good chance of making it back to the Transkeian side. Now, a hundred metres from the bridge and well into Ciskei, we could easily be cut off.

The tension, the pressure, the fear of the unknown, turned me into a nervous wreck. I was gripping my AK-47 so hard that my hands hurt. I was trying to look everywhere at the same time, expecting to see members of the Ciskei army behind every bush while simultaneously hoping to see none. Everything seemed to be happening in slow motion. Lungs burning, legs stretched, heart pounding, the last five metres to the relative safety of the car seemed to take a lifetime.

Suddenly I was there! I pressed my back against the front door. My nerves were stretched to breaking point, my senses were straining, my body was taut, my muscles were braced for the impact of the bullets I was sure were on their way. Seconds turned to minutes – and nothing happened. I began to relax. Maybe this was my lucky day.

It was now midday so it was extremely hot and sticky, the road was full of potholes and progress was slow. Pete and I were on our way back to Port St Johns. Driving the vehicle that had belonged to the head of the Ciskei intelligence, we were relaxed and happy to be alive. Adding to our happiness, without a doubt, was the fact that in the boot of the car was a suitcase containing one million rand. I was told to hang on to the suitcase, which I did. It was hidden under the bed in the bedroom of the house I was using in Port St Johns. It stayed there for three days, unnoticed among my other suitcases, before I handed it over to Major Curtis. My cut was fifty thousand rand, a lot of money in those days.

Two days had passed since I had been dropped off by Pete. I had heard nothing of the progress in trying to turn the captive but two days was two days too long. I knew deep inside that the whole operation was doomed. Time, it was all about time. There was no way on earth that the Ciskei government would not know that their head of intelligence was missing. He was the man of the moment; he was the man who was going to deliver Charles Sebe, their enemy, into their arms. He would be in constant contact with his president, informing him of the latest developments. For two days, however, nobody had seen him, let alone heard from him and to think this would not cause alarm bells was nothing short of complete and utter stupidity.

Now the serious waiting began. Port St Johns is a lovely place, situated at the mouth of the Umzimvubu River on the Wild Coast; it is generally peaceful, quiet and an easy place to relax in. I tried everything I could think of – fishing, drinking, playing golf and diving for crayfish – to take my mind off what I now considered a disaster in the making. Nothing seemed to help. I could not sleep, even after a couple of beers. I could not shake the feeling of impending doom.

On day three still nothing had happened. It was eight o'clock in the morning. I was sitting on the steps leading to my house, beer in hand, trying to figure out what was going on. I was living by myself and I had no one to talk to, no one to tell me everything was alright, so I tried to convince myself that everything was fine. The bottom line was I failed dismally, I could find no positives and my brain kept on repeating, "It's all about time, time that ran out two days ago. Wake up!"

It was pretty clear by this stage that our captive had not been convinced that selling out his government was the right thing to do. Surely, the powers that be could see the attack on the palace was no longer feasible, that in fact the whole Ciskei operation should be abandoned. Sitting there on the steps, beer in one hand, cigarette in the other, I looked across the valley at the hill where the detention barracks were situated and which was now the new home of the Ciskei intelligence chief. I knew with utter certainty that the attack was going to take place. Regardless of the consequences, it was too far gone to stop. Too many military reputations were at stake, political careers on the line, never mind the money spent. If men had to die in the process, so be it. Pride, arrogance, stupidity, greed, ego and desperation are a dangerous combination. And always in the background, the paymaster, the puller of strings: the security services of the South African government.

27

The attack on the presidential palace: Ciskei, 19 February 1987

Finally, but oh so late, we got the word to proceed with the raid on the presidential palace and the capture of Lennox Sebe.

I was stressed-out and could not sit still. I had lost count of how many headache tablets I had taken, yet my head still throbbed. I had not slept for days, my eyes were red and swollen, my ears filled with a continuous high-pitched buzz. I should have been in hospital but, instead, here I was sitting in the front seat of a car driven by Pete Mac. It was a warm evening and we were still in the Transkei heading for the main high-level bridge over the Kei River on our way to the presidential palace in the Ciskei.

Pete Mac and I had the dubious honour of being the advance guard. Our task was to make sure the road ahead was clear of roadblocks for the main force that was following. It was a nightmare of a drive. The fact that our vehicle was old and prone to breaking down only added to the tension. Every corner we went round I expected to see a roadblock, and when there was none, instead of relaxing, I just got more and more stressed. By the time we got to King William's Town and gave the all-clear to the main column, I was one throbbing, raw nerve end.

It was starting to get cold. We were parked on the side of the road about five hundred metres short of the presidential palace, waiting for the rest of attack force. Time seemed to stand still, the minutes passing agonizingly slowly. I was not saying much and nor was Pete. An almost spiritual silence settled over the car: we were like two condemned men waiting to climb the steps to the gallows, hoping for a reprieve but knowing deep inside there was no chance. How do you put into words the feelings that flash through your mind in circumstances like these, the utter all-encompassing, soul-destroying loneliness, the flashes of irrational anger, the feelings of remorse, the willingness to accept fate calmly without anger, but at the same time have a determination to survive, no matter what the cost?

I was continually shifting from left cheek to right cheek: we had been sitting in the car for a while and I felt like I had no skin left on my behind and my legs were getting pins and needles. My headache was worsening from the stale air. I needed a bit of fresh air and a couple of trips around the car to get my blood moving again.

Getting out, I had a good look around. It was a clear, cool evening, strangely quiet; the silence only broken by the occasional sound of a car in the distance, but you could have heard a pin drop. It should have registered but it did not. I had been sitting on my behind for far too long, had drunk too many beers, smoked too many cigarettes and in the process had lost the touch. It was too quiet. There was no sound of frogs from the nearby stream, no flash of a bat as it hunted for insects, not even a rustle in the grass as the pack rats went about their business. My senses that had been honed to perfection in the Rhodesian bush war were now a poor shadow of their former self, compliments of the easy life. I was now about to pay a hefty price.

The sound of approaching vehicles caught my attention. It had to be the column. If it wasn't then Pete and I were in big trouble. We were unarmed, our weapons were with the column; if the vehicles turned out to be either the Ciskei army or police then we were on our way to jail. The sound got closer and closer but there was still no sign of headlights. It had to be the column. Who else would be driving around at two o'clock in the morning without lights?

Twenty minutes later we were in extended line, advancing towards the Ciskei presidential palace. My brain was no longer functioning. I was like a robot, a mass of unthinking, unfeeling flesh, stumbling through the thick grass, trying to keep abreast of the people on either side of me. We must have sounded like a herd of buffalo as we tripped and lurched our way forwards.

Lying flat on my stomach, chest heaving, arms stinging from the numerous cuts inflicted by the grass, clutching my AK-47 for dear life, I watched as two vehicles approached the palace gates. I was no more than thirty metres from the gates and under the floodlights. I could see quite clearly.

The front vehicle was without doubt the one owned by the Ciskei intelligence chief, the second a camouflaged Toyota Land Cruiser. Unable to distinguish any faces, I assumed the first vehicle contained the intelligence boss and a driver, with possibly one or two Transkei Special Forces soldiers hidden in the boot. Major Curtis, the co-commander of the operation, was in the second vehicle, together with his Transkei Special Forces counterpart Major Africa, plus several black Transkei Special Forces in the back. This then was the team that was going to overrun the guards and open the gates to let the rest of us in. A Trojan horse affair, I thought to myself, with the horse being the head of the Ciskei intelligence. The palace had been a gift from the government of Israel to the people of Ciskei and, knowing the Israelis, getting in was one thing, getting your hands on the occupant was another. Luckily for us, we never got into the grounds, never mind the palace.

This was it: the moment of truth. Everything would be decided in the next couple of seconds. The silence was oppressive. I lay close enough to hear the gravel crunching under the wheels of the vehicles as they passed my position, my body trembling in hope, barely breathing, with my eyes unblinkingly fixed on the two vehicles as they came to a halt in front of the gate.

Nothing happened. I stared in disbelief Perhaps the palace guards were obliviously asleep, but before I could think of any further reason, the silence was shattered by a burst of automatic fire. Instantly my brain turned from a blob of grey matter into a full-blown survival machine, desperately trying to figure out the reasons for the burst of fire, and their consequences for me.

"BLOWN!" my brain screamed. "Get the hell out of here ... back to the vehicles."

"No," countered the optimistic, never-learn side of me, "it might have been an accident, a new guard who did not recognize the car as that belonging to the head of his intelligence service."

The never-learn side of me lost hands down. Tracer bullets streaked across the sky as our vehicles to the rear came under fire. The killing had begun. And as usual it was the pawns, the people who had no clue why they were attacking the presidential palace in the Ciskei in the first place, who were to die. It was an attack that should never have happened. Under normal circumstances, it would have been abandoned. These were not normal circumstances. Reputations, careers and a whole pile of money were on the line. If people died, so be it.

All my worst fears had come true: we were blown, sold out, compromised, call it what you will and, to make matters worse, our only means of escape, the vehicles, were under fire. Among all the confusion and bullets, the driver of the vehicle containing the head of the Ciskei intelligence managed to turn the vehicle around and speed away down the road towards the column that was also under fire. He managed to run the gauntlet of fire only to be caught in one of the many roadblocks set up in the area by the Ciskei police. The Land Cruiser stood alone and deserted in front of the palace gates. Indecision and chaos were the order of the day. We had no plan B. What was happening was not supposed to be happening. One minute I was helping to push the stranded Land Cruiser away from the palace gates, the next I was advancing with everyone else towards the captured vehicles. I had no idea why; I was just following everybody else.

Gradually, out of the chaos, order started to return. Pete and I ended up lying in a shallow depression in the ground facing the palace. The hundred or so metres between us and the gates were flat, having recently been mowed, and brightly lit by floodlights, probably in anticipation of our visit. To our right, approximately three or four metres away, were Major Curtis and Major Africa. As to the whereabouts of the rest of the attacking force, I had no clue. How long we lay there, I have no idea. The firing had stopped and a peaceful, almost serene, silence settled over the area.

I was agitated. Why were we still hanging around the palace? I knew Major Curtis: he was a very experienced officer who knew just as well as I that it was time to get out. There was nothing for us here, we had been set up, the whole of the Ciskei knew we were coming, and when I say the whole of the Ciskei, I mean the whole of the Ciskei, including the tea lady working in the palace. Then again, I was not present at the briefing Curtis had received from Reid-Daly and did not know what additional pressures he might be under.

Sold out, set up, and with the sense of betrayal came a blinding, all-consuming, irrational anger. Looking to my rear, I could see several figures, who could only be members of the attack force, drifting away. Not that I could blame them: there was nothing left here, only death.

As I lay there trying to control my anger, a new sound caught my ear, the sound of approaching vehicles. Emerging slowly out of the darkness came the first of several armoured vehicles, commonly known to military and police members as Buffels. They would literally be unstoppable if they attacked us, armed as we were with AK-47s. Attack us they did not; instead they parked in front of the palace gates, as if daring us to do our worst. It was a stalemate; the only difference was that they were winning hands down.

Still we stayed, but the longer we stayed, the more chance we had of getting cut off when we tried to break contact and escape. Major Africa was looking at Pete and me, gesturing towards the armoured vehicles with his pistol. I stared in stunned disbelief. Surely he did not seriously think that we should engage the Buffels? At this stage I was in the 'live and let live' mode: they had not attacked us and there was no reason on earth that I could think why we should attack them. Looking at Major Africa, I shook my head, at the same time mouthing the words, "No chance." Ignoring me, he continued to point at the two armoured vehicles. There was no chance in hell that I was going to run a hundred metres over open, floodlit ground to attack two armoured vehicles that were doing me no harm. My chances of survival would be nil.

Something inside my head snapped: what was the matter with the man, the show was over, we had been sold out, they had been waiting for us, our intended victim, Lennox Sebe, was most probably sitting in a safe house miles away laughing himself silly. What did Major Africa not understand, for God's sake? It was time to cut our losses, break contact and get the hell out of here before it got light.

The Ciskei army had gone into defence mode, showing no signs of aggression, as if to say, "Get the hell out of here, there is nothing left here for you, enough people have died already." What the fuck was I doing here? I must be one of the most stupid people around. This was my second attempt to assist in the overthrow of a government. The Lesotho effort had ended in disaster. Had I not learned anything? Obviously not: I was as thick as two short planks. And here I was lying in a small depression on the open, floodlit ground surrounding the palace of the president of the Ciskei, trying to do the same thing again.

Staring at the armoured vehicles, I decided to take them up on their mute offer and get the hell out of there. I had had enough. I was a civilian, hired by a security company to train people to become soldiers, not attempt to overthrow governments. Yet here I was, AK in hand, trying to kill people. This was not Rhodesia; this was not my war, especially not for my meagre salary of five thousand rand a month. Refusing my chance at immortality by attacking the armoured vehicles, I warily got to my feet, my eyes fixed on the Buffels. I was exhausted and light headed, my legs were shaking, my head felt like it was in a vice and, even though it was a cool morning, I was sweating. It had been a long couple of hours. The only thing keeping me going was my anger, providing me with the strength to continue. Keeping my eyes on the two vehicles, I turned to Pete, who was my best friend. We had worked together many times and had been in some pretty awkward positions in the past, but we had always managed to come out in one piece and I trusted him with my life, yet such was my anger that none of these things entered my mind. Bending down, I offered him my extra ammunition, told him I'd had enough of this crap and was out of here. He said nothing, just stared at me.

Straightening up, I had one last look at the armoured vehicles then turned and walked away. I walked slowly, concentrating hard on putting one foot in front of the other. My feet felt heavy, as if my shoes were made of lead and my back muscles were as taut as guitar strings. With every step I took I expected to feel the impact of bullets in my back. What I was doing was probably wrong but at the time I was consumed with anger, not only at myself for not having learned anything from my experiences with the Lesotho Liberation Army but also at the hierarchy for believing that a man in the position of head of security of a country could go missing for four to five days without arousing suspicion or causing alarm. Arrogance, pride and, lurking in the background, greed were the factors that influenced our superiors in their decision to go ahead with the attack. Whether it was feasible or not had nothing to do with it. Whether we had been compromised by the stream of visitors during training was neither here nor there. And, as ever in the back of my mind, I wondered where Big Daddy, the puller of strings, the paymaster, the security services of the South African government, fitted in.

As I concentrated on putting one foot in front of the next, I started to cool down a bit and debated going back. I stopped and turned around. But it was already too late; I could see several people moving in my direction. The retreat, withdrawal, call it what you will, had begun. Turning again, I continued in the direction I was going. I had no plan other than to get as far away as I could from this disaster. To my left and right I could see survivors of the attack heading basically in the same direction.

It was starting to get light and I was stuck waist deep in mud, trying to cross a small river. I had not seen or heard any of my co-attackers for over an hour; somehow we had got separated and I was now alone. Being alone did not worry me, however the police sirens, the gunshots and the increasing visibility did, for as soon as it got light, aircraft would take to the air, making escape all the more difficult. I had to get out of this river and quick. Under normal circumstances, the mud would not present much of a problem. These, however, were far from normal circumstances. The adrenalin and anger that had kept me going had long since departed, replaced by total exhaustion. I had been battling the mud for three or four minutes but it seemed like three or four hours. I no longer had the strength to lift my legs and my breathing sounded like a ruptured boiler. I struggled to keep my eyes open, my head one mass of pain. I was in big trouble as my body was starting to shut down.

A couple of desperate lunges later, I was lying on the riverbank trying to get my breathing back to normal. I had to keep moving: the area was flat and open, offering little or no cover. I needed to find a place where I could lie up and try to come up with a plan.

Half an hour later, I was lying in a clump of rough on the King William's Town golf course. It was full daylight. I was struggling to keep awake, my whole system screaming for sleep. In the distance I could hear the sound of heavy firing and the occasional sound of helicopters. My friends were getting airlifted out. I was too far away and too tired to attempt to join them. I was on my own and needed to come up with a plan.

I decided that the first thing I needed to do was to get rid of my weaponry, so I dug a shallow trench-like hole then buried my Galil, the Israeli version of the AK-47 I had claimed during my time in Lesotho, chest webbing and magazines. All the while I was talking to myself, as if there were two people inhabiting the same body, the one wanting to give up, the other determined to fight and survive.

Staggering across to a nearby water trap, I did my best to remove all the mud from my clothing and, using sand, the black camouflage cream from my face. The sound of helicopters and firing had ceased and it was now strangely quiet. My comrades had gone and I was now completely and utterly alone. Clean as I ever was going to get, dead on my feet, still lacking a plan, I headed towards King William's Town itself.

Wet from the waist down, water squirting out of my shoes, blood running down the side of my face courtesy of the piece of glass from a broken Coke bottle that I had tried to shave with, I must have looked like an escapee from a lunatic asylum. All I could think was that I needed to get to a phone as soon as possible. While trying to get the mud off my clothing and make myself presentable, I had checked the contents of the little plastic bag I always carried on this type of operation. I had enough money to buy something to eat but, more importantly, telephone numbers of people who might be able to help me. It is amazing what a bit of good fortune can do. My morale was no longer dragging in the dust behind me, the craving for sleep had disappeared and my confidence was the highest it had been in weeks, so I figured I was in with a chance of surviving this disaster, providing I did not lose my nerve.

The way I figured was that all the police and army for miles around would be engaged in searching the bush and patrolling the roads between King William's Town and the Transkeian border, so one of the safest places in the area to be would be King William's Town itself. If I was wrong I hoped I would at least get a chance to get something to eat and drink before being arrested, or shot.

After leaving the golf course, the first road I came across was the main tarred dual carriageway. I had no intention of using it as a route into King William's Town; it was too dangerous as it was bound to be patrolled. What I was looking for was a dirt road or track, one that was seldom used and where there was little or no chance of running into an army patrol or police roadblock.

From where I was lying in the thick grass, the dual carriageway seemed a kilometre wide. I needed to cross it, and quickly. Lying in the warm sun was making me sleepy which was a bad sign. I needed to keep moving before I made excuses to stay where I was. It was now or never. Taking a deep breath, throwing caution to the wind, arms and legs pumping like a world-class sprinter, I made a dash for the other side of the highway. Time and distance ceased to exist, my feet pounded down on the tarmac, my arms pumped, my muscles strained, yet I seemed to be getting nowhere.

Suddenly, bruised and bleeding, gasping for breath, I was lying in the ditch on the other side of road. Forty minutes later, I found myself in a quiet suburb. Everything seemed normal, dogs were barking at every gate, sprinkler systems were watering the lawns, no police cars were patrolling and I could not hear any sirens in the distance. It was just a nice, quiet morning in a nice, quiet suburb. As peaceful as it was, it was not the place to hang around in. I would be noticed, I did not fit in. My dress alone was enough to send some old lady hurrying to the phone to report the fact that she had seen a strange man dressed like a hobo lurking around. The last thing I needed was a visit from either the police or the local security company.

Concentrating hard, I tried to act natural which, under the circumstances, was a lot easier said than done. I had managed to get rid of the stiff-legged robot walk and had got the jerky head movements under control. Now all I needed to do was eliminate the headache, the tired, aching legs, the red, burning, glazed eyes, the sweating for no reason, the feeling of utter loneliness and, most of all, the constant fear eating away at my confidence and determination, and it would be a walk in the park.

I bought a Coke, which tasted amazing; I could feel the energy returning to my body. Leaning against the wall of the small take-away shop, I had a good look around. Everything seemed normal, no huddled groups of people talking in hushed voices, no police cars riding up and down, no soldiers patrolling the streets, as if the attack on the palace had never taken place. It was a normal day as far as the citizens of King William's Town were concerned.

From where I stood, I had a good view of the police station. It was completely deserted as far as I could see: no vehicles, no policemen standing outside in the sun smoking, no locals come to report the crimes of the previous evening. There was absolutely nothing out of the ordinary. Maybe my hunch that the police would be out manning roadblocks and scouring the countryside looking for the palace attackers was right.

Coke in hand, I crossed the road to take a closer look. My heart sank and my world came crumbling down: the only public telephone booth in King William's Town was directly opposite the police station. I had no plan B – everything, my whole plan, focused on being able to use a public phone.

My mind raced trying to come up with another plan. I briefly considered asking one of the local shopkeepers to use their phone, but looking and smelling as I did the chances of success were not good. Morale in my boots, shoulders slumped, I returned to the take-away. As I stood there, empty Coke can in hand and trying to come up with plan B, I noticed a tall church steeple not too far away. Many years ago I had read an article in a magazine trumpeting the virtues of the Christian church. The one item that had really caught my attention was that if ever you found yourself in serious trouble and nobody was willing to help you, the church was the place to go. The way I figured, I was in serious trouble. I had just tried to replace a government by force of arms, which was bad enough, but the fact that we had failed only made things worse.

Like a drowning man clutching at straws, I headed for the church. St John's cathedral in King William's Town is a very big and impressive building. Twenty minutes later, hands shaking and breathing as if I had just run a marathon, I tried to open the massive doors. They refused to budge. I pushed, I pulled, I swore. I was so tired and confused that it took a while for me to register they were locked. On unsteady legs I made my way round to the back, where I could see a large, fancy house. This, I thought, must be the priest's residence. I had never met a poor priest in my life and, looking at the size of the house, this one was not an exception.

Climbing the small flight of stairs up to the back door, I took a deep breath and knocked. There was no response. I knocked again. "God," I thought "what if he's on leave?" but before I could continue with that line of thought the door opened. Standing in the doorway was a man in his late forties, balding and on the plump side. Standing behind him was a woman, most probably his wife. He took one look at me in my dirty, torn clothing and my half-blackened, blood-stained face and came to the conclusion that he did not want to be my friend. Before I could say a word he started screaming. I couldn't really comprehend what he was saying but the hate, the anger and the fear in his voice was like a punch in the chest. I staggered back in surprise as he slammed the door in my face. I had not expected to be welcomed with open arms but nor had I expected this kind of reaction from a priest. It just goes to show, you should not believe everything you read.

Things were going from bad to worse, so I pulled myself together and walked back to the centre of town. It was a long and lonely walk. Every step I took I expected to hear a police siren. Leaning against the wall at the same take-away, I had another long look at the police station. I was tired of being scared, tired of sneaking around, tired of the situation I found myself in, tired of the headaches, tired of being tired. I was now pissed off and determined to sort out this mess one way or the other.

The police station still appeared deserted. Working on the principle that fortune favours the bold, I straightened up and, Coke in hand, walked across the road to the telephone booth. I approached it slowly, keeping an eye on the police station. There was nothing, no movement, it was deserted. I sat down on the bench next to the phone, the feeling of relief overpowering. The tension drained from my body and I did not know whether to laugh or cry. Maybe, just maybe, the gods were back on my side.

Once again, time was of the utmost importance. How long the police station would remain deserted I did not know; I had to use whatever time there was available quickly and wisely. The distance between me and the entrance to the police station was no more than ten to twelve metres. I checked again. The windows were closed, as was the door: it was definitely deserted. I just hoped the time I had wasted at the church was not going to cost me too dearly.

Putting my can of Coke on the ground next to me, I dug around in my pocket and removed my small plastic bag. The seven rand it contained was not going to help but the list of telephone numbers most definitely would. Picking up the phone with shaking hands, I hoped and prayed that it was working. With a dry, croaking voice I gave the operator the phone number of a contact who lived in Port St Johns. It was a reverse-charges call. I could hear the phone ringing on the other side. It rang … and rang.

"Please God," I said to myself, "please let someone answer."

"Hello." It was the voice of my contact.

My throat was dry, my jaw muscles locked. I could not talk. "Speak, for God's sake, speak," I muttered to myself. After a pause, having croaked a dry hello, I gave him the number of where I was phoning from and hung up. I had explained, as best I could, my situation, asking him to pass it on to my superiors.

Now all I could do was wait. I was not happy sitting outside the police station but I was afraid to move. The telephone was my lifeline. I needed to be around to answer it when it rang. I knew the caller would try only once and if I failed to answer, he would assume I had been captured. I would be back where I started. I could not afford to take the chance. I had to stay where I was.

It was a warm, pleasant morning, I was relaxed and at peace with myself. I was confident I had taken the right decision by phoning. Pushing all the doubts to one side, I sat there dozing in the sun, waiting for my friend to call me back. As I waited, my mind drifted back to the Rhodesian bush war.

28

Fallout and aftermath

I was brought back to the real world by the sound of a ringing telephone. It had to be my contact from Port St Johns.

I listened in dismay at my superiors' suggested plan. I was to move, in broad daylight, in a countryside crawling with Ciskei troops looking for stragglers stupid enough to be abroad during daylight hours, and proceed to the main Kei River road–rail bridge where they would meet me on the Transkeian side. I was so angry I could hardly speak, not at my superiors but at myself. How stupid I could I get: I was the man on the ground, I knew what was going on better than them. It was my problem, not theirs. I needed to come up with a solution, not them. As I half-listened to what my contact was saying, a sense of helplessness and defeat replaced my earlier optimism. My sluggish brain struggled to come up with an alternative plan. All I knew was that I had to get out of town before it got dark and the police returned. The thought of capture was ever-present. I could imagine the beatings, the parades through town, the appearance on national television, the humiliation of having to beg for forgiveness from the people of the Ciskei for the bad thing that I had tried to do, never mind having to sing the praises of their president, Lennox Sebe. Any fate would be better than being captured.

The alternative plans hastily put together by my overworked, fear-encased brain were not much better than those of my superiors. The thought of approaching one of the many white-owned farms in the area, especially at night, was enough to cause an outbreak of goose bumps and heart palpitations. The chances of being shot while I sneaked around a maize field trying to get to the farmhouse without the local black workers seeing me were very good. Then, of course, there were the dogs, and local farms favoured huge Rottweilers, big and strong enough to kill you. I did not even bother going down that road: I was trying to get out alive, not commit suicide.

Through the murky mists of defeat that shrouded my brain, I heard my contact say, "Give me ten minutes. I have a plan. I'll phone you back," but before I could reply he hung up.

My morale went through the roof, the feelings of defeat and helplessness disappeared. It was like Christmas and my birthday all wrapped in one, the huge weight of having to make a decision lifted from my shoulders. I felt light-headed, happy and at the same time nervous and apprehensive. Looking down at my shaking, bloody and bruised hands, I muttered, "Please God, I need a bit of help."

I don't know how long I had sat on the low crumbling wall outside the garage, staring down the road. A lifetime later the phone rang, sounding shockingly loud. I lunged to my feet and on the second attempt managed to get a shaking hand on the receiver. "Hello," I croaked. My contact's plan was simple. It had to be simple: my brain was past figuring out anything complicated. I was to sit at the garage, at the entrance to King Williams' Town, where I would be picked up by his wife's father. The wait, he assured me, would be short as my lift was already on its way.

My mind was blank. I could not even remember the colour or type of car that was going to pick me up. I seemed to be looking at everything from a distance, from another world. I could see myself sitting on the wall, the cars going by, the people walking by. Everything was in slow motion without sound. It was as if my mind had taken all it was going to take of the continual pressure and uncertainty and had left my body for a moment's rest.

The car arrived. I opened the door and got in. I was in an exhausted stupor. It still seemed as if I was watching events unfold from a distance, as if my mind was trying to make sure all was well before returning to my body. Of the journey to safety I remember little. One second I was getting into the car and the next I was having a shower.

The next morning broke bright and clear. Like a punch-drunk boxer, my mind tried to put the events of the past day into some kind of order. Two hours later, as I climbed aboard the helicopter sent to collect me and take me back to Port St Johns, I was still trying to put some semblance of order to all the thoughts that flashed through my mind. I could not believe my eyes: there, sitting in the helicopter, looking somewhat worse for wear, dressed in full uniform shining like a new pin, was the brains, the architect behind the disastrous palace attack, the abuser of trust, the king of greed, arrogance, pride and stupidity, Ron Reid-Daly. I stared at him. He stared back. I did not acknowledge his presence nor did he acknowledge mine. He was dressed as if he was going to attend a parade, business as usual. The fact that people had died trying to carry out his stupid plan seemed to have no effect on him. He did not seem to realize it was all over. Did he seriously think that after such a disaster there would be no price to pay, that everything would return to normal?

A stiff British upper lip was one thing but arrogance, pride, greed and stupidity were another. The paymaster was going to be deeply disappointed with his two failures. First the Lesotho Liberation Amy débâcle and now this: heads would roll and first on the list would be his. As I watched the blue sea and yellow sand flash past beneath, I wondered who was going to be the scapegoat for this misguided, costly effort. Reid-Daly had gambled everything on one roll of the dice. He had lost. We had all lost. Now all we could do was wait. Of one thing I was sure, the repercussions of this failure would be far-reaching and nasty.

The helicopter dropped me at Port St Johns. The town was strangely quiet. It was as if the entire population was walking around on tiptoes, talking in hushed voices, expecting something to happen but not sure what. I could not find any of the advisers. I began to worry. I had expected at least a week to pass before any action would be taken against us. Looking around the town, it appeared I was wrong: the clean-up had already started.

I was to learn later that all the advisors had been called to Umtata for a so-called meeting. On arrival, they were arrested and thrown in jail. The Transkei military, effectively the government, had had enough of the advisers. The training, the discipline, the embarrassment on the international stage … enough was enough. They were much happier before we arrived, growing and smoking *dagga* and using their army-issue weapons to fight their endless tribal feuds and spreading AIDS like there was no tomorrow.

I was arrested two long, nerve-wracking days later while buying food in the local supermarket. In a strange way it was a relief. I had spent the previous two days drinking and smoking myself stupid, wandering around undecided on what to do: go or stay. Now I no longer had to decide.

I knew and had trained the three soldiers who arrested me. Dressed in full camouflage uniform and armed to the teeth, they looked ready for whatever came their way. If they were expecting trouble from me, they were going to be deeply disappointed. I was a white man in a black man's world. Survival was what it was all about. Anger, pride, arrogance and a big mouth had no place in this situation.

I was not too worried about anything happening to me while in the shop, not with the locals and tourists looking on with big eyes and bated breath. Once out of sight of the gathering crowd, however, who could tell what would happen. The corporal in charge gestured to the door with his rifle. The message was clear: the party was over, living off the fat of the land and the life of luxury and ease was about to come to an end. The shoe was now on the other foot. It was payback time. We were on our way out of the land of milk and honey.

With a sickly smile on my face, I walked slowly to the door. I was dripping with sweat, it was a hot day, my legs felt heavy and I was having difficulty walking normally. My back muscles were throbbing and felt like they were about to explode. The tension was incredible. I expected at least a good whack in the kidneys with a rifle butt, for show if nothing else. I was in a crowded supermarket but you could have heard a pin drop. It seemed to take forever to reach the exit.

Once outside, I was ordered into the back of a modified 'dog-carrying' Land Rover. The silent crowd gathered around the vehicle did nothing to dispel the feeling of impending doom that had settled on me. "Hello darkness, my old friend," I muttered to myself. I had not exchanged a single word with my captors. All instructions were conveyed to me by hand signals. The lack of verbal communication only added to my unease.

Port St Johns is not a big place, more like a village. The drive to my house took no more than three minutes; short yes, but ample time for the imagination to run wild and all the devils to return. My house was situated on top of a grass-covered sand dune and was somewhat isolated. As we started climbing the steps to the front door, with me in front, I tried to start a conversation with my captors. I was desperate to find out what was going on and, if nothing else, break the uneasy silence. All my questions went unanswered.

I was extremely nervous. My legs seemed made of steel and refused to bend at the knees. I kept tripping on the steps. The climb took forever. By the time I got to the top, I was sweating. It was a hot day, yes, but this was the cold, rancid sweat of fear. The simple task of unlocking the front door became a mission. My hands were shaking and wet, and it took several attempts before I finally got the key out of my pocket. Like a drunk, I struggled to get the key into the lock. I dropped the key at least four or five times before I finally got the door open. Angry, desperate, alone, scared but determined to survive, I stepped to one side and let my escorts enter.

It was a large, three-bedroomed house, with two bathrooms, a kitchen and a sitting room. The entire contents of the house consisted of a couple of chairs, a pot or two, a knife, a fork, one old television, a bed, a couple of blankets and my personal belongings. These were the fruits of six years of hard work.

Standing quietly in the corner of the bedroom I called home, I tried to relax as I watched my captors begin their search. What they were looking for I do not know and did not ask.

While the search was taking place, I tried to get my thoughts in order. Any thoughts of escape were put on the backburner. My number-one priority was survival. Even though the search was in full swing, my captors still kept a wary eye on me. They need not have bothered: I was not going anywhere. I had already weighed up my chances of escaping from the house, surviving the thirty-yard dash down the open sand dune, to reach the vehicle that had brought me here, as sadly lacking. Besides, the keys were held by my escorts. My only other option was to take on three well-armed, well-trained soldiers but I was no Rambo and knew nothing about karate and less about boxing.

The fact was I was scared to death. My stomach was churning, my legs felt heavy and the smell of cold, rancid sweat filled the room. I was struggling to keep on my own two feet let alone attacking anyone. So far I had been well treated, with no threats of violence, no slapping or kicking. The more I thought about it the more convinced I became that going with the flow was the best way to go.

Watching my few belongings and much-loved books being thrown around the place, I started to get a bit pissed off. "Steady, calm down," I said to myself. "Play it cool, it's all about survival." Unfortunately, before the message could reach my fear-drenched brain, I took a step forward. The sudden movement on my part brought a halt to the search and all three weapons swung in my direction, steadying on my stomach. I froze, literally scared stiff. "Stupid, oh so stupid," screeched my kick-started brain. My pounding heart felt close to bursting as my body braced itself for the impact of the rounds. I wondered if I had I opened my big mouth once too often. My throat was dry, my Adam's apple bobbed painfully as I tried to speak. After several attempts, I managed to croak, "What are you looking for?" The sweat poured down my back and face as I wondered if I had overstepped the mark. My three captors stared back at me, their faces expressionless, their weapons steady, levelled at my stomach.

"Kiss your ass goodbye," I said to myself. "You've really done it this time." Time seemed to stand still, I tried to relax: what would be, would be, it was in the hands of the gods.

Suddenly, the corporal in charge smiled. The tension drained from me like I had received a new lease on life, like a huge adrenalin rush. The feeling returned to my legs and arms, my senses were like new, I could hear better, see better, smell better, my headache disappeared and my stomach settled down. My morale climbed several notches. The gods were smiling upon me.

"The money, sergeant-major, the money; that is what we are looking for."

At first I did not register what money and my sense of well-being started to fade. Was I being kept alive to locate money I knew nothing about? If so, I was in line for some serious beatings and they were in line for a serious let-down. Then it dawned on me: the only money they could be talking about was the million rand that we had received, or rather had taken, from the head of the Ciskei intelligence on his capture. A lot depended on my being able to convince the corporal that I no longer had the money or knew of its whereabouts. Failure to do so could result in a severe beating.

Speaking slowly and carefully, my throat and mouth once again dry, I tried to explain that I no longer had the money, that it had been taken to Umtata by Major Pete Curtis. An hour later they admitted defeat. It had been a long hour. I had been dragged, pushed and prodded with rifle barrels from one room to the next.

We were now all standing outside next to the rainwater tank. As the search had progressed, I had relaxed a bit and regained some of my confidence. Looking at my staring escorts, my confidence evaporated and the uncertainty returned, complete with dry throat, croaking voice, sweaty body and legs that refused to function.

The moment of truth had arrived.

Now was the time. If any beatings or shootings were going to happen, they would happen now. I knew from experience that a black man is extremely unpredictable. One day he would be sitting down talking to you, the next he would be hacking you to death with a panga. However, no man is crueller to a black man than another black man, as experience in the Rhodesian bush war had shown. My three escorts were huddled together talking softly. I could not make out what they were saying, but every now and then they would stop talking and look at me. This carried on for several minutes. As I stood there watching, I tried to relax and get my brain working again. Things could be worse. I was alive and uninjured and I intended to stay that way. Realizing that all my escape plans were just a shortcut to getting myself killed, I decided to keep with the flow.

Back in the enclosed vehicle I started to feel better. The sweating had stopped and the shaking had almost disappeared. My throat was still dry, my eyes still red, swollen and burning and I had a headache from hell, but hey, I was alive. As the vehicle bounced from one pothole to the next on the badly maintained roads to Port St Johns, I wondered what would happen next.

After a short trip through town, with hooter blowing, lights flashing and me crouched in the back of the vehicle to show the locals who was in charge, we headed out of town towards the sea. How the mighty had fallen. Two weeks ago I was the boss but now I was in a cage on the back of a Land Rover being paraded through town. Was I angry? Did I feel humiliated? Hell yes, but I was still alive.

There was only one place we could be going: the newly constructed army detention barracks. Modern, costly and unnecessary, it was situated on top of the cliffs overlooking the sea, with a breath-taking view of the Transkei Wild Coast. The view was the last thing on my mind as the vehicle struggled up the narrow track leading to the complex. Clinging to the bouncing vehicle for dear life, I wondered if Captain Zulu was still in charge. If he was, my chances of coming out of my present mess in one piece would be greatly improved. After about ten minutes of grinding gears and wheel spinning, we arrived at the top. It was flat, devoid of vegetation and, as usual, the wind was blowing up a storm. I could hear the sea smashing against the rocks below and feel the spray on my face. There was not a cloud in the sky and you could see for miles. I had spent many a relaxing hour at the bottom of this same cliff diving for crayfish. Paradise lost indeed.

A rifle barrel in the ribs brought me back to reality as I stumbled forward to the office indicated by my captors. All the way from my house until the time we reached the top of the cliff, they had paid me little attention, laughing and chatting among themselves. Now, all of a sudden, they were all business, trying to impress the captain. On reaching the door to the captain's office, I was told to stop. My legs felt like lead. I was sweating again and my throat was extremely dry. I had had nothing to drink for hours and my eyes burned as if two mountain climbers were using their ice picks just behind them.

It is difficult to explain what I felt. I was alone, I had nobody to talk to and I was scared to death. I was not sitting in a cell with people around me. I had no one to tell me not to worry, that everything would be alright. There is safety in numbers. I was alone and if anything happened to me no one would know and few would care. Never in my life had I felt so helpless. Over my immediate future I had no control. Coupled with the uncertainty of not knowing what was going on, was an overwhelming feeling of despair. I felt like lying down and saying, "Fuck you, I've had enough of this shit, do what you want."

The will and instinct to survive is very strong in humans and mine had been honed to a fine edge during my years in the Rhodesian Light Infantry and the Selous Scouts. So I stood there, in front of the door to the office of the commander of the detention barracks, still determined to somehow survive.

Knocking, the corporal in charge entered, closing the door behind him. Several minutes passed before the door re-opened and the corporal reappeared. Gesturing to me to come forward, he stepped to one side. Moving slowly, I concentrated on putting one foot in front of the other, determined not to trip over my own feet. Suddenly it was important to show my captors that I might be down but I was not out. Coming to a halt in front of the captain's desk, I lifted my throbbing head and, trying as hard as I could to stop swaying, I managed a croaking, "Good afternoon, captain."

He stared at me for a couple of seconds, saying nothing. Then shaking his head, he said, "Sorry about this, sergeant-major. I am just obeying orders from Defence Headquarters in Umtata."

Captain Zulu was a short, plump officer with an open, friendly face, more suited to the quartermaster stores than running a detention barracks. He appeared more amused with the situation than anything else. Taking a chance, I asked for some water as my throat was so dry I could hardly talk. Studying me closely, he ordered one of my captors to get me some water, while at the same time indicating that I should sit down. Concentrating hard, I lowered myself onto the straight-backed wooden chair. I did not want to trip over my own feet or, worse, miss the chair completely and end up lying on the floor, which was quite possible as my legs still felt as if they were made of lead.

After I had accomplished the miracle of sitting down without injury, I took a chance. Clearing my throat in an effort to make it easier to talk, I asked the captain what was happening. He did not reply. Before I could repeat the question, the water arrived. Taking the large tin cup from the soldier, the captain handed it to me. As I reached for it, I noticed my hands were still shaking. "Gently, gently," I said to myself as I tried to control the shaking that was not only embarrassing but, more importantly, might cause me to drop the cup. I did not think the chances of getting another one were good. Holding the cup as steadily as I could, I lifted it to my lips. Then disaster struck. Instead of slowly sipping the water, I tried to gulp it down. The captain was not impressed as water sprayed all over his desk and papers, never mind the floor.

I tried desperately to bring my coughing under control and at the same time not fall off the chair. There was still a bit of water in the cup and I needed to drink it before the cup was taken away. Taking a deep breath, I forced the remaining water down my throat. Somehow it stayed down. Little did I know it but that was the last water I was to see for a while. Relieving me of the empty cup, the captain informed me that I was to be held in detention barracks in the solitary-confinement cell.

⚘

Sitting in the darkness of the soundproofed cell, with the bucket I had been given to use as a toilet close at hand, I struggled to control my feelings. I felt like crying. The feelings of isolation, loneliness, fear and hopelessness were overpowering. This was all about mental strength. Muscles meant nothing in this game. Sitting on top of the bucket, I started talking to myself. I talked as if I was chatting to an old friend, giving myself encouragement, building up my morale, convincing myself I was going to come out of this alive. Five or ten minutes later, feeling more confident, I started to think of other things.

First and foremost I was very lucky to be alive. Without the help I had received from my friend and his wife's family, I most likely would have been caught, beaten half to death, put on television, humiliated and ended up in jail. Sitting there in the darkness, I tried to figure out what had gone wrong. I had been hired as an adviser, not a revolutionary: my name was Andy, not Che Guevara. Yet I had crossed over from being an adviser to a government overthrower, as it were, without a second thought.

I let my mind drift back to when Pete Mac and I were offered the job of helping train the Transkei Defence Force. Included in the brief was setting up a Transkei Special Forces unit. It was a job we could do, no problem. We had each spent some fifteen years in the Rhodesian army, the last five in the Selous Scouts. After that we had ended up in 5 Reconnaissance, a South African Defence Force Special Forces unit. We subsequently left that unit after a pay dispute. We had been working in Secunda at the Sasol oil-from-coal refinery, trying to set up an informer network. For whom and why, I do not know; I never asked, though probably for the same bosses I ended up working for in the Transkei. When the Transkei offer came, it sounded great compared to Secunda.

I tried to pinpoint when my job had changed from advising and training to trying to overthrow governments. Or, to put it bluntly, when did we start working for the South African security services. And working for them we definitely were. There was no way a group of advisers could take on tasks of the magnitude of overthrowing or replacing governments without the support and knowledge of the South African security services. We did not have the support, money or the connections. I do not know who approached whom, or when, but after three years of training and advising, we moved into the big time. We were to attempt to replace governments for our new bosses.

The decision to change course was taken by the directors of Scouts Security International. We, the advisers, did not have to follow but we did, like lambs to the slaughter. The reason for the change could only have been money, and lots of it. Where it went and to whom I do not know, but it certainly did not filter down to the rank and file. I started on five thousand rand a month and six years later I was still earning five thousand rand a month. That the Transkei government knew and backed the Ciskei coup was obvious; their soldiers were used in the attempt

For the life of me, I could not see what the South African government would gain by replacing the Lesotho government with one more friendly to them, no more than I could see the reason for the attempted change of Lennox Sebe for Charles Sebe. Then again, I was not a politician. Were these attempted overthrows in any way connected to the upcoming release of Nelson Mandela, I wondered. The more I thought about it, the more confused I became. The one thing that did emerge as clear as daylight was that I was as stupid as they come. I deserved to be locked up.

Lying next to the bucket, I tried to get some sleep. I was mentally and physically exhausted and sleep was one way to stop my imagination from running wild. The last thoughts to cross my mind as I drifted off were not of me, but of the previous occupant of this cell, the head of the Ciskei intelligence. I wondered what hell he had suffered. Where was he now? Was he dead or alive? I could not help but feel sorry for him; life had not been kind.

The door opened and sunlight flooded in, blinding me. It took several seconds for me to register where I was. With the realization came the uncertainty, the fear and at the same time hope. I did not know what to expect. Was it payback time? Like a drunk, I staggered to my feet, averting my eyes from the blinding light, trying to steady myself. Through the confusion, I could hear someone calling.

"Come, white man, time to go."

It took a while for the words to register. But when they did, they also brought with them a ray of hope. I stumbled to the door, a smile on my face and hope in my heart. Nothing could be as bad as the soul-destroying, soundless, all-enveloping darkness I was leaving behind me. At the door, I was met by the same soldiers who had arrested me. How long I had spent in the cell I did not know and did not care. All I knew is that, after feeling the sun on my back and the sea breeze on my face, they would have to kill me to get me back into that mind-destroying hell.

Sitting in the same cage on the back of the same Land Rover, bouncing over the same potholes, holding on for dear life, we headed down the same winding track to Port St Johns. After another quick trip round the town with the hooter, we headed for the main road to Umtata.

It was dark when we finally arrived in the capital. I was freezing cold and my hands were blue from hanging on to the sides of the cage. Shorts and T-shirts were fine in Port St Johns, but Umtata was a lot colder. It had been a long and stressful journey. My captors refused to talk to me and with nothing to occupy my mind, my imagination ran wild. Every time the vehicle slowed down or I saw a side road coming up, my body would tense up and my brain would ask the inevitable question: is this where I am going to be beaten or, worse, shot and left for the vultures and hyenas? Time to think is a soldier's worst enemy.

I was taken to the HQ building at 1 Transkei Battalion and questioned by several officers, most of whom I knew. The atmosphere was friendly and the room warm. I started to relax once again. The questions revolved around the advisers' latest calamity, the disaster, the fuck-up that was the Ciskei palace attack!

As I sat there answering the questions as best I could, I felt embarrassed. I got hot and sweaty and could not sit still. The more questions I was asked, the more obvious the flaws in the plan became.

"Surely," I was asked, "you did not think you would succeed. It took you four days to convince the high-ranking Ciskei official you kidnapped to come on side. Four days! He was the head of their intelligence services and a close friend of Lennox Sebe. His disappearance for a couple of hours would have set off alarm bells. Four days! No wonder they were waiting for you."

Where the group of officers got their information from, who knows. Talk about sloppy security, never mind the fools rushing in where angels fear to tread – and old fools at that!

Twenty minutes later I was dropped off in a nearby suburb. The suburb was occupied mainly by advisers working in Umtata. The place appeared deserted. The houses were lit up, street lights were on but nothing moved, no dogs barked, no sounds of music, no cars driving around. It was like being in a cemetery. I was to find out later that most of the advisers had been arrested and thrown in jail. The houses were occupied but by their families, hence the strange silence.

Cemetery or no cemetery, I needed to find a phone, and quick. Continuing down the road, I started looking for a house where something was happening. Barely five minutes later, I found myself standing outside Major Sam's house. The doors were open, the lights were on and I could see someone moving around. The answer to my prayers.

I stuck my head through the door and there, busy packing, were Major Sam and Major Rex. Why they had not been arrested and thrown into jail with everybody else I did not know and cared less. I needed to use the phone. After a quick chat, I was dialling my brother-in-law's number in Johannesburg, some nine hundred kilometres away. It was already dark outside. Once again it was all about time. I briefly explained the situation to him, emphasizing the need for speed. I had to be out of Umtata before it got light the following morning.

"No problem," he replied. He knew the area well from his car-rally days; all he needed was my address, eight or nine hours and he would be there. For once, being single was an advantage. I had only myself to worry about. The other advisers' hands were tied: they had families.

Now all I could do was wait and hope that he would have a trouble-free trip and arrive before dawn. As I sat there staring into the darkness, my mind wandered.

✂

A barking dog snapped me back to the present. A quick look at my watch told me it would be at least another two to three hours before I could expect my brother-in-law. How times had changed. We had arrived amid much fanfare and handshaking; now, six years later, we were leaving like whipped dogs, tails between our legs. Time dragged on. Each hour seemed like a day. I was tired, hungry and cold and could hardly keep my eyes open. Standing up to get my blooding flowing into my feet, I noticed a set of car lights heading slowly down the road towards me. It could only be my brother-in-law. Who else would be driving around at this time of morning? I did nothing. I did not wave, I did not walk towards the car; I just stood there and stared. My brain was having a problem accepting what my eyes were seeing. After the last week of hell, I did not blame it.

The car stopped next to me and I got in. We made for the South African border. It was as simple as that. No hugging, no handshakes, no greetings, no smiles. I was too far gone to show or feel emotion. I was mentally and physically drained.

The feeling as we crossed the border into South Africa was very similar to the time when we crossed back into Rhodesia after a raid into Mozambique. The feeling of relief was indescribable and I could feel the tension drain out of me. It had been a very bad week. First the Ciskei palace attack disaster and the escape from King William's Town. Then the solitary confinement and the trip from Port St Johns to Umtata that I thought would be my last, the questions from the Transkei officers, waiting for my brother-in-law. Enough was enough. I needed to have a couple of strong drinks, a couple of good nights' sleep and I would be as good as new.

This had to have been one of the worst times in my life. As I sat relaxing with a stiff drink – the first time I had been able to do so in a very long time – I reflected on the path my life had taken and the experiences I had had leading up to this last disaster.

Epilogue: Indaba Hotel, Sandton, Johannesburg, 1988

Pushing my empty beer glass to one side, I stood up, put a smile on my face and thrust out my hand. God, I hoped this would work out. I needed a job and a change of luck. I had been unemployed for a long time – but not due to the lack of trying in finding a job. Every job I'd applied for, I was either overqualified or too old and not having a driver's licence was not helping my cause. Prior to this, I had spent two weeks down in Durban with my old friend Joe Bresler, looking for a job on the docks. I was not fussy: anything would do. I was broke and needed to make some money. It was while I was in Durban that I received a call from another friend saying that he knew of an organization looking to recruit a couple of guys and they wanted to talk to me. I was not sure what it was all about but I needed a job and I was prepared to listen. Saying goodbye to Joe and his wife, I had headed back to Johannesburg, not realizing at the time that that was the last I would see of Joe: he was to die in a car-bomb explosion in Iraq.

An hour later, after numerous questions, I had at long last got myself a job. Now, grinning like a Cheshire cat, on my fourth beer, my morale going through the roof and my pocket full of money – money did not seem to be a problem with my new employer and he was not shy handing it out – I was ready to face the world. Life was good.

Six months later I would be wishing I was still broke and unemployed, but it would be too late. I was alive, however; I as sure as hell hadn't learned anything, but that is another story!